The Library of American Biography
by Jared Sparks

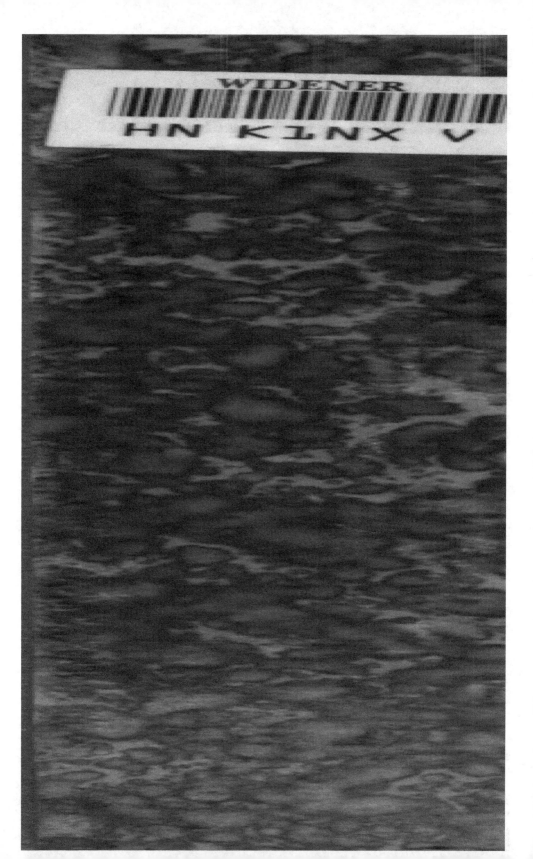

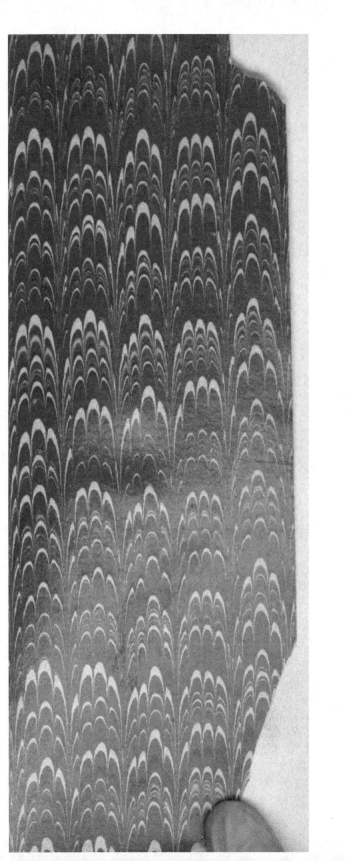

THE

LIBRARY

OF

AMERICAN BIOGRAPHY.

CONDUCTED

By JARED SPARKS.

VOL: II.

BOSTON:

HILLIARD, GRAY, AND CO.

LONDON:

RICHARD JAMES KENNETT.

1834.

5 - 12

LIVES

OF

ALEXANDER WILSON

AND

CAPTAIN JOHN SMITH.

BOSTON:
HILLIARD, GRAY, AND CO.
LONDON:
RICHARD JAMES KENNETT.
1834.

CAMBRIDGE:
CHARLES FOLSOM,
PRINTER TO THE UNIVERSITY.

CONTENTS.

LIFE OF ALEXANDER WILSON,   Page
    By WILLIAM B. O. PEABODY. . .   1

LIFE OF CAPTAIN JOHN SMITH,
    By GEORGE S. HILLARD.

Preface. 173

CHAPTER I.

His Birth, early Adventures, and brilliant
Achievements in the Turkish Wars. . . . 177

CHAPTER II.

His Captivity, Escape, and Return to England. 194

CHAPTER III.

State of public Feeling in England in Regard to Colonizing the Coast of America. — Smith becomes interested in the Subject. — Establishment of the Virginia and Plymouth Companies. — An Expedition sets Sail from England. — Dissensions on the Voyage. — Arrival in Virginia. 204

CHAPTER IV.

Early Struggles of the Colony. — Active Exertions of Captain Smith in providing Food and suppressing Insubordination. 216

CHAPTER V.

Captain Smith's Captivity among the Indians. — His Life is saved by Pocahontas. — His Return to Jamestown. 229

CHAPTER VI.

Arrival of Newport from England. — His Visit to Powhatan. — His Return. 243

CHAPTER VII.

Captain Smith explores the Chesapeake in two Expeditions. — He is chosen President of the Colony. 256

CHAPTER VIII.

Second Arrival of Newport. — Abortive Expedition to explore the Interior. — Injudicious Conduct of the Council in England. — Their Letter to Captain Smith. — His Reply. . 278

CHAPTER IX.

Difficulties in procuring Provision. — Captain Smith's unsuccessful Attempt to obtain Possession of Powhatan's Person. 293

CHAPTER X.

Captain Smith's Adventures with Opechancanough, Chief of Pamunkey. — His Return to Jamestown. 308

CHAPTER XI.

Troubles with the Indians. — Scarcity of Provisions. — Mutinous and treacherous Disposition of some of the Colonists. — Arrival of Captain Argall. 317

CHAPTER XII.

New Charter granted to the Virginia Company. — Expedition despatched to Jamestown. — Confusion which ensues on its Arrival. — Captain Smith returns to England. . . . 332

CHAPTER XIII.

Remarks on Captain Smith's Administration in Virginia. 345

CHAPTER XIV.

Captain Smith's first Voyage to New England. 353

CHAPTER XV.

Captain Smith sails a second Time for New England. — Is taken by a French Squadron and carried to France. — Makes his Escape. — Arrives in England. — Publishes his Description of New England. 358

CHAPTER XVI.

Visit of Pocahontas to England. — Captain Smith's Interview with her. — Death of Pocahontas. 367

CHAPTER XVII.

Captain Smith's Examination by the Commissioners for the Reformation of Virginia. — His Death. — His Character. 384

NOTE.

Account of Captain Smith's Writings. . . 398

Pittsburgh Feby. 22d 1818.

I have refused to navigate a steam
Battean which I have bought, & name the
Cincinnatti, down to Cincinnatti, 528 miles,
respectfully —

Yours most sincerely
Thos Wilson

LIFE

OF

ALEXANDER WILSON;

BY

WILLIAM B. O. PEABODY.

ALEXANDER WILSON.

THERE are some men in the world, who are sufficiently intellectual in their tastes, but too active in their habits, to submit to the restraint of quiet literary labor; their minds never exert themselves to the best advantage, except when the body is in action; and certainly it would seem, as if the employment, which engages at once the physical and intellectual powers, must be best suited to the present nature of man. The pursuit, in which ALEXANDER WILSON acquired his great reputation, is of this description; it combines within itself many circumstances, which give it surprising attraction; it requires the self-complacent skill of a sportsman, and the wild romance of an adventurer; it opens a field for the beautiful powers of an artist, and the fine discriminations of a man of taste; moreover it adds the dignity of science to the exciting consciousness of danger. When we think of the ornithologist, the imagination does not present him to us in the safety and repose of a study; we think of him, as leaving the abodes of civilized man, launching his canoe on unbroken waters, depending on his rifle for subsistence, keeping on his solitary march till the bird has sung its evening hymn, and then lying down to rest, with no society, but the sound of his fire, and no shelter but the star-lighted skies.   Accordingly, this pursuit has interested minds of a very high order, and enlisted in the service of science those, who would otherwise have been engaged in fields of blood.

Wilson, and some others like him, have a right to be considered as benefactors of mankind.   It is wisely ordered, that happiness shall be found everywhere about us ; we do not need to have a rock smitten to supply this thirst of the soul ; all we want, is an eye to discern and a heart to feel it.   Let any one fix his attention on a moral truth, and he will find it spreading out and enlarging beneath his view, till, what seemed at first as barren a proposition as words could express, becomes an interesting and exciting truth, of momentous bearing on the destinies of men.   And so it is with all material things ; fix the mind intently upon them ; hold them in the light of science, and they continually unfold new wonders. The flower grows even more beautiful, than when it first opened its golden urn, and poured its earliest incense on the air ; the tree, which was before thought of only as a thing to be cut down and cast into the fire, becomes majestic, as it holds its broad shield before the sun in summer, or as it stands in winter, like a gallant ship, with its sails furled and all made fast about it in preparation for the storm. All things in nature inspire in us a new feeling; and the truth is, that ignorance and indifference are almost the same; as fast as our knowledge extends, we are sure to grow interested in any subject whatever.

This explains, why men of powerful minds, like Wilson, grow so deeply interested in what are ignorantly regarded as little things; how they can watch, with the gaze of a lover, to catch the glancing of the small bird's wing; and how they can listen to its song, with as much interest as if it breathed thoughts and affections; how the world can be so spiritually bright to them, while to others the bird is only a flying animal, and the flower only the covering of a clod. If any man's labors tend to give interest and meaning to the things of the visible world, we consider him as one who has rendered good service to mankind.

But there is no need of spending time in attempting to establish the claim of Wilson to public regard; for, although the history of his life abounded with depressing circumstances, his name, since his death, has been constantly gaining renown; and the place which his chosen science holds in the public favor, must be considered as principally owing to his exertions. All his powers were concentrated upon this single purpose; he engaged in it, not as an amusement, nor even as an employment, but as the great business of his life; and with a deep and determined spirit, which few men can imitate or even understand. He considered the subjects of his art, not as playthings; he loved them as familiar friends; their voice was not music, but language; instead of dying away upon the ear, it went down into the soul. To many his interest in these things no doubt seemed senseless and excessive; but he is one of those, who never smile at the depth and earnestness of their own emotions. When he described the birds, he spoke of their habits and manners, as if they were intelligent things, and has thus given a life and charm to his descriptions, which will make his work the chief attraction of the science in our country for many years to come.

ALEXANDER WILSON was born in Paisley in Scotland, on the 6th of July, 1766. His father was a distiller, poor in his fortunes, but is said by those who knew him to have been a man of active and sagacious mind. He outlived his eminent son, and perhaps enjoyed the reflection of his fame, which was already widely extended in

1816, the year when the father died. Wilson was so unfortunate as to lose his mother at the early age of ten, and was left, one of a large family, without that tender and judicious care, which a mother alone can give. Young as he was at the time, they had probably detected something intellectual in his tastes and habits; it was their intention to educate him for the ministry; a purpose, which implied a high opinion of his power; since the Scottish peasantry, who look upon every thing connected with religion with unbounded reverence, seldom, in their wildest imaginations, form a higher wish for their children, than that of seeing them lead the devotions of a Christian assembly, and bear the message of salvation to men.

His father, not long after the death of his wife, formed another connexion; and it has been repeatedly stated, that the unkindness of his stepmother compelled Wilson at that early age to seek another home. But his Scotch biographer, who is perhaps most likely to know the truth, tells us, that his new mother sustained that most difficult and delicate of all human relations, to the perfect satisfaction of all parties; and that, when Wilson did leave his father's house, it was only as an apprentice to reside with his master. Wilson was a man of strong feelings; and had he been thus ill-treated, would probably have

expressed himself with some asperity in regard
to it, when speaking of his early days ; but he
is said to have mentioned her with respect and
gratitude, though not with the affection he felt
for his own mother, who was a woman of a superior order, and who probably did something in
his infancy to elevate his mind.

As to his father, if he was illiterate as he has
been represented, he was not without a taste for
intellectual improvement ; for we find Wilson, in
one of his latest years, declaring with energy,
that for all he had done, and all he had been in
the world, he was indebted to the kindness of his
father, whose judicious attention directed his
mind, at he time when it was most open to
receive such impressions, to the excellence of
learning, and the elevating effect of a familiarity
with the grand and beautiful of nature ; these
tastes, thus early formed, had made him a wan-
derer in the world, but they had been the sources
of his best enjoyment, and had enabled him to
sustain to the last the character in which he
gloried, that of a respectable and honest man.
Such a testimony to a father, proceeding from
one whose words were always severely true,
proves conclusively, that, whatever his advantages may have been, he was more than an ordinary man, and probably much of his character
was inherited by his son.

To this early period of his life, then, may be traced that admiration of all that is high, which distinguished his later years. The young mind is exceedingly apt to throw its own brightness upon the scenes and prospects before it ; and as the rose-colored tints disappear on the least acquaintance with the world, as the reality seems so poor and cold, compared with the imagination, the young mind, not having learned that discrimination which saves high thoughts and feelings from sinking in the dusty path of life, often retreats to the ideal world which poetical inspiration reveals to its view. A mind of inferior power will be wholly enervated by this intellectual seclusion ; its effect will resemble that of sensual indulgence ; but, a mind that has energy and principle, will be the better for this occasional retirement ; the effects are as different, as those of the devotion of the closet and of the cloister ; the former sending out a man to active life, better fitted and disposed to discharge its duties, the other encouraging a languid, life-long worship, useless to man and unacceptable to God.

Wilson fortunately had the sort of character which is improved, because it is softened and exalted, by poetical musing ; of energy he had enough and to spare ; but gentleness and purity might possibly have been wanting, had he not thus early been conducted to the sources of high and tender feeling, which poetry sometimes opens in the wilderness, that would else be very dry. Scotland, even before the days of Scott, was a romantic and inspiring region.   Her hills and valleys, desolate though they seemed to the eye, were always animated with powerful associations of self-devotion, of glory, and of love ; in such a country, and with such a spirit as Wilson's, it is not surprising that he became a poet ; and that, finding little sympathy in those about him, and thus being constantly driven back upon his own resources, he kept the fire burning to the last in the very centre of his soul.

The first employment in which he engaged, was not certainly of a very poetical character. In the thirteenth year of his age, he was bound apprentice to William Duncan, his brother-in-law, to learn the business of a weaver.   He contin-ued an apprentice three years, during which time he was faithful to his employer, but never became reconciled to the confinement which the employment required.   In all his leisure mo-ments, he was trying his skill in the composition of verses, in which, however, he never succeeded. In what the Antiquary called the mechanical part of the poet's profession, the clashing of rhymes, he always failed ; and this is a little singular, when it is remembered, that his de-scriptions of birds abound with touches and pas-sages of great poetical beauty.

In that day, the world had not reached the discovery, that poetical inspiration could be breathed in more dialects than one. We smile at the simplicity of him, who had been speaking prose all his life without knowing it; but it is equally true, that many have written poetry all their lives, without suspecting it themselves, or receiving credit for it from others, because their inspirations were not breathed with measured cadence and in regular form. Perhaps it is well, that Wilson never was acquainted with the fact, that there is poetry without verse, as well as verse without poetry; since, had he succeeded better in that which he set his heart upon, he might never have discovered that great field of *poetical action*, in the new world, which his adventurous foot was the first to tread.

Wilson's term of apprenticeship expired at the end of three years; but, not having chosen any other business, and probably disliking the loom less, when he was no longer chained to it by the authority of another, he continued to work as a journeyman weaver, at intervals for four years, residing sometimes with his father, and the remainder of the time with his brother-in-law. His application was not so close at this time, as to prevent his rambling in the neighborhood, and making attempts at descriptive poetry. One of his poems, written at this time, is called " *Groans from the Loom*"; it expresses, with more force than taste, his aversion to his sedentary employment, and his hope that a better destiny awaited him in future years. It is evident from his writings at this time, that he had many hours of despondency and gloom; and it is honorable to his character that, while he felt that he was made for better things, and yet saw no prospect of a favorable change, he should never have sunk into that sullen discontent and sickly sensibility, into which minds of less energy are so apt to fall. It is man's duty, no doubt, to be content with his condition, so far as Providence has assigned it, and taken it out of his own discretion; but, so far as it is left to himself, it is right to wish and endeavor to change it for the better, only taking care not to sacrifice the present to the future, — not to sacrifice the sure and present to that which is uncertain and to come. His poetical attempts at this time were given to the world in the " Glasgow Advertiser," and soon became the subject of much discussion, in the clubs and bookshops of Paisley. Since to astonish the natives of one's own city is, to the youthful poet, a success far more inspiring and triumphant than any that crown his later years, this civic honor doubtless did much to confirm Wilson in a pursuit, in which, however sanguine and determined, he was fated never to succeed.

He did certainly make a change in his circumstances about this time, but whether it was for the better, may be doubted by some readers. His brother-in-law, Duncan, in the hope of improving his fortunes, determined to abandon the loom, and to make trial of the life of a travelling merchant, as it is called in Scotland, but in plain English, a pedler, a character not wholly unknown in this country. Wilson delighted in the prospect of accompanying him ; and they went forth rejoicing, on a tour through the eastern districts of Scotland. Perhaps, with the solitary exception of Wordsworth's philosophic pedler, the profession never numbered in its ranks a more singular disciple than Wilson. He cared much more to behold the beauties of nature, than to display the contents of his pack ; his first feelings were those of wild rapture, on escaping from confinement, to move with perfect freedom over the glorious world of nature ; and the expressions of delight, which burst from him, were such as pedlers seldom use, at least in our day. " These are pleasures," he says, " which the grovelling sons of interest, and the grubs of this world, know as little of, as the miserable spirits, doomed to everlasting darkness, know of the glorious regions and eternal delights of Paradise."

His course was not determined solely by considerations of gain. He states, that he went much out of his way to visit the village of Athelstaneford, at one time the residence of Home, the author of "Douglas," and of Blair, the author of "The Grave." But his tours were not wholly unprofitable; since, though his pocket became no heavier, his heart grew lighter; he became more familiar with men, and gained perhaps what he valued more, a greater familiarity with nature. Of the ways of men he was a keen and sarcastic observer; but to the contemplation of nature he gave himself up with entire devotion of heart; and in a country where the scenery is wild and romantic, and where every hill and valley, if they had language, could tell some story of the past, he could not but strengthen that solemn and affectionate feeling, which the grand and beautiful of the visible world always inspired in his breast. Besides, in the intervals of his journey, he found time, not only to indulge such feelings, but to record them; and he indulged them more safely, thus thrown into daily contact with men, than he could possibly have done in retirement; and learned, better than he otherwise might, the proportion which they may properly bear to active claims and duties.

It does not appear, that he gave any attention at this time to that pursuit, which is now inseparably associated with his name. He tells us in his preface to his great work, that birds had

engaged his attention from his childhood ; but
he probably noticed them as parts of the scenery,
not as subjects of particular interest and description. His thoughts were given at this time almost wholly to poetry ; many of the poems, which
were subsequently published, show by their dates
and incidents, that they were suggested, if not
written in these rambles ; these perhaps were the
most profitable results of his enterprise, and these
were few and small.

While Wilson was thus engaged, Burns was in
the blaze of his fame, at least in Scotland ; for
in England his extraordinary merits were more
slowly felt and acknowledged. The Scottish dia-
lect, which is now so pleasing, then sounded barbarous and uncouth to English ears ; but, in his
native land, it was the language which went most
directly to the heart. The sudden and perfect
success of Burns was not without its effects upon
the ardent mind of Wilson. There were many
points of resemblance between the two ; both
were men of warm feelings and passions, and of
strong and manly understanding ; both had the
same contempt for what was mean, and the same
admiration for all that was high ; they resembled
each other in their poetical feeling ; but, in poetical expression, Burns was as decidedly superior
to Wilson, as Wilson was in moral respects to
him. It must be said, to the praise of Wilson,

that he never acquired those habits of dissipation, into which his melancholy feelings and accidental companions might, to appearance, have so easily betrayed him; but, though he and Burns had similar difficulties to contend with, which they met with equal resolution, the trial of prosperity, which the history of human life assures us is the hardest of all to bear, was one which Wilson was never called to meet.

Burns's success was like a short arctic summer, which threw a deeper gloom, when it departed, upon all the winter of his years; Wilson, perhaps fortunately for his virtue, was compelled to struggle with difficulties to the very last; and thus, strengthened by continual exertion, grew more virtuous as he advanced in years, never failed to command the respect of all around him, and when he died, left the enviable memory of a life, full of difficult and depressing circumstances, but unstained by the least excess. When Wilson, in his youth, sighed for success like that of Burns, he might have been comforted, could some prophet have assured him, that he should lead a life more excellent and honored, and leave a name of equal renown.

Inspired by this example, Wilson resolved to publish his poems; and, in 1789, contracted for the purpose with a printer in Paisley. But the means to defray the expenses of the press were wanting ; and he had no resource, but to take up his pack, and proceed again upon an expedition to sell his wares, or get subscribers for his poems, as the case might be. He was not very successful in either attempt, but he was not overcome by his disappointment ; he kept a journal during this excursion, which is said by those who have seen it, to breathe a spirit of fierce independence and a detestation of everything low; feelings, which doubtless appeared in his manner, and had their effect in preventing his success. The ex racts from it, which are given, are not so free and natural as his usual style, and seem rather prepared for publication, than a familiar registry of incidents and feelings.

Like most other men of decided character, he did not seek advice, nor follow it when it was given. It is recorded, that he submitted his poems to critical friends before they were published, and paid no more deference to their suggestions, than is usual on such occasions. Finding that subscriptions were not to be obtained, he had the book published, and took it with him on another expedition. A judicious adviser might have told him, that the character of a pedler is not one that inspires much confidence, even in mercantile transactions, and that, in matters of literature, they are among the last of the human race, to whom one would look for any other poetry, than such as

might be made to sell. It is true, that he had
merit; still, to human eye, he was nothing but a
pedler. He was afterwards convinced by his
own experience, that the two pursuits are incom-
patible; each is too engrossing. The man must
either be all poet or all pedler; neither of these
interesting occupations is satisfied with a divided
heart. In one of his letters, he speaks on the
subject, more in sorrow than in anger, and seems
quite convinced, that a pedler is a character, whom

> " there are none to praise ;
> And very few to love."

Having found himself wholly unable to dispose
of his work, he seemed determined to renounce
his poetical profession as well as the other; but
it is a curious fact, that, while there is no pursuit,
in which a man is so easily wounded by failure,
there is none in which it is so utterly impossible
to break, either the passion, or the heart in which
it dwells. As soon as the unfortunate candidate
for fame recovers from the stunning effect of the
blow, he rises and hopes again, trusting to have
either better success, better judges, better subjects,
or some other circumstances in his favor, which
were against him before. Wilson had quietly returned to his loom; but having learned from a
friend, that a debating society in Edinburgh had
proposed for discussion the question, whether
Fergusson or Allan Ramsay had done most honor

to Scottish poetry, he was seized with a desire to distinguish himself on the occasion.

He had never read the poems of Fergusson, and had but a few days for preparation; but he borrowed the work from a friend, made up his mind on the subject, labored harder than ever to provide the means for his journey, and arrived in the city, just in time to bear his part in the discussion. The poem which he recited, called the "*Laurel Disputed*," though it assigned the palm to Fergusson, contrary to the opinion of the audience, appears to have had sufficient merit to gain for him considerable respect and favor.

At this time, in 1791, he recited in public two other poems, and published the "Laurel Disputed"; but his success, though it seems to have been sufficient to satisfy his ambition, brought him no permanent advantage. He contributed occasionally to a periodical work called "The Bee," published by D. Anderson; but The Bee, though it profited by the honey, could not save from withering, the flowers from which its resources were drawn.

He came near securing an object of much higher interest and ambition, an acquaintance with Burns. Soon after the poems of the latter were published, Wilson wrote to the author, objecting to the moral tendency of some of the pieces, and stating his sentiments with freedom, though no acquaintance existed between them. Burns returned for answer, that he was so accustomed to such salutations, that he usually paid no sort of attention to them; but that, as Wilson was evidently no ordinary man, he should depart from his usual course, and vindicate the passages in question. Shortly after, Wilson went to Ayrshire, to visit Burns, and he always spoke of the interview in terms of great delight. It has been said, that Wilson was envious of Burns, and that their intercourse was suddenly terminated by some offensive criticisms on the part of the former; but this story is not confirmed by any good authority, and it is moreover inconsistent with the character of Wilson, who, though fiery and passionate at times, always abounded in admiration of excellence, and in every manly and generous feeling. His poem called *"Watty and Meg"* was published without his name, and was at once ascribed to Burns; an acknowledgment of his merit, which gave Wilson great satisfaction.

The work which he had previously published, was called *"Poems, Humorous, Satirical, and Serious, by Alexander Wilson."* The book went through two small editions in octavo, the second of which appeared in 1791. He does not seem to have gained any thing whatever by this publication. Many years after, he wrote in a blank leaf of one of the copies, "I published these poems when only twenty-two, an age more abundant in sail than ballast. Reader, let this soften the rigor of criticism a little. Dated Gray's Ferry, July 6th, 1804." The great difficulty, in all his attempts, is the want of grace and freedom in poetical expression. It is true, that he never could have succeeded like Burns in lyric poetry ; but he had considerable powers of humor, strong feeling, and a correct observation of nature, which, had he not been deficient in language, must have made him successful in some departments of the art.

The next passage in his history is unfortunate, if that can be regarded as a misfortune, which was the principal cause of his coming to America. The town of Paisley was shaken to its centre by a dispute between the manufacturers and the weavers. Wilson was induced by his position to join the party of the weavers ; and he engaged in the conflict, with that determined spirit, which formed a leading feature in his character. Fierce and violent were the satires which began to appear, and if they had not wit in proportion to their fury, they were probably not less acceptable on this account to his own party ; they expected no light touches to be given by the weaver's beam. Naturally indignant at what he believed to be oppression, he set no bounds to his vengeance, and went so far as to write a most severe personal satire on an individual in the place, who was represented by some as a monster of avarice and extortion, though others speak of him as a respectable and well meaning-man.

Wilson doubtless considered him as deserving the full outpouring of his vial, for he was not the man to do injustice to any, except when carried away by excessive feelings. But even those, who make a point of taking jokes, are very apt to make a distinct exception of all of which they happen to be the subject; and, accordingly, he who was the victim of the lampoon, was much less delighted with it, than the weavers. The piece was published anonymously; and though Wilson was suspected of having written it, the fact could not be proved; till one night, as he was returning from the printer's, he was seized by some spies, and papers were found upon him, which threw sufficient light upon the birthright of the poem. He was immediately prosecuted before the sheriff, sentenced to a short imprisonment, and compelled to burn the libel at the public cross of Paisley with his own hand; which last infliction, his tormentors, knowing the natural affection of a poet for his own productions, thought, and probably were correct in thinking, the unkindest cut of all. The printer was also fined for his share in the publication.

Wilson had no enduring malice in his composition; and on this occasion he probably never reflected, that what was sport to him and his companions, might not be equally agreeable to the other party. He was also fully convinced that the weavers were suffering under gross oppression, and felt that the extortioner deserved all the chastisement, that he was able to give. But he never thought of these productions with any satisfaction in his later years. Nor indeed was it long, before he was sensible that he had injured others; for before he left Paisley for America, being even more ready to acknowledge than to inflict the injury, he waited on some of those whom he had satirized, and asked them to forgive any uneasiness, which his attacks might have occasioned. Whether, like Parson Adams, they told him, that they would rather be the subject than the author of such satires, does not appear; but it seems clear, that the only permanent harm, that was done by them, consisted in the unpleasant recollections which were left in his own mind.

Many years after, he sent for his brother David to join him in America. When David came over, he made a careful collection of these pieces, thinking that the author would be gratified to see them again. But he received slender thanks for the pains he had taken. The moment he had placed them in his brother's hands, Alexander threw them into the fire, saying, "These were the sins of my youth; and, if I had taken my good old father's advice, they would never have seen the light." This anecdote is creditable to the father's good sense, and equally so to Wilson's moral feeling. A great proportion of men are innocent, simply because they never were tempted; but the man, who can see and confess his transgression, and instead of palliating it to himself, make use of it as a warning to humble his pride, and guard himself from similar offences, seems far more deserving of honor, than many who never have fallen; and gains wisdom from his unpleasant experience, which he never would have had without it.

This incident was associated with other causes, which had some influence in effecting this transgression, and combined with it to produce a disgust with his situation and prospects at home. The Revolutionary spirit was spreading from France throughout the nations; and the star of reform, which afterwards turned into blood, was at this time, hailed like the star which led the eastern sages to the Savior's feet. Thousands of men, who were not over-sanguine on other occasions, believed that the time was come, when every valley of poverty and depression should be exalted, every mountain of wealth and tyranny be brought down to a common level, and the reign of equal rights and universal peace and happiness be at once established in the world. Wilson associated himself with the friends of popular rights, and entered into the cause with his usual disinterested and unculculating zeal ; and as his former offence, not yet forgotten, had caused him to be looked upon with a suspicious eye, as he was detested by many, to whom it must be confessed he had given sufficient cause, and as he was known to be resolute and daring in every thing which he undertook, his situation became more and more unpleasant every day. Like other sons of toil, he was not bound by any very strong ties of sentiment to his native land ; and, what is a little remarkable, he does not seem to have formed any attachment of the heart, such as bind men to their home.

Here perhaps we may trace one cause of his want of success in poetry. Burns was always in love, and the passion never failed to kindle the fire of his genius ; he was enthusiastically attached to his native land, as appears from his expressions at the time when he was expecting to leave it for ever. But Wilson was more a man of enterprise and action, and therefore was a stranger to many of those fine feelings and associations, which give men success in poetry, and unfit them, in about the same proportion, for the active business of the world. Wilson does not often touch upon the subject; and, when he does, it is with the same composure, with which he would speak of the discoveries in the Arctic regions. It is said, that he once kept up a correspondence with a young lady of some rank and accomplishments; but it does not appear that his heart was ever interested in it; if it was, it certainly was not broken.

Having heard favorable accounts of America, as a land of plenty and freedom, he determined upon the plan of emigrating, some time before he put it in execution. But, with a foresight not by any means universal among emigrants, he considered beforehand by what means he should subsist in a foreign country. One of his plans seems to have been, to qualify himself for some mercantile business, and for this purpose he applied to a friend, who kept a school, for instruction in the requisite branches; but after studying one day, he went his way, and his teacher saw him no more. The fact was, that he had not the means to pay his passage, and the only way in which he could supply them was by applying himself to the loom. With his characteristic determination, he gave up every other pursuit, labored with incessant industry, and lived upon a system so rigidly economical, that, for four months, his whole expenditure did not exceed one shilling a week.

By this exertion he raised the amount required, and then waited on his friends, among others on the aforesaid teacher, for the purpose of bidding them farewell. When this duty had been performed, he went on foot to Port Patrick; thence, he crossed to Belfast, in Ireland, where he engaged a passage to America, on board the ship Swift of New York, bound to Philadelphia. When he arrived at Belfast, the vessel had her full number of passengers; but, rather than give up the opportunity, Wilson consented to sleep upon the deck, through the whole passage.

Of his passage, which, under this arrangement, could not have been a very confortable one, we know nothing, but that he arrived on the 14th of July, 1794, and began his American life, almost as poor as he began his mortal existence. It is difficult to tell, whether the light or the strong heart is best suited to encounter such difficulties as this. Wilson's was never light; but, however it may be in the moment of trial, those who have forced their way through obstacles by their own manly strength, feel a satisfaction in the remembrance, which the light-hearted, who have glided over them, can never know.

When Wilson landed in this country, he had but a few shillings in his pocket, and those borrowed from a fellow-passenger; he had not a single letter of introduction, nor one acquaintance, to diminish the feeling of solitude, and give him advice and society in a land of strangers. He had not even a decided object in view, upon which he might concentrate áll his exertions. But the feeling, that he was in a land of freedom, prevented his being oppressed with these embarrassments, which often weigh so heavily on men in his situation, that, like birds escaped from their cages, they sometimes return to their bondage.

He first touched the American soil at Newcastle, and, with his fowling-piece in his hand, prepared to walk to the city. He was delighted with every thing he saw, and his attention was most strongly arrested by the birds, which he met with in his way. He shot one of them, a red-headed woodpecker, the first which met his eye, and often, in later years, he described his delighted surprise at the sight of this beautiful stranger. This was certainly a fortunate meeting; for there is not, in all the forest, a bird more likely to attract and engage attention. Nothing can exceed the richness of its plumage, of pure white contrasted with black with blue reflections, and surmounted by the bright scarlet of its head. Its playful habits of intercourse with its own race, and its comical pranks in its concerns with man, or rather with the works of man, are very amusing to an observer; and if, as Wilson did, he goes on to investigate its peculiar structure, he finds much to reward philosophical investigation. The long, barbed tongue, which it darts into the worm-hole of the tree, to bring out the mining grub; the gland, from which the tongue is moistened in such a manner, that the insects which it touches are lost; the strong tail-feathers, with which it supports itself as it strikes the rattling tree with its hammering bill, these, and other peculiarities of this bird, would excite reflection in a man like Wilson.

That he did become thus interested in this bird, is evident from the wrath with which he repels Count Buffon's libel upon the Woodpecker. That naturalist, writing in this case wholly from imagination, represents these birds, as condemned to lead a mean, gloomy, and hard-working life, in a sphere which is bounded by the narrow circumference of a tree. Wilson resents the misrepresentation, as if one of his friends had been the subject of it; and really, if the Count had seen this bird, triumphantly stripping the ears of green Indian corn ; rapping on the shingles of the house, as if to perplex the inhabitants within ; chasing its fellows, with loud laughs, round the branches of a dead tree ; or striking its bill in the ripest apple of the garden, and bearing it off exulting, he would have been satisfied, that Nature had not neglected the Woodpecker, in its liberal provision for the wants of the feathered race. This incident certainly inspired in Wilson a desire to know more of these natives of the wood ; but it was a taste which he could see no possibility of gratifying at that time, if ever. It was necessary to provide for his own subsistence ; for even in the land of plenty, food does not supply itself; and the first question was, how this should be done.

We presume that the taste, for which he was afterwards so distinguished, was formed at this time, because in the year after his arrival, being desirous to see the country, he found no means of gratifying his curiosity, except by resorting to his old employment of a pedler. In the tour, which he made in this capacity, he kept a journal, as he had formerly done in Scotland ; and it shows, that while he took note, as before, of the manners of the people whom he met, and the scenery which he saw, he was more minute in his account of natural productions, and the birds came in for their share.

But when he first arrived in Philadelphia, unwilling to return to the loom, he applied to Mr. John Aitkin, a copper-plate printer, who gave him employment in his own business. This he soon relinquished, and resumed his trade of weaving, having made an engagement with Mr. Joshua Sullivan, who lived in Pennypack Creek, ten miles from the city. Having learned that favorable prospects were opening to settlers in Virginia, he removed to that state, and took up his residence in Sheppardstown. He was disappointed in his success there; and, finding that he must weave, wherever he was, he returned to Mr. Sullivan at Pennypack. His peripatetic experiences in this country, though they were not more honored than in his native land, were attended with somewhat more success; but the profit did not tempt him to persevere; and when he returned from the tour which has been mentioned, in which he traversed the state of New Jersey, he quietly seated himself upon the throne of a village school.

It is honorable to Wilson, that, while thus beset by troubles of various kinds, he never failed to speak well of the country of his choice. His Scotch biographer believes that " he did this, on the principle of the fox who had lost his tail;" and evidently thinks, that the part of wisdom would have been, to return to the trap, where peradventure he might lose what little yet remained of that appendage. But either this pleasing alternative never occurred to Wilson, or he thought it certain, that there was no part of the habitable globe in which man can be wholly secure from vexations. In his very first letter in 1794, he says to his friends, that, though the country is not wholly Elysian, it offers great advantages to those who are disposed to improve them; and that a weaver from Scotland, if disposed to be industrious, could save at least as much as at home, while he lived ten times better.   Among other things, it was a pleasure to live where good fruit of all kinds abounded, and was not under the guardianship of mastiffs, spring-guns, and stone walls.   They must expect, he says, that transplanting a tree will check its growth a little; but those, who persevere, will do well, and may reach independence and even wealth at last.   Whenever he looked on the abundant tables everywhere spread, and remembered the fare of his countrymen, he could not help being sad, to think how poorly they were provided.

Though some of his countrymen might think it his patriotic duty to be dissatisfied, there is a plain good sense in these observations, which is better than any amount of sentiment and romantic feeling.   And they show, that, however enthusiastic he was in every pursuit that engaged him, he was no visionary in the common affairs of life.   In these communications to his friends, he gave perfectly just impressions of the country of his adoption; and, had all emigrants been equally sensible and candid in describing what they had gained by the change, it would have prevented much disappointment and suffering; for many, misled by the accounts of those who conceal their mortification under expressions of delight, have been induced to follow them, and on their arrival, not finding that our institutions have broken up the necessary connection between living and labor, have found themselves as miserable and helpless as if drifting in the open sea.

The profession of a teacher, though not commonly regarded as a subject of human ambition, and by no means honored as the interest of society requires that it should be, was not without its benefits to him. His first experiment was made upon the Bustletown road, a short distance from the town of Frankford, in Pennsylvania. Not contented with his situation here, he removed to Milestown, where he remained thus engaged for several years, adding something to the income of his school by surveying land for the farmers in the neighborhood. No situation, into which he could have been thrown, would have served so well as this, to make him sensible of the defects of his early education, or to put him in the way to repair them. Accordingly in his leisure moments, he applied himself with great diligence to several important studies, and, among other attainments, acquired a considerable knowledge of mathematics. The employment was not sedentary, compared with that of a weaver, and above that of a pedler it was highly exalted.   He submitted, with a good grace, to the labor which it required, and while professing to instruct others, was in fact educating himself for the great undertaking, which has made his name immortal.

While Wilson resided at Milestown, he seized an opportunity to make a journey on foot to the Genesee, in the state of New York, in order to visit his nephew, William Duncan.   Wilson had been enabled, by the aid of Mr Sullivan, to buy a small farm in that country, in conjunction with Duncan, who lived upon the estate.   Mr. Duncan's mother, and her family of small children, having come over to this country, needed some such asylum ; and Wilson, who had aided, with that feeling which distinguishes his countrymen, to procure this home for his relations, took this journey on purpose to visit them, and do what he was able for their welfare.   A walk of eight hundred miles in that country, even now, would hardly be proposed as a jaunt of pleasure ; but Wilson commenced his journey with strong heart, in a day when roads and accommodations were different from what they are now, and returned after an absence of twenty-eight days.   Mr. Duncan's farm was in the town of Ovid, in Cayuga county.

Many of his letters to this young man are preserved, and are exceedingly interesting as exhibitions of his manly character and feeling.

Sometimes they are sufficiently short and sarcastic. Speaking of one of their acquaintance, he says, " P. continues to increase in bulk, money, and respectability ; a continual stream of *eleven-penny-bits* running in, and but few running out." At other times he bursts forth in indignation, where some others might have been tempted to smile. " When I told R. of his sister's death, ' I expect so,' said he ; ' any other news that's curious ? ' So completely does absence blunt the strongest feelings of affection ! May it never be so with you and me, if we never should meet again. On my part, it is impossible, except God, in his wrath, should deprive me of my present soul and animate me with some other." His letters show that his nephew had much to contend with ; for Wilson tells him, that a fireplace must be made without delay, and advises him to undertake to build one himself, if masons are not to be had. He tells him, that he makes such suggestions, not from a doubt of his exerting himself, but because he is anxious for the health of his sister ; and he exhorts Duncan, to do every thing in his power, by his own cheerful attentions, to reconcile her to her many hardships and privations.

It would seem, as if his sister's sons, William and Alexander, began to be discontented with their station ; for he often urges upon them the necessity of bearing up with manly firmness under their difficulties. "It is more healthy, more independent, and agreeable, than to be cooped up in a dungeon, surrounded by gloomy damps, and breathing an unwholesome air from morning to night, shut out from nature's fairest scenes and the pure light of heaven. When necessity demands such seclusion, it is noble to obey ; but when we are left to our choice, who would bury themselves alive ? Were my strength equal to my spirit, I would abandon my school for ever for such an employment as yours." He tells them, that when his quarter-day arrives in the spring, he will immediately put all the money which he receives into their hands. " But Alexander can get nothing but wheat and butter, for all his *hagging* and *slashing !* Never mind, my dear namesake, put up awhile with the rough fare and rough clothing of the country. Let us only get the place into good order, and you shall be no loser by it." It is delightful to hear the manly but hearty and affectionate tone, in which he encourages these young men, at a time, when his own condition was far from being the most inspiring in the world.

At the same time that he animates them to exertion, he urges the eldest, his " dear friend and nephew," to give instruction to the younger every evening, and not to be discouraged because their progress is necessarily slow. He enjoins upon him, also, to be the counsellor of the little colony, and to do all in his power to aid, encourage, and make them happy ; for to have a mother, sisters, and brothers looking up to him in the solitude of a foreign country, places him in a dignified point of view, and if he is faithful to them, the remembrance will come in later years, as an angel of peace to his soul. " Now," he says, " do every thing in your power to make the house comfortable ; fortify the garrison at every point, stop every crevice that may let in the roaring northwest, heap up fires big enough for an Indian war-feast, keep the flour-barrel full, bake loaves like Hamles Head, make the loom thunder, and the pot boil, and your snug little cabin reëcho nothing but sounds of domestic felicity." This letter breathes the very soul of generous affection, and concludes with, " my best love to my sister, to Isabella, Alexander, John, the two Maries, James, Jeanie, little Annie. God Almighty bless you all ! "

Wilson amuses himself very much with Alexander's expressions of his feeling. In reply to him he says, " I have laughed on every reading of your letter. I have now deciphered the whole except the blots ; but I fancy they are only by way of half-mourning for your doleful captivity in the back-woods, where you can get nothing but wheat and butter, eggs and gammon, for *hagging* down trees. Deplorable! what must be done?" But he begs his nephew to consider, that, while an old weaver shivers over rotten yarn and an empty flour-barrel, the old farmer sits in his arm-chair, before a blazing fire, with his barns and storehouses full. While he writes in a playful manner, he does not make light of the young man's uneasiness, which was so natural in his situation; he allows that there are many and great difficulties, but endeavors to impress upon him the truth, that he could not escape them by change of place; the only way to escape was to resist them.

In a subsequent letter to the elder Duncan, who complained that he had but little grain to carry to market; Wilson makes an interesting allusion to Burns, which he well knew was touching a key-note, to which every Scotch heart would respond. It also shows by its tone, that Wilson had not that feeling with respect to Burns, with which Cromek has charged him. He tells his nephew, that if Robin, when the mice nibbled his corn, said,

> "I 'll get a blessin with the lave,
> And never miss 't,"

his nephew, whose corn had been expended in the support of a mother with her children, might expect a thousand blessings to Robin's one.

" There is more true greatness in the affectionate exertions which you have made for their support, than all the bloody catalogue of heroes can boast of." No reader whose heart is in the right place can ever be weary of these beautiful expressions of interest and affection ; and it must not be forgotten, that while he was thus sustaining others, his own condition was depressing. Peter Pattieson was not the only teacher, who left the stifled hum of the school with trembling nerves and an aching head. At the time that Wilson was complimenting his nephew upon his exertions, he himself was straining every nerve to contribute to the support of those friends, his nephew among the rest. One would suppose, that, if any were discouraged, he would be the first to sink under a burden, which he bore in addition to no trifling weights of his own.

While he was thus engaged in the service of these relations, who had like himself emigrated to this country, he never was unmindful of those, whom he had left at home. In one of his letters to his father, written while he resided in Milestown, after describing at large the state of society and manners around him, which, as has been already mentioned, he did with a judgment and impartiality not often found in those who are situated as he was, he says, " I should be very happy, dear parents, to hear from you, and how my brothers and sisters are. I hope David will be a good lad, and take his father's advice in every difficulty ; if he does not, he may regret it bitterly and with tears. This is the advice of a brother, with whom he has not yet had much time to be acquainted, but who loves him sincerely. I should wish also, that he would endeavor to improve himself in some useful parts of learning, to read books of information and taste, without which man in any country is but a clodpole ; but, beyond every thing else, let him cherish the deepest gratitude to God, and affectionate respect for his parents. I have thought it my duty, David, to recommend these amiable virtues to you, because I am your brother, and very probably I may never see you. In the experience I have had among mankind, I can assure you, that such conduct will secure you many friends, and support you under all your misfortunes ; for, if you live, you must meet with them ; they are the lot of life."

Letters like this afford such unquestionable proof of the goodness of Wilson's heart, that it seems hardly necessary to speak of his character, so far as respects the kind and social affections. But the truth was, that like many other men of energy, who have met with difficulties and forced their way through them by main strength, he had an occasional roughness and severity in his manners, which sometimes misled careless observers. Like many others, who know their own worth, and feel that they are condemned to a station in life below their merits, he sometimes made exhibitions of his independent spirit to those who treated him lightly. Knowing that he must stand self-sustained, he was not forward to give his confidence to others. These circumstances and traits of character often gave an incorrect impression to those who were not familiar with him. But all agree that he was upright and generous; that, in his dealings with others, he was the very soul of honor; that he was always ready to acknowledge his faults, and, as far as possible, to repair them. Such were the substantial virtues of his character, as they appeared to common view; and from these letters, it appears, that the parts of his history, which, while he was living, the world did not know, were consistent with those which were seen, and equally worthy of applause.

The benevolence of those, who give what they can easily spare, whose liberality resolves itself into a mere indulgence of feeling, which costs them nothing in comparison with the pleasure it brings, is thrown into deep eclipse, by the generosity of one, who, feeling that he had great resources within himself, submitted to the weary confinement of a village school through many of the best years of his life, and allowed others to share, or rather to enjoy all the slender profits of his labor. To all who have a right perception of moral distinctions, he appears even greater, in these humble and unseen exertions, than when he was afterwards engaged in laying the foundations of his fame.

Wilson, after he had remained several years in Milestown, removed to the village of Bloomfield in New Jersey, where he again taught in a school. Soon after, hearing of a situation more to his mind, he applied to the trustees of Union School, in the township of Kingsessing, a short distance from Gray's ferry on the Schuylkill; his services were accepted, and he was thus established within a few miles of Philadelphia.

From this time, must be dated the beginning of his history as an ornithologist; and it is worthy of remark that Audubon whose name is now so distinguished, and who is proud to bear testimony to the merits of Wilson, caught the same inspiration upon the banks of this river. Wilson's school-house and home happened to be near the Botanical garden of Bartram, a name well known to science. The family which bore this name, were by inheritance lovers of nature. John Bartram, whose history ended before the Revolution, was pronounced by Linnæus, "the greatest self-taught botanist in the world." It is said, that the taste was first inspired in him, while he pursued his labors as a farmer. One day when wearied with ploughing, he was resting under the shade of a tree, and his eye fell upon a daisy, which excited in him a train of reflection. Desiring to know something of its history, and of the power which made it, he applied himself to the study of Botany, with such aids as he could procure, which in that day and in his situation were of course very few. The taste for improvement thus kindled, became powerful and engrossing; in the intervals of his labor, he made pilgrimages in various parts of the country, and even at the age of seventy, he undertook a journey to East Florida, which at that time, was equal in hardship and danger to a journey at present to the Rocky mountains. Hector St. John describes the patriarchal appearance of his domestic establishment, particularly when assembled at dinner, with the venerable master, his family and guests, on one side of the table, and an array of lighthearted Africans on the other.

When he died, his son William succeeded him in his tastes and his gardens; he, like his father, did not confine his studies to Botany, but took an interest in every department of natural history. Before Wilson became a master of Ornithology, William Bartram was probably better acquainted with birds than any other man in this country; and was thus qualified to offer that assistance and sympathy which Wilson needed, and which fortunately for both of them and for the world, Mr. Bartram had the heart to give.

It has been said, that Wilson, ever since he arrived in the country, had taken an interest in the subject of birds; but his own observations must have been extremely limited, and there were very few who could assist him. It is surprising to see, how little is generally known concerning them now, after all that Wilson, Audubon, and Nuttall have done. Most persons are acquainted perhaps with the blue-jay, who comes near the house in winter, sounding his penny-trumpet as a signal, that, since the forest is no longer a place for him, he is disposed to be on good terms with man as long as the case requires. Every miller and vagrant fisherman knows the belted kingfisher, who sits for hours on his favorite dead branch, looking with his calm bright eye far into the depth of the waters. The robin also is familiarly known and everywhere welcome, not only from the tradition of the kindness shown by his European relative to the Children in the Wood, but by his hearty whistle, lifted up as if he knew all would be glad to hear that the winter is over and gone. The solemn crow, who is willing to place confidence in man, taking only the simple precaution never to come within shot; the quizzical bob-o-link, or rice-bunt-

ing, who tells man in so many words, that he
cares nothing about him, not he ; the swallow,
that tenants our barns, or the more domestic one
that thunders in the chimney ; the purple martin, that pays his house-rent by waking us hours
before sunrise ; the snow-bunting that comes riding
on the northern storms ; the baltimore, that glances
through the foliage like a flame of fire ; the
thrasher, that pours his note of rich and delightful
fulness ; the goldfinch in his black and yellow
livery ; the bold-faced little humming-bird ; the
cat-bird, that groans with reason at the sight of a
boy, or, when he thinks himself alone, breaks out,
like Davie Gellatley, in wild snatches of song ;
these birds, and the whip-poor-will, whose sor-
rows add solemnity even to the night, almost complete the list of those, which are familiarly known
to man.

There are many birds, which are supposed to
be known, but which, had not the voice of the
ornithologist been eloquent in their favor, would
have been perpetually misunderstood, and even
now are very far from receiving the encouragement and protection which they deserve. The
farmer, for example, accuses the woodpecker of
boring his trees, as if mischief was the bird's only
object ; when he only enlarges with his bill the
hole which the grub had made, darts in his long,
arrowy tongue, brings out the unhappy offender,

and teaches him effectually never to do so again. Many a poor bird, in like manner, after having slain his thousands of insects, which were laying waste the garden, is sentenced to death for the very offences, which he has spent his life in preventing. Complaints are annually increasing in every part of the United States, that some insect or other is increasing with such rapidity, as to render hopeless the cultivation of the plants and trees which it infests; and perhaps the very men, who make these lamentations, are sending out their children, in rejoicing ignorance, to destroy the very means, which Providence has appointed to abate the nuisance they deplore. It is said by Kalm, that the planters in Virginia, succeeded by legislative bounty in exterminating the little crow. But it was not long before their joy was changed into mourning; the insects increased in such numbers, that they would have been glad to recall the exiled birds; but this, though not inconsistent with state rights perhaps, was far beyond state powers. This ignorance is illustrated by an incident mentioned by Wilson; the legislature of New York passed an act for the preservation of the Pinnated Grous, by its common name of Heath-hen. The chairman of the Assembly read the title of the bill, " An act for the preservation of the Heathen; " a thing, which, he says, astonished some of the members, who could see no propriety in preserving Indians, to whom alone the name would apply.

There is so much, that inspires curiosity, in the various tribes of birds in this country, that it is difficult to account for the ignorance which has prevailed in respect to them, except by ascribing it to the want of a student of nature like Wilson, who had industry to collect the observations of others, and compare and combine them with his own. The periodical migration of birds is curious enough to call the most intelligent attention to the subject. When the days shorten and the leaf grows red, an uncommon movement is seen among them. Some, like the great snow-owl, delight in the prospect of moonlight, shining in deathlike stillness upon the icy plain; others, like the snow-bunting, rejoice to accompany the storm, as it rushes down from the Frozen Ocean. But most birds choose a mild climate and perpetual verdure, and therefore retreat before the coming winter, with a fleetness greater than its own.

Some, like the swallow, which was formerly thought to plunge into the mud, though one would think that a bird which can fly sixty miles an hour, could find more agreeable ways of passing the winter, fly only by day; while others, like caravans in the sandy deserts, rest by day, and travel by night. They move in singular regularity. The wild geese, whose word of command is so often heard in the silence of night, form two files meeting in a sharp angle at the head, where the leader cleaves the air and guides the procession, giving his place when he is weary to the next in order. Every thing is subordinate to the great work they have in hand; the swallow snatches his insect and the kingfisher his prey without suspending their flight; and, if they are late in their journey, they allow themselves hardly a moment of rest. Hard times are these for birds of large size and little wing; on they must go; partly by trudging, partly by swimming, they relieve the labor of flying, till they reach their place of rest. Wilson was no stranger to the wish which Logan sang, and a thousand hearts have echoed, — to travel and return with the cuckoo, "which knoweth her appointed time," an inseparable companion of the spring.

It is interesting also, to observe the provision which birds make for their wants, and to see how, when reason sometimes falters, instinct always acts with certainty and success. The nut-hatch opens nuts, or the stones of fruit, by repeated blows of his sharp, horny bill. The butcher-bird, which lives on insects and little birds, is said to attract the latter by imitating their call, and has a habit of impaling on thorns such insects as he does not need at the moment. It is a comfort to see, that the trick of gathering what he does not

want, and keeping it till it is useless, is not confined to man. The whippoorwill sits on the
fence or the door-stone, singing as if his heart
was broken ; but, if any unguarded insect trusts
that his appetite has failed, the bird rises and
swallows him, and then proceeds with the song.
The raven and the gull, fond of shell-fish, but
unprovided with oyster-knives, are said to carry
them high in the air, that they may fall on rocks
to break the shell.

The eagle, haughty as he seems, supports
himself in no honorable way. He sits in gigantic
repose, calmly watching the play of the fishing
birds, over the blue reach of waters, with his
wings loosly raised, and keeping time with the
heaving sea. Soon he sees the fish-hawk
plunge heavily in the ocean, and reappear with
a scream of triumph, bearing the struggling fish.
The gaze of the eagle grows fiery and intense ;
his wings are spread wide, and he gives chase to
the hawk, till he compels him to let fall his prize ;
but it is not lost ; for the eagle wheels in a
broad circle, sweeps down upon the edge of the
wave, and secures it, before it touches the deep.
Nothing can be more majestic than the flight of
this noble bird ; he seems to move by an effort
of will alone, without the waving of his wings.
Pity it is, that he should descend to robbery ;
but if history says true, this circumstance does

not wholly destroy the resemblance between the king of birds and the kings of men.

The art which birds display in making their nests, is another curious subject, which attracts and rewards the ornithologist's attention. The nest is not the house of the bird; it is nothing more than the cradle of the young. Birds of mature life are exposed to all the changes of climate, but are provided with oil to spread upon their plumage, which secures it from being wet by the rain. It is remarkable, that this supply ceases, in a great measure, in such birds as are sheltered by the care of man. The nest of the delicate little humming-bird is the choicest piece of work that can be imagined; being formed and covered with moss in such a manner, as to resemble a knot of the tree in which it is built. But even this is surpassed by the tailor-bird of India, which, living in a climate where the young are exposed to all manner of foes, constructs its nest, by sewing together two large leaves at the extremity of the bough, where neither ape, serpent, nor monkey would venture for all beneath the moon.

There is something resembling this in the nest of the Baltimore Oriole, a common and favorite bird. It is formed, by tying together some forked twigs, at the end of a drooping branch, with strings, either stripped or stolen from a graft or a window. These twigs form the frame-work, round which they weave a coarse covering to enclose the nest, composed of thread, wool, or tow. The inner nest is at the bottom of this external pouch, where it swings securely in the highest winds, and is sheltered by the arbor of leaves above it, from both the rain and sun. This is the most remarkable structure of the kind in this country; but, if certain accounts may be credited, there is a bird in India, which makes a similar nest, with several apartments, which it lights up with fire-flies by night. Other birds construct their nest with less delicacy, but more labor. The woodpecker chisels out its gallery in the wood of the tree, by repeated strokes of its powerful bill. The kingfisher scoops out a tunnel in the bank of his favorite stream. The little sand-martin, in its small way, follows the kingfisher's example. The purple martin, and the republican swallow, which is now emigrating from the west to the east, defend their tenements with a mud wall. Some birds manifest a perfect indifference on this subject. The common hen, though so motherly in her habits, merely scratches a place for her nest. The sea-birds, naturally rough and hardy in their habits, leave their eggs lying loosely on the sand. But the duck, the eider particularly, which is one of the northern visiters of New England, strips the down from its

own breast to line the nest for its young. The
natives plunder the nest; again it is lined, and
again it is plundered. Many an individual in civilized countries thus feathers his nest at the expense of this unlucky bird. There is one singular exception to the rule of honest industry; the
cow-blackbird follows the example of the European cuckoo, and, to avoid the trouble of rearing
its young, imposes the burden on others. The
American cuckoo is free from this reproach, and
actually patches up a construction, which, considering that it is honestly made, may perhaps deserve the name of a nest. But the cow-bird
lays its egg in the nests of other birds, without
much care in the selection; and when the young
foundling is hatched, it either stifles or throws
out the other young. It is difficult to account
for this strange deviation from the common order of nature.

The means of defence and security which birds
enjoy, are not the least interesting subject to
which the ornithologist's attention is directed.
Various provisions of nature are necessary to save
the weak from the strong. The structure of the
eye gives an advantage to the cannibal, as well as
to his victim, being suited in a wonderful manner
to the wants of the animal, and to the element in
which he lives. It has an apparatus, by which the
bird can push it out or draw it in, and thus adjust

it, like a telescope, to the distance of the object; the nictitating membrane covers it with a semi-transparent curtain, when it would reduce the light without closing the lid; the nerve is quick in its sensibility to every impression, and birds are thus enabled to discern insects close before them, and look abroad over miles of earth and sea. The fish-hawk sees the fish at an immense distance beneath it in the waters; and others discern their prey on the ground or flying, where a similar object would be wholly invisible to the human eye.

In order to save the nest of the smaller birds, the females are generally of a color the least likely to attract attention; the female of the brilliant Scarlet Tanager, for example, is of a yellowish green, which would not be noticed among the leaves. Some of the smaller birds borrow resolution from their danger. The graceful kingbird, whose military tastes are intimited by the red plume under his crest, will face the largest tyrant of the air; and not only crows and hawks, but even eagles, have been known to retreat before him. When the smaller birds think it unwise to do battle, they retire under hedges and brushwood, while the hawk looks after them, as the British frigates did after the little Greek corsairs, not knowing whether they had passed into the earth or the air; while they were quietly sunk near the shore, ready to float again, as soon as the danger was past.   Sometimes they rush out to meet the bird of prey, and, by crowding round him with all possible uproar, they bewilder him, in such a manner that he retreats in confusion.

Some birds are protected by their resemblance to the bark of the tree; the nighthawk and whippoorwill escape unpleasant observation in the day-time, by their resemblance to earth and stones.   The quail gives the alarm of approaching danger to her numerous family, who secure themselves by remaining quiet, and the closest search can hardly detect them, such is their likeness to the dead leaves among which they nestle.   In desperate cases, birds will put themselves under the protection of man; but they evidently consider this a choice of evils.   It is this fear of man, whom they certainly have reason to distrust, which makes it so difficult to trace the characters of many birds.   The crow in his wild state is suspicious and reserved; every string near the cornfield, seems to him like a snare; he keeps beyond the reach of a man with a fowling-piece, while he shows no fear of one who is unarmed.   When domesticated, he lays aside his solemnity, and becomes as mischievous as a monkey; showing, in all his pranks, astonishing sagacity in selecting the subject and occasion.

The voice is the power which gives most general attraction to the feathered race ; and this depends very much on the quickness of their hearing, in which respect they excel most other animals. Their lungs are large in proportion to the body, which is so formed as to receive copious admissions of air, which increases the energy of the sound. The distance at which the soaring bird can be heard is almost incredible. The cry of the eagle reaches us from his most towering height, and the wild scream of the sea-bird is distinctly heard over all the thunder of the beach. The variety of tones is not less surprising ; the common barn-door fowl, by far the most distinguished in this respect, is ludicrously *human* in its tones, which run through all changes expressive of passion, and are most eloquent in discontent, anxiety, sorrow, and despair. But the smaller birds are those which fill the forest and the garden with their spirit-like song. Their strains are poured out to swell that stream of blended melodies, which is called the voice of spring ; a voice, full of pleasing and tender associations, which comes upon the ear, reminding us of all we love to remember, and often fills the soul with rapture and the eyes with tears. No country is richer in melody than this. The European nightingale has long been considered unrivalled ; but it is now conceded, that his strain owes something of its charm to the thoughtful hour when it is heard, when the sounds of the day are over, and all is breathless and still. But the American mocking-bird, so unworthily named, since he introduces imitations of other birds into his voluntary, not from poverty of invention, but rather from wantonness, and to show how much his own power surpasses them all, seems more like a rapt enthusiast, than a performer ; as those know, who have seen him in his matins with every nerve apparently trembling with delight, and resembling St. Ignatius, who, as Maffei says, was often lifted some feet above the ground, by the intenseness and spirituality of his devotions.

These fine powers of song are not confined to one or two birds ; where the mocking-bird is never heard, there are strains, not so various and striking perhaps, but equally plaintive, original, and sweet. The clear piping of the baltimore, and the canary-like whistle of the goldfinch, are as pleasing to the ear, as their fine colors to the eye ; the glowing redbird, is not more distinguished by the splendor of his dress, than the wealth and fulness of his song. The brown thrasher excites the delighted surprise of all who hear him ; and nothing perhaps exceeds the delicious note of the warbling vireo and the red-eye, whether heard over the rattling streets of the city, or from the quiet elm that overhangs the cottage door. Every one enjoys the song of the bluebird and the robin ; in part, perhaps, because they come as heralds of the spring.

So little attention has been paid to the subject of Ornithology, that the remarks just made for the purpose of giving an idea of its attractions, will not be thought unnecessary by many readers. Mr. Bartram seems to have possessed but few works upon the subject; but he had, what was more important to Wilson, taste and judgment to assist and advise him in the pursuit to which his mind now began to be directed. Wilson's work was afterwards enriched with many of his observations, and they are often given with considerable descriptive power. For example, in speaking of the White Ibis, Mr. Bartram says, "It is a pleasing sight, at times of high winds and heavy thunder-storms, to observe the numerous squadrons of these Spanish curlews, driving to and fro, turning and tacking about high in the air ; when, by their various evolutions in the different and opposite currents of the wind, high in the clouds, their silvery white plumage gleams and sparkles like the brightest crystal, reflecting the sunbeams that dart upon them from between the dark clouds." It is easy to understand how Wilson should be interested by the example of such an observer. But, with all the respect which he paid to the opinions of his venerable friend, Wilson was not the man to rely on any observations but his own, or such as he had himself confirmed.

Mr. Bartram had been in the habit, for example, of considering the nighthawk and whippoorwill as the same bird, and Professor Barton of Philadelphia agreed with him in that opinion. Wilson, instead of considering the point as established, took pains to shoot thirteen nighthawks, all which he carefully examined and dissected. Nine were males, and four females. He found that they all corresponded in the markings and tints of their plumage, with a slight difference between the sexes. He also shot two others as they rose from their nests or rather their eggs, which are laid without much formality on the naked ground; and these were also examined and dissected. He then proceeded to shoot four whippoorwills, two males and two females, all which he examined, together with the eggs of the latter. In this way he ascertained that the whippoorwills all had bristles by the sides of the mouth, while the nighthawks had none; that the bill of the whippoorwill was more than twice as long as that of the nighthawk; and that, while the wings of the nighthawk were large and long, such as favored it in its habit of feeding in its flight, the wings of the whippoorwill, when folded, did not reach within two inches of the end of the tail. Thus Wilson satisfied himself upon the subject, and was fortunate enough to bring his friend to acknowledge that they were two distinct species of birds.

As another instance of the little respect which Wilson was disposed to pay to mere authority, his remarks concerning the torpidity of swallows during winter may be mentioned. The opinion was very general in his time, that swallows, at the approach of the cold season, plunged into mill-ponds and rivers, and passed the winter beneath the waters, whence they emerged in the spring, not drowned as might be supposed, but, on the contrary, much refreshed by their long slumber. There are papers in the Transactions of our learned societies, which show that this opinion was sustained by some enlightened observers; and even now, though it is known that swallows have organs of respiration similar to those of other birds, and though no bird is better able to encounter the labor of migration, since it collects its food while on the wing, and is never weary in its flight, there are those in many parts of this country, who are ready to die in the belief, that they bury themselves under the waters. A thousand stories are told, of vast numbers of swallows which are found in draining mill-ponds; and this circumstance is thought sufficient evidence of the fact of their submersion, though it does not appear, that the labors of any Humane Society ever restored one from this state of suspended animation, and the natural inference would be, that it was suspended for ever.

Wilson had no patience with this credulity; that this lively bird, the gayest herald of spring, should share the winter-quarters of eels and turtles, or even herd with toads and serpents on the shore, seemed to him like an enormous heresy in the religion of nature. That the chimney-swallow, in the early part of the season, had been found in great numbers in hollow trees, he did not deny; but he accounted for it satisfactorily, by supposing, that soon after their arrival, they might be chilled by the cold mornings of spring, and thus have been driven to some such retreats; but he demanded an example of one, which had been found torpid *in the winter*. Millions of trees, such as afford them shelter, have been cut down at that season, and not a single swallow has ever been found. If it were said, that they resorted to caverns, he had explored many of them, particularly the great caverns in the Barrens of Kentucky, and had conversed with the saltpetre-workers in them, but never could hear of a single swallow, which had made them the place of its winter residence. Wilson also explored hundreds of the holes of the bank-swallow, but never could find one in them in the winter, living or dead; after many researches and inquiries of the kind, he declared that he would no more believe such stories, than he would believe that there were Indians who passed the winter at the bottom of the great rivers, and came to life again every spring. Though Aristotle and Pliny in old times, and sundry modern naturalists, believed in the torpidity of swallows in trees and caves; though Linnæus had faith in their wintry submersion; though Wallerius asserted that he had often seen them, after singing a funeral dirge, embrace each other and plunge beneath the water, these great authorities were nothing to him; his experience and observation were his only guides.

The marvellous power of fascination, by which serpents were said to make birds their victims, was another popular opinion, in which he had no faith whatever. He had seen many conflicts between the cat-bird, which is the one supposed to have suffered most from this power, and the black snake, which is supposed to have exerted it; and so far from being disabled by fear, the cat-bird provoked the battle, and was often victorious. His explanation was, that serpents have a strong partiality for the eggs and young of birds, and that the nests of cat-birds, which build near the ground, are most exposed to their depredations. When the poor bird sees the snake plundering its nest, it may well exhibit the agony of despair, as it often does on less important occasions; but that it is *sucked down* from the tops of trees (which by the way it seldom visits) by the yawning mouth of the snake, he declares, is "an absurdity too great for him to swallow." He admits, that the serpent sometimes wounds birds, and that they are stunned or paralysed by the blow; and he believes, that this is sufficient to explain all the strange accounts that have been given of this imaginary power. This, as Lacepède supposes, may cause its agitation, and its helpless fall at last.

Some naturalists of high distinction at the present day are disposed to regard the subject as not quite determined, and to suppose that birds may be affected, not by any power in the serpent, but by a passion of dread; but in answer to this, it is sufficient to say, that the cat-bird is bold as a lion, and gives battle to his enemy, without the least fear of the result. Mr. Bartram witnessed an action in his garden between these two contending parties; and after the engagement had lasted some minutes, the snake was seen in full retreat. The conclusions, to which Wilson was led by his own good sense and accurate observation, are generally adopted at this time by the learned world.

It is not to be regarded as a misfortune, that Mr. Bartram's library did not abound in works on ornithology, since those which it afforded were sufficient to give Wilson an idea of the science, and to direct him in making observations for himself. Facts, not theories, were wanted; the science, in this country, presented a field almost entirely untrodden; and the best, indeed all, that the first adventurer could be expected to do, was to collect his own observations, to be corrected or confirmed by subsequent researches, as the case might be. It appears that the system of field-study was suited to Wilson's health, as well as to his improvement; for his confinement to the close air and weary routine of a village school had begun to wear upon his nerves and spirits. His Edinburgh biographer ridicules the idea of Wilson's depression, thinking doubtless, that the brilliant prospects of fortune and fame presented by a country school, would have prevented any such sinking of the heart; but, however plausible his view of the subject may be, it seems probable, that Wilson's daily associates would be most likely to know his situation. His friends say, that he was melancholy and despondent, and that this tendency was increased by his devotion to poetry and music, in which he spent most of his leisure time.

Mr. Lawson, the engraver, judiciously advised him to give up the flute and the pen for a time, and to study the art of drawing, as well adapted to his habits and inclinations, and suited to restore the health of his mind. Wilson mentioned afterwards to one of his friends, that, while he was one day rambling in the woods with his gun, it accidentally slipped from his hand, and as he attempted to recover it, the piece was cocked, and the muzzle fell against his breast, in such a manner as to endanger his life; and that he afterwards shuddered to think of the reproach, under which his memory would have labored, had he been found dead in that retired spot. This induced him to make exertions to throw off the burden from his mind; he applied himself with spirit to his new employment, copying prints of landscapes, animals, and men. For a long time, he was condemned to that misfortune, so grievous to beginners, of being compelled to laugh at his own productions; but, when he made trial with birds, he met with more encouraging success, and soon became able to execute such drawings with considerable grace and power.

That he succeeded to his own satisfaction in these attempts, appears from a note to Mr. Bartram in 1803, in which he says, " I have attempted two of those prints which Miss Nancy, [Mr. Bartram's niece] so obligingly, and with so much honor to her own taste, selected for me. I was quite delighted with the anemone, but I fear I have made but bungling work of it. Such as they are, I send them for your inspection and opinion ; neither of them is quite finished. For your kind advice towards my improvement, I return my most grateful acknowledgments." But he wrought under many disadvantages, not the least of which was the necessity of drawing by candle-light, the duties of his school consuming almost all the hours of day. He was obliged also to give up social enjoyments for the purpose of improving in his new vocation.

At first, his attention was turned to natural history in general, as appears from a letter to Mr. Bartram, in which he describes the state of his own apartment crowded with opossums, squirrels, snakes, lizards, and birds, in such numbers, that they gave it the appearance of Noah's ark, though Noah had a wife in it, and was in that respect more favored than he. While others were busy in getting money, his heart was bent on gaining a familiarity with the works of nature. Though specimens did not come of their own accord to his ark as to that of the patriarch, he found that small donations, judiciously applied, had sufficient power to attract them ; and he says, in proof of it, that one boy, knowing his taste, had brought him a whole basketful of crows. One little incident is so beautifully illustrative of his character, that it must be given in his own words. "One of my boys caught a mouse in school a few days ago, and directly marched up to me with his prisoner. I set about drawing it that same evening ; and, all the while, the pantings of its little heart showed, that it was in the most extreme agonies of fear. I had intended to kill it in order to fix it in the claws of a stuffed owl ; but happening to spill a few drops of water where it was tied, it lapped it up with such eagerness, and looked up in my face with such an expression of supplicating terror, as perfectly overcame me. I immediately untied it and restored it to life and liberty. The agonies of a prisoner at the stake, while the fire and instruments of torture are preparing, could not be more severe than the sufferings of that poor mouse ; and, insignificant as the object was, I felt at that moment the sweet sensations that mercy leaves on the mind, when she triumphs over cruelty.", Doubtless there are readers who would laugh at such feelings ; but, if they will reflect, they will see, that it is no subject of rejoicing, that they have not been created with minds and hearts, capable of sympathizing with such a man as Wilson.

It seems to have been in the year 1803, that the plan of an American Ornithology first dawned upon his mind ; not however in its full extent and magnificence, for these could hardly have entered into his wildest imaginations. He writes to a friend in Paisley, that his health had suffered from confinement, his former habits not having prepared him for the severe regularity of a teacher's life, and that, after trying various kinds of amusement, he was engaged in making a collection of the finest American birds. He first stated his plan to Mr. Bartram, who had full confidence in his ability and perseverance, but doubted whether he would find sufficient patronage or mechanical skill in the country, and could not conscientiously advise his friend to involve himself in embarrassments, which he might never be able to struggle through. Wilson also disclosed his intentions to Mr. Lawson, a name which has long been honorably associated with his own ; he also, being from his profession better qualified to judge of the practicability of the enterprise, freely stated to Wilson the precise difficulties he would have to encounter. But his objections were completely overruled by the ardor of his friend, who felt fully able to remove the obstacles that rose like mountains before him.

His Edinburgh biographer complains of this discouragement, saying that such is always the case, when ordinary men undertake to decide what men of genius are able to perform. But when Wilson was so excited on the subject, that he treated their cautions as the result of " cool, calculating, and contemptible philosophy," it was evidently the part of friendship and good sense, to let him know the measure and magnitude of the undertaking ; and, when he was poor in circumstances and depressed in spirits, to prevent his being hurried, by his enthusiasm, into efforts beyond his power. It is plain, that they encouraged him in his attention to the science, and the only question was, in what form the results could be given to the world, with the least injury to his fortunes, and the greatest advantage to his fame. He seems afterwards apprehensive lest Mr. Lawson should think him unfriendly, and takes pains to explain to him, that the passion for drawing, which he had caught from himself, consumed every moment of time, not required by the drudgery of the school. In the same communication, he begs Mr. Lawson not to *throw cold water* upon his plan of making a collection of all the North American birds ; for, visionary though it may appear, it has become a " rough bone," upon which he employs himself to fill up his vacant hours.

His letters to Mr. Bartram at this time show how fixed was his determination to proceed ; and while it is evident that their advice, under the circumstances, was such as any friend would have given, no one can help admiring the quiet confidence in his own resources, which his purpose discovers. He tells Mr. Bartram, that the face of an owl and the back of a lark have proved entirely beyond his graphic powers ; and, after having spent a week on two drawings of the last named object, he has destroyed them, and must resort again to the aid of Miss Nancy, finding it much easier to copy her painting, than to copy directly from nature. His collection of native birds, he says, is growing ; but, at the same time, he requests Mr. Bartram to write the names of all the birds upon the drawings which he sends, *since, with the exception of three or four, he does not know them.* Surely, for one, who makes this request, to be at the same time engaged in projecting an American Ornithology, would have been thought presumptuous enough, if the attempt had not succeeded.

In another letter, he offers his sympathy to that gentleman, who was suffering under a severe domestic loss. He is sorry, he says, that the misfortune has fallen on such a man, while the profligate and unthinking so often pass through life without such visitations ; but he reminds his friend, that the affliction is meant in kindness by Him who sent it ; he begs him to remember, how many beautiful flowers have withered under his eye, and how often an untimely frost has destroyed the early promise of the year ; and, while the feelings of nature cannot be repressed, the duty of man is to receive gratefully what Heaven bestows, and what it has left us, and not to mourn, as without hope, for those blessings which are taken way.

This religious feeling was not assumed for the occasion; there is evidence enough, though he was not forward to express his deeper emotions, to show, that these sentiments were familiar in his breast. In truth, he would have been unequal to his undertaking without them, both as a naturalist and as a man. For it is the glory of modern science, that it is decidedly religious in its character. The philosopher is not even satisfied with finding marks of *design* in the subjects of his investigation; he does not consider himself as acquainted with their nature, till he has sought for what he is sure of finding, some design of benevolence, such as might be expected from a merciful Father. Wilson had this qualification for his undertaking, and it is pleasing to find the same trait in Audubon, his worthy successor. In the same letter, to which allusion has just been made, he rejoices in the return of spring with its music, its foliage, and its flowers. He says that the pencil of nature is at work, and outlines, tints, and shadows, that baffle all description, will soon be spread out before the eye of man, by this unwearied kindness of his Father. He calls on his friends to look upon the millions of green strangers, just starting into life, as so many messengers, come to tell the power and greatness of

Him who made them; for himself, he says, he was always an enthusiast in such things, but now he discovers new beauties in every bird, plant, and flower, and finds his ideas of the First Cause continually more and more exalted.

As he grows more familiar with the science to which he has given his heart, his religious reverence enlarges in proportion. He says, that our ornithology, with its rich display of splendid colors, from the humming-bird with its green and gold, to the black, coppery wings of the condor, that sometimes visits our northern regions; — a numerous and powerful band of songsters unsurpassed on earth for melody, variety, and sweetness; — an everchanging scene of migrations, from torrid to temperate, and from northern to southern regions; — such a diversity in habits, forms, dispositions, and powers, each exactly suited to the wants and happiness of those that possess them; — all these circumstances, he says, "overwhelm us with astonishment at the power, wisdom, and beneficence of the Creator!"

Before proceeding to the history of Wilson's life, which here assumes a new aspect, and takes a new direction, it may be well to give a more minute account and illustration of this, and other traits of mind, heart, and character, by which he was eminently qualified for his enterprise; nor can such an account be said to interrupt the course

of a narrative, the purpose of which is, to give
as correct an idea as possible of the man. The
religious feeling, which has just been referred to,
is exhibited, not by direct expression, not by
censuring the offences of other men, but in the
most appropriate way, by gathering wherever he
can find them, and setting in as striking a light as
possible, those marks of the adaptation of the
world to its inhabitants, and again of those inhabitants to the world, which inspire admiration
and praise.

He was struck with a circumstance of this kind
in the Ruffed Grous, which is called the Partridge
in the Eastern States, while the real owner of
that name is called the Quail. In walking one
day in the woods, he started a hen pheasant with
a single young one. In common cases, the bird
flutters as if wounded, to attract the attention of
the sportsman, while the young conceal themselves in the withered leaves. But on this occasion, the parent, after fluttering before him for an
instant, suddenly sprang to the young one, seized
it in its bill, and bore it safely away, leaving him
fixed to the ground with surprise. It seemed
like an effort of reasoning, and that, too, judicious
and conclusive. If the bird had been attended,
as usual, by a large brood, it would have been
impossible to save all in this way, nor would it
have been natural to save one, leaving the rest to

die. But in this case, she adopted the most simple and effectual means to preserve the single one, that . was endangered. This effort of instinct filled him with admiration, and he probably speaks the feelings of his readers, when he says, that this affectionate parent would never have been injured by him.

Once, when travelling in Tennessee, he was struck with the manner in which the habits of the Pinnated Crous are suited to its natural residence on dry, sandy plains. One of them was kept there in a cage, having been caught alive in a trap; it was observed that the bird never drank, and seemed rather to avoid the water; but a few drops happening one day to fall upon the cage, and to trickle down the bars, the bird drank them with great dexterity, and an eagerness, that showed that she was suffering from thirst. The experiment was then made, whether she would drink under other circumstances, and, though she lived wholly on dry Indian corn, the cup of water for a whole week was untouched and untasted; but the moment water was sprinkled on the bars, she drank it eagerly as before. It occurred to him at once, that in the natural haunts of this bird, the only water it could procure was from the drops of rain and dew.

He gives yet another example, which, like the former, would form a valuable accession to a work on natural theology. It is the formation of the sheerwater's bill. This has been pronounced by some writers a "lame and defective weapon." But Wilson declares this opinion to be dictated by ignorant presumption. The sheerwater, or black-skimmer, is formed, he says, for skimming the surface of the sea for its food while flying, and in this way it collects shrimps and other small fry, whose haunts are near the surface and the shore. That the lower mandible, when thus cleaving the water, may not oppose resistance to its flight, it is thinned and sharpened like the blade of a knife; the upper mandible, which is out of the water, is not so long, but tapers gradually to a point, that, when shutting, it may offer less opposition; and it shuts into the lower, like the blade of a penknife in its handle. To prevent inconvenience from the rushing of the water, the mouth is confined to the mere opening of the gullet, and, the whole office of mastication being thus left to the stomach, it is furnished with a gizzard of uncommon hardness and power. By explanations of this kind, of which he furnishes many, he affords many beautiful examples to be added to the evidence, which now exists, of the perfection of the works of the Almighty hand.

Another characteristic, not unallied to this, and one which also qualified him in a remarkable manner for his undertaking, was the delicacy and kindness of his feeling. He regards the subjects of his art as friends, not as victims ; and, in all his writings, takes every opportunity of recommending them to the kindness and forbearance of men. The interest, which he manifested in behalf of the injured woodpecker, has already been mentioned ; this pleading is several times repeated ; he asks, why the benevolent provision of Scripture, which reserved to the ox a right in the corn which he trod out on the threshing-floor, should not be extended to these birds, which are constantly engaged, each in slaying its thousands of destructive vermin, and thus securing the field and garden from depredation. He shows that the curious perforations, which the little downy woodpecker makes in the bark of fruit-trees, are of service to its growth and bearing ; and, so far from exhausting the sap, as is commonly thought, these holes are made, never in the spring, when the sap is abundant, but late in the autumn, when it is ceasing to flow.

In favor of the orchard-oriole, he shows, that, while he destroys insects without number, he never injures the fruit ; he has seen instances in which the entrance to his nest was half closed up with clusters of apples, but so far from being tempted with the luxury, he passed them always with gentleness and caution. He enters into a deliberate calculation of the exact value of the services of the redwinged blackbird, which certainly bears no good reputation on the farm; showing, that allowing a single bird fifty insects in a day, which would be short allowance, a single pair would consume twelve thousand in four months; and if there are a million pairs of these birds in the United States, the amount of insects is less by twelve thousand millions, than if the red-wing were exterminated.

He was delighted to see the hospitality, which the Indians extended to the purple martin, hanging up gourds and calabashes to receive them; and to find, that the slaves on the plantations followed the same good example, setting up the same retreats on canes near the doors of their cabins, where the martins resorted with great familiarity.

He once encountered an old German, who accused the kingbird of destroying his *peas*. Wilson indignantly denied the charge, maintaining that they never eat a pea in their lives; but the old man declared, that he had with his own eyes seen them "blaying about the hifes and snapping up his pees." The fact of their depredations on the bee-hive he could not honestly deny; but he contends, that there is no reason why man should enjoy a monopoly of murder, and shows, that the charge comes with an ill grace from those who destroy the same insects by thousands, in order to steal the fruits of their labor. He undertakes to combat the prejudice, which is so common against the harmless cat-birds, and evidently thinks them much better members of society than the idle boys, who make it their business to destroy them. He says, that the only reason of this prejudice, ever offered to him, was, that *they hated cat-birds* ; so, he says, some will say, that they hate Frenchmen, &c., thereby showing their own narrowness of understanding and want of liberality. In his opinion, all the generous and the good will find in the confidence which this familiar bird reposes in them, in the playfulness of its manners, and the music of its song, more than a recompense for what little it destroys.

On one occasion, a wood-thrush, to whose delightful melody he had often listened, till night began to darken and the fire-flies to sparkle in the woods, was suddenly missing, and its murder was traced to the hawk, by the broken feathers and fragments of the wing ; he declares, that he solemnly resolved, the next time he met with a hawk, to send it to the shades, and thus discharge the duty assigned to the avenger of blood.

When he was on the voyage to this country, he labored to convince the seamen, that the little petrel, which walks the waters with so much more confidence than the Apostle Peter, after whom

Buffon tells us it is named, is innocent of all accession to the storm. In some cases he seems quite willing to suffer vulgar prejudices to subsist, because they are on the side of humanity. A German, whom he encountered in one of his rambles, told him, that no barn which the swallows frequented, was ever struck with lightning, and that if they were shot, the cows would give bloody milk ; he took special care not to disturb him in his superstition. He delights to approve acts of delicate humanity in others. He once, in passing through the woods, caught a young scarlet tanager, that had but just left the nest ; he carried it with him about half a mile to show it to Mr. Bartram, who placed it in a cage near the nest of some orchard-orioles, hoping that they would be induced by charity to provide it with food. They, however, thought, as men are too apt to do in such cases, that charity begins at home. It would receive no food from him, and was in a fair way to perish, when, after the lapse of several hours, a scarlet tanager, doubtless its parent, was seen trying to open the cage. Finding this impossible, it went away, and returned with food, and fed it till after sunset, when it took up its lodgings in the same tree. In the morning, it fed the young again, and continued, undisturbed by the abuse of the orioles, to do the same throughout the day, roosting at night as before.

On the fourth day, it appeared so anxious for the release of the young one, and made so many appeals to the sympathy of the naturalist, that he could not resist it ; he therefore released the prisoner, which, with songs of exultation, flew off with its parent to the woods. The happiness of the naturalist was hardly less complete. Wilson remarks, " if such sweet sensations can be derived from a simple circumstance of this kind, how exquisite, how unspeakably rapturous, must the delight of those individuals have been, who have rescued their fellow-beings from death, chains, and imprisonment, and restored them to the arms of their friends ; surely, in such godlike actions, virtue is its own most abundant reward."

Besides these qualifications for engaging with interest in the pursuit, he had other requisites for pursuing it with success. He had a strong taste for experiment ; and, as he was never willing to admit any uncommon facts, except when confirmed by his own experience, he was constantly engaged in experimental researches. Even in cases where there were no doubts in his own mind, he made experiments for the satisfaction of others. An instance of this kind is found in his account of the beautiful Carolina parrot, which is thought to poison cats, that are unfortunate enough to eat it, though it is certain that the cats betray no such apprehensions, as one might expect from an interested party. When he was at Big Bone, he wished to try the experiment, but after procuring the parrots, the cat was sent for, and was reported missing, being probably engaged in other business of the same kind. The accidental death of a tame parrot afterwards gave him an opportunity to make the trial with a cat and her kittens, which soon despatched every part of the bird that could possibly be eaten, but betrayed no signs of uneasiness, either of body or mind.

This bird seems to have been a favorite with him. He carried one with him in one of his most laborious journeys in the Western States; by day, it rode in his pocket, and at night, it rested on the baggage, dozing and gazing into the fire. Happening to catch another, which he had slightly wounded, he placed it in the cage with this, who was delighted to gain the accession to her society; she crept up to the stranger, chattering in a melancholy tone, as if expressing sympathy for its misfortunes, stroked its head and neck with her bill, and at night they nestled as close as possible to each other. On the death of her companion, she appeared inconsolable, till he placed a looking-glass near her, by which she was completely deceived. She seemed delighted with the return of her companion, and often during the day, and always at night, she lay close to the image in the glass, and began to doze with great composure and satisfaction. He was so unlucky as to lose this interesting bird in the Gulf of Mexico, where she made her way through the cage, left the vessel, and perished in the waves.

Another experiment was to ascertain, whether the young of the knavish cow-bird, which imposes its offspring on other birds, would actually receive that attention to which it was not entitled. He took a young cow-bird, which he carried home with him, and placed in the same cage with a red-bird. The cardinal examined it for some time with great intentness, and, when the young bird became clamorous for food, kindly answered its demands. When the red-bird found that the grasshopper he had brought was too large for it to swallow, he broke it into small pieces, chewed them a little to soften them, and then put them separately into the young bird's mouth. The young one, as it grew older, seemed to be grateful for this parental kindness, and acknowledged it by exerting all its powers of song, of which, however, the cardinal did not seem to have any great opinion. It seemed to Wilson, like a negro fiddler treating Handel with a touch of his art.

He tried somewhat similar experiments with a blue-jay which he accidentally caught in the woods. He put it into the cage with a gold-winged woodpecker, which almost beat it to death. He then removed it to the cage of an orchard-oriole, which seemed to consider it an intrusion, while the jay remained perfectly still. After a time, seeing the jay pick up a few crumbs very quietly, the oriole did the same; they soon entered into conversation, and became fast friends. Wilson rejoiced very much in being able to show, that the blue-jay, which rather inclines to the cannibal in its propensities, had a heart not unsusceptible of kind and affectionate impressions.

Wilson had no patience with the marvellous, where the subject admitted a more natural explanation. Mr. Heckewelder had published an account of the butcher-bird, in which he said that its well known practice of impaling insects upon thorns, was intended to offer a bait to small birds, which it makes a prey. But Wilson remarked, that it impaled small birds themselves in the same manner; and says, that to suppose the butcher-bird to be employed in this way, with such views, is like believing that the farmer hangs up dead crows, by way of invitation to the living. Grasshoppers, he says, are a favorite food of the butcher-bird, but those which these insects are thought to be intended to decoy would leave them untouched for ever.

Pennant had observed concerning the migrations of the worm-eating warbler, that it did not return by the same way it went, but took a winding course round the western mountains. On this Wilson remarks, that the bird no doubt extends its tour, supposing the fact to be established, for the purpose of finishing the education of its young by travel. He laments that the ducks and geese have never discovered what an internal improvement can be made, by leaving the shore and sailing down the Mississippi and Ohio rivers; but they never have; and, on the contrary, all the birds of his acquaintance return as they went, without varying their direction.

The impression prevailed with respect to the Carolina rail, which disappears at the first severe frost, that the bird buries itself in the mud, and some inquirers believed that they change into frogs. He was told by a person living near the mouth of James River, that his negroes had once brought in a creature which appeared neither like a rail nor a frog, but something between the two; and that he and his negroe' 'n council unanimously concluded, that it was a rail in its intermediate state between the bird and the frog. Wilson suggests that this grand discovery is fully established by the fact, that the frogs cease their vociferations as soon as the rail comes in the fall of the year. He says, however, that he was informed by a Captain Douglas, that on his voyage home from St. Domingo, when he was a hundred miles off the Capes of the Delaware, several rails came on board by night, one of which dashed through the glass of the binnacle; and many others have testified to the fact of meeting them at a great distance from the shore; so that this pleasing superstition must be abandoned, both as respects their transformation and their winter-quarters in the mud.

When singular facts can be established by competent authority, Wilson delights to repeat them. He dwells with pleasure on the bird called the tell-tale, from its friendly attention in giving notice to the ducks and other game, in time for them to escape the sportsman. So well do the ducks understand the matter, that while this bird is silent, they feed without the least apprehension; but the moment they hear its shrill cry of alarm, they retreat from danger, and the gunner retires, dolorous and malecontent, bestowing left-handed benedictions on this never-sleeping sentry.

The credulity, which gives most annoyance to Wilson, is that of Buffon, whose eloquence gives currency to his errors. He says, that the Count's eternal reference of every animal of the new world to that of the old, would leave us in doubt, whether the katy-dids of America, were not European nightingales, degenerated in voice by their residence in this country. Equally beautiful is the theory, by which Buffon accounts for the wood-thrush's deficiency of song (though our readers probably know, that it is one of our finest musicians); it has degenerated, he says, by change of food and climate, and its cry is become harsh and unpleasant, by reason of its living among savages. Dr. Latham comes in for a share of Wilson's patriotic indignation. "Blue-birds," says the doctor, "are never seen in the trees, though they make their nests in the holes of them!" "The Americans," says Wilson, "are never seen in the streets, though they build their houses by the sides of them!"

As for Wilson's earnestness in the pursuit of facts and subjects, some idea may be formed of it, from his own description of his chase of a pied oyster-catcher. Near a deep and rapid inlet in the sea-beach of Cape May, he broke the wing of one of these birds, and, having no dog with him, he pursued it himself into the inlet to which it fled. Both plunged at the same instant; but the bird being more at home in that element, escaped his grasp, and he sunk beyond his depth; on rising to the surface, he found that the fierce current was sweeping him out to sea, encumbered all the while, with his fishing apparatus and his gun; he was therefore compelled to give up the bird, and with great difficulty he escaped to the shore, which he reached in safety, though not without the loss of all his powder, in addition to his mortification, which was not allayed by seeing the bird rise and swim away with an air of unconcern.

The last of his qualifications which it is necessary to mention at present, was his power of description, which has done so much to recommend the science to his readers. His language is nervous and expressive; he apprehends so strongly, and selects so happily the circumstances most likely to interest his readers, that the attention is always arrested by the truth and beauty of his descriptions. The cedar swamps of the south, for example, took fast hold of his imagination, and he succeeds in giving to every one, a vivid impression of their desolation, wildness, and gloom. These swamps appear as if they occupied the bed of some lake or stream which has been filled up by the vegetable matter that gathers in the course of ages. The stranger sees tall trunks, straight as arrows, with their tops woven together into an impenetrable shade, rising out of the water, which takes its color from the roots and fallen leaves of the cedars which it steeps. Here the ruins of the ancient forest are heaped together in confusion; the roots, and the logs, which lie wild and disorderly, are covered with green mantling moss, while an undergrowth of laurel makes it almost impossible to force a passage through. If he attempts to advance, he is caught by the laurels, stumbles over the fallen timber, and sinks to the middle in ponds, which the green moss conceals from his sight. A few rays of broken light only struggle through the perpetual shade ; nothing but his own step breaks the deathlike stillness, except when he occasionally hears the heron's hollow scream. When a breeze rises, it sighs mournfully through the tops of the trees, till the tall cedars begin to wave and grate upon each other, producing sounds resembling shrieks and groans.

The manner in which he describes the movements of the red-wings also brings the sight and sound at once before the reader's mind. Sometimes they appear like a vast black cloud, varying its shape every moment as it drives before the storm ; sometimes they start up in the field with a noise like distant thunder, and the glittering of the vermillion upon a thousand wings produces a splendid effect to the eye ; then, sweeping down, they cover the tree-tops of a grove, and set up a general chorus, which can be heard at a great distance ; and when listened to with about a quarter of a mile between, with a slight breeze to swell the flow of its cadences, the sound is grand and even sublime.

In the same manner, he describes the large crow black-birds, which sometimes gather in such hosts that they darken the air with their numbers. They rush up, with thundering sound, from the fields, and then descending on the road, fences, and trees, cover all with black; when they gather on the boughs of a naked forest in winter, all appears hung with mourning, their notes meantime, resembling the roar of a great waterfall, swelling and dying away on the ear as the breeze rises and falls.

But while Wilson excels in the grand and solemn, he is equally excellent in the beautiful and familiar; his accounts of the domestic habits of birds, of their playful manners, their expressive music, and the traits of character by which they are distinguished from each other, are so admirable, that his great work will be the text-book of the science in our country, and none will be so ready to do justice to his excellence, as those who become eminent in the same pursuit, and are thus best able to judge of his accuracy and power.

While Wilson was thus qualified for his undertaking by his character and natural feeling, his circumstances were against him, and he attempted to find some employment, which would suit his taste better, and leave him more leisure time. He directed his attention to the "Literary Magazine," then conducted by Charles Brockden Brown, a man of talent, whose reputation would have stood very high at present, had he not been misled, by the success of Godwin, to adopt subjects and a style which enjoyed a certain degree of popularity for a time, but which no man of taste can permanently approve. The only advantage which Wilson could have proposed to himself by writing for this magazine, must have been that of making himself favorably known, with a view to some other employment; for, in the present day, the rewards of literary labor in this country are not splendid, and in those days there were none; writers by profession were soon starved into silence, and the periodical publications seemed, by a law of their being, to start into life and pass into forgetfulness, in rapid and orderly succession. Wilson published in it his "*Rural Walk*" and "*Solitary Tutor*"; but it does not appear that he received any recompense for his contributions. Mr. Ord is somewhat severe upon Dennie, the editor of "The Portfolio," for republishing the "Rural Walk," with a commendation of its beauties, which, he himself says, he found it impossible to discover. He should have remembered, that supposing the poetry to be bad, it was not the editor of a magazine abounding in poetical enormities, who could be expected to act the part of a severe critic; and the presumption is, that Dennie, who was certainly a man of literary pretensions, discovered, under the harshness of the numbers, a real poetical feeling, and a passionate love of nature, which, in his view, formed the soul of poetry, and was not to be scorned, because it dwelt in a lame and misshapen form.

It is curious to see Wilson, in a letter to Mr. Lawson, apologizing for his vanity in asking his kind offices to procure the publication of these pieces in the magazine. The sharp eye of biographical history is sometimes shut in despair as it attempts to discover the dark corners, in which men of genius counted it a privilege and honor to make a first appearance before the world. In many cases of productions given to the world, the world unhappily remains for ever in ignorance, both of the bounty and of its benefactor.

Having no great facility in versification, Wilson was embarrassed by the exactness of his observation of nature, and failed, not from want of poetical mind and feeling, but from want of easy and natural power to express them. His accuracy in matters of fact was such, that he seems to have been hardly willing to see them colored in the least by imagination. In a letter to Mr. Bartram, written about this time, he criticizes a Geography, in which it was asserted that the people of Scotland are prejudiced against swine, and eat no pork, because that animal was once the subject of demoniacal possession. The fact, according to Wilson, was, that Scotland, though abounding in pastures, was but poorly cultivated, and of course supported sheep and cattle in great numbers, while it afforded but little food for swine. It was therefore needless to go to the Scripture, to account for the origin of a prejudice which never existed. Wilson has often inserted specimens of his poetry in his ornithological descriptions; and every reader is struck with the fact, that the prose is poetical, while the poetry inclines to the prosaic; the explanation is, that he was able to express himself in prose with much greater freedom, and therefore with greater power.

It was not till October, 1804, that Wilson commenced his first pilgrimage; he set out for Niagara on foot with two companions. It was very late in the season to undertake such a journey, in what was then so desolate a country; they met with hardships which they had not expected, and, while they were still in the western region, were overtaken by winter, and compelled to proceed on their way through a considerable depth of snow. He was more persevering than the companions of his way; one of them remained with his friends near the Cayuga Lake; the other chose an easier mode of travelling; but Wilson, who was too proud and hardy to give out, went on alone, carrying his gun and baggage on his shoulders, and reached his home on the 7th of December, after an absence of fifty-nine days, in the last of which, he walked forty-seven miles.

He published an account of this journey, first in "The Portfolio," and afterwards in a separate form.   It was called "*The Foresters, a Poem,*" and had considerable merit, though strongly marked with the prevailing faults of his poetical style; some parts are written with great truth and energy, particularly the account of the schoolmaster, which was dictated by his own experience, and would appear to advantage among the strong descriptions of Crabbe. He was powerfully affected by the sight of Niagara ; and it is interesting to observe, how his favorite pursuit is associated with every striking scene. When he describes the cataract, with its stupendous column of spray, rolling up from the gulf into which it falls, and floating away in large, dark masses upon the wind, he is not so much engaged with the grandeur of the scene, as not to observe the eagle towering at an immeasurable height above, unawed by any thing but man, looking abroad over an immeasurable reach of forest, field, and sea, sailing on slow and majestic pinion, but capable of outriding the storm ; sometimes moving in graceful circles, like a dark point in the bright heaven, then bearing away with steady flight, till he is lost in the deep blue sky.

Wilson seems to have regarded this journey as a trial of strength for the hardship which he was afterwards to undergo. In a letter to Mr. Bartram, he expresses his satisfaction at the result of the experiment, saying, that, although he had just finished a journey of more than twelve hundred miles on foot, through deep snows; passing through uninhabited forests, dangerous rivers, and wild mountains; moving over rough paths by hurried marches, and exposed to all kinds of weather,— he is so far from being satisfied with what he has accomplished, or discouraged by what he has encountered, that he feels more earnest than ever to enter upon some new and more extensive expedition. He feels the most perfect confidence in his own perseverance and resolution; and, having no family to chain his affections or to suffer from his desertion, no ties but those of friendship to break; having a constitution which fatigue only hardens, a disposition sociable and familiar, and as much at home by an Indian fire in the woods as in a city apartment; having moreover the most ardent affection for his chosen country, he feels persuaded that he might do something as a traveller, both for himself and others. But his ignorance of botany, mineralogy, and other sciences, hangs like a millstone upon him, and he asks advice from his venerable friend, as to the best manner of supplying his defects and accomplishing his designs. It is worthy of remark, that when he was writing in this manner, the whole amount of his personal property was three quarters of a dollar!

It is so difficult for one who now passes through the country, to which Wilson refers in this communication, to conceive of hardships and dangers, that it would be interesting to give an account of it in his own words, did the limits of this narrative permit. He describes it in a letter to William Duncan, which begins with this characteristic remark ; " My school this quarter, will do little more than defray my board and firewood. ' Comfortable intelligence truly,' methinks I hear you say ; but no matter." Mr. Duncan had left them at Cayuga Lake, and Wilson informs him how they proceeded after their separation. He and Isaac, his remaining companion, passed the night at a miserable dram-shop, half stunned by the noise of a drunken party. They left the house at five in the morning ; stopped at Skeneateles Lake, dined on pork-blubber, and bread, and passed the night in Manlius Square, a village of thirty houses. He was obliged to sing, to drown the groans of his disconsolate companion, who could hardly make his way through the depth of snow and mud. He took every opportunity of shooting birds, and collecting information. When they came within fifteen miles of Schenectady, his companion got on board a boat, while he kept on till it was so dark that he could hardly rescue himself from the mud-holes ; and thus he persevered, till his pantaloons were matters of history, and his boots were reduced to legs and upper leathers.

On the night of his arrival, he found that a child had been named in compliment to him ; this honor cost him six dollars, and left him with the sum which has been mentioned. He gave an account of this journey in a letter to his father, which he concludes with the following words ; " I have nothing more to say, but to wish you all the comfort which your great age, and reputable, and industrious life, seem truly to merit. In my conduct to you I may have erred ; but my heart has ever preserved the most affectionate veneration for you, and I think of you frequently with tears. In a few years, if I live so long, I shall be placed in your situation, looking back on the giddy vanities of human life, and all my consolation in the hopes of a happy futurity." In Wilson's character, energy and manly tenderness were always united in their just proportions ; his tenderness never degenerated into unmeaning sentiment, nor did his uncommon energy give coldness, either to his manners or his heart.

The leisure hours of the winter succeeding this tour, seem to have been spent in preparing " The Foresters " for publication. He did however complete drawings of two birds which he shot upon the Mohawk river, and which he took much pains to preserve, supposing them to be wholly new to naturalists, though one of them, the Canadian Jay, was known before. These he presented to Mr. Jefferson, then President of the United States, who acknowledged the attention in a very civil and kind reply. There were few in this country at the time, who had attended more to ornithology than Mr. Jefferson. He had been led to it, by preparing his Notes upon the Natural History of Virginia ; but one of our common birds presented an impenetrable mystery to him, and he proposed the investigation to Wilson, as matter of curiosity. The bird, he said, was heard in every forest, singing with notes clear and sweet as those of a nightingale ; but he was never able to get a sight of it, though he had followed it for miles, except on one occasion ; when he observed that it resembled the mocking-bird in size, was thrush-colored on the back, and greyish white on the breast. Wilson needed no more to quicken him to unwearied researches, and after most diligent inquiry, it appeared, that this wonder of the wood was no other than the Wood Thrush, sometimes known by the name of Ground Robin, though it is not seen, as Mr. Jefferson says, on the tops of the tallest trees, nor does its plumage answer with much exactness to his description.

It is due to Mr. Bartram to state, that, when Wilson proposed the question to him, he sug-

gested that the Ground or Wood Robin, as it is
sometimes called, was the bird in question. It
is a little singular, that such a musician as the
wood-thrush should not have been more early
and generally known. It is retiring in its habits, it is true ; but, though a lover of solitude,
it can be found by those who search for it in
shaded hollows among the wild vines and alders.
Wilson describes its performance with his usual
beauty. He says, that, from the top of a tall tree
that rises above the deepest shade of the forest,
this bird pipes his clear notes in seeming ecstasy ;
the prelude or symphony resembles the double-
tonguing of a flute, and sometimes the tinkling of
a little bell. The whole song consists of several
distinct parts, at the close of each of which, the
voice is not sunk, but suspended ; and the close
is managed with such charming effect as to
soothe and tranquillize the mind, and to seem
sweeter and sweeter, every time it is repeated.
In dark and wet weather, when other birds are
melancholy and silent, the notes of the wood-
thrush thrill through the dropping woods, and
his song grows sweeter in proportion to the sad-
ness of the day. Though this bird had been
described by naturalists, no one had taken notice
of its melody, and Buffon, in particular, had, as
has been mentioned, applied his favorite theory,

to account for its entire want of all musical power.

But these judicious attentions, though they served to flatter and encourage him, could not supply the means for his support.   In the spring of 1805, he says, that the sum of fifteen dollars was all that he could raise from his school, consisting of twenty-six scholars.   This would not answer the purpose ; he therefore called together the trustees, and stated to them, that it was necessary for him to retire from their service. Their movement on the occasion, shows, much to his credit, that he was faithful in this uninviting employment, though his heart was all the while set upon another.   Two of them offered to pay of themselves one hundred dollars a year, rather than permit him to go ; a meeting was immediately called ; forty-six scholars were subscribed for, and he remained in his humble vocation. The embarrassment arose from the unusual severity of the winter, in which the Delaware was frozen for two months, and the poor, throughout the country, suffered much with hunger and cold.

While he was thus engaged in the essential business of securing a subsistence, he endeavored to interest others in his favorite pursuit, and many touches of his own enthusiasm appear in his letters.   He exhorts his nephew, Mr. Duncan, if he finds any curious birds, to take pains to preserve them, or at least their skins, which will answer his purpose nearly as well; and, by way of relief to his labors on his farm, Wilson begs him to keep an account of every thing that strikes him as new or interesting; he tells him, that, with the great volume of nature open before him, he can never be at a loss for amusement. "Look out," he says, "now and then for natural curiosities, as you traverse your farm, and remember me as you wander through your woody solitudes." All his correspondence with this relative expresses a strong attachment; the farm, their joint purchase, not having turned out to be profitable, Wilson wishes him to dispose of it in some way, if possible, that they might not be separated from each other. But he cautions him, not to let his desire to leave the place induce him to submit to imposition. He observes, "more than half the knavery of one half of mankind is owing to the simplicity of the other half." If his nephew is inclined to low spirits, Wilson suggests to him, that his dress, compared with that which he formerly wore, would, if tolerably well described, afford a picture that would make a mourner smile. But it is no sufficient cause for depression; for he is dressed like those about him. Wilson specially notes, that a worthy, whom he saw in that country, wore a hat which had lost every particle of the brim, which had either been eaten by rats, or cut off for soles to his shoes; but the exhibition was so common in that region, that no one took the least notice of the decoration.

He was now entered upon his profession as an Ornithologist beyond recall. The spring of 1805 saw him seriously commencing operations; and at the close of a month or two, he tells Mr. Bartram, that he has completed twenty-eight drawings of birds, either resident or occasional visiters in Pennsylvania, which he shall submit to his inspection, though he trusts they are far from being equal to his future exertions. These sketches he begs Mr. Bartram to criticize freely, since there is no one whose judgment is so valuable, and no severity will depress him. Wilson seems to have judged himself truly, when he thought, that what would be discouragements to others, would serve as so many springs to him. His letter closes with these words, so interesting when one remembers his subsequent history. "Accept my best wishes for your happiness; wishes as sincere as ever one human being breathed for the happiness of another. To your advice and encouragement I am indebted for these few specimens, and for all that will follow. They may yet tell posterity that I was honored with your friendship, and that to your inspiration they owe their existence." Posterity will be inclined to reverse the obligation, and, while it does justice to the merits of Mr. Bartram, will think that these works may be more properly said to inform the world, that Bartram was honored with the friendship of Wilson.

Having learned, that the plates for the Natural History of Edwards were prepared by the author himself, a practice which modern improvements and the example of Cuvier and Bell have rendered common of late, Wilson examined them with much attention, and succeeded in persuading himself that he could execute prints as good, and give more spirit and life to his illustrations than an engraver, who mechanically followed the drawing set before him. Mr. Lawson was of course applied to, not, as may be presumed, so much to give his advice, as to lend his aid and instruction. Having procured the tools and copper, Wilson began to learn the art of etching, with as much zeal, as if his life depended on his success. The next day, after he had taken the first lesson, Mr. Lawson was astonished to see Wilson rushing into his apartment, shouting that he had finished his plates, and they must proceed to business at once, for he must have a proof before he left town. The good-natured engraver complied with his request; the proof was furnished, and though evidently the work of an artless hand, Wilson was so

well satisfied with it, as to transmit it at once to
his oracle, Mr. Bartram.   He then proceeded
to execute another ; but his deliberate judgment
was not satisfied with the result of his labors.
The first two plates only of the Ornithology
were etched by his own hands.   He was soon
convinced, that nothing but the *graver* would
give proper effect to his illustrations.

But engraving seemed beyond his reach.   A
proposal which he made to Mr. Lawson to engage in the work with him was declined, and the
whole aspect of things was unpromising ; still, so
far from being disheartened, he solemnly declared,
that he would proceed with his plan, even if it
should cost him his life.   " I shall at least leave,"
said he, " a small beacon to point out where
I perished ! "   No one can help admiring this
manly spirit, which no failure could depress, and
no obstacle withstand.   But the close of the year
1805 found him nearly where he was when it
began ; for it appears that his second attempt at
etching was sent to Mr. Bartram, with a note
containing the wishes and salutations of a new
year.

While he was in this undecided state, and the
object was growing more dear to him, as it seemed
more difficult to attain it, every thing excited his
ardent imagination.   When in Philadelphia, he
sought acquaintance with a person, who, in 1804,

went down the Ohio, in a small batteau, with a single companion. He was told that the country was exceedingly beautiful, and that the travelling was not uncomfortable; they had an awning, and slept on board the boat, and by sailing night and day could move at the rate of seventy miles in the twenty-four hours. One solitary adventurer in a small boat, going from Wheeling to New Orleans, was the only person whom they met upon the river! Wilson wished to arrange the plan of a similar expedition, and to prevail on Mr. Bartram to bear him company; but he soon after saw by the newspapers, that a party was to be sent out by the government, to explore the valley of the Mississippi, and it occurred to him at once, that the west would be the best field for his labors. His friend agreed with him in opinion, and advised him to write an application to the President, which he would enclose in a letter of his own. This was accordingly done, and his application contains so distinct a statement of what he had already done, and what he hoped to accomplish, that the reader will not be displeased with its insertion. It was addressed to "*His Excellency*, Thomas Jefferson, President of the United States."

"Kingsessing, February 6th, 1806.

"Sir,

"Having been engaged these several years in collecting materials and furnishing drawings from nature, with the design of publishing a new Ornithology of the United States of America, so deficient in the works of Catesby, Edwards, and other Europeans, I have traversed the greater parts of our northern and eastern districts, and have collected many birds, undescribed by these naturalists. Upwards of one hundred drawings are completed, and two plates in folio already engraved. But as many beautiful tribes frequent the Ohio, and the extensive country through which it passes, that probably never visit the Atlantic states; and as faithful representations of these birds can only be taken from living nature, or from birds newly killed, I had planned an expedition down that river, from Pittsburg to the Mississippi, thence to New Orleans, and to continue my researches by land, in returning to Philadelphia. I had engaged as a companion and assistant, Mr. William Bartram, of this place, whose knowledge of Botany, as well as of Zoology, would have enabled me to make the best of the voyage, and to collect many new specimens in both those departments. Sketches of these were to have been taken on the spot, and the subjects put in a state of preservation, to finish our drawings from them, as time would permit. We intended to set out from Pittsburg about the beginning of May, and we expected to reach New Orleans in September.

"But my venerable friend, Mr. Bartram, taking into more serious consideration his advanced age, being near seventy, and the weakness of his eyesight; and apprehensive of his inability to encounter the fatigues and privations unavoidable in so extensive a tour; having, to my extreme regret and the real loss of science, been induced to decline the journey; I had reluctantly abandoned the enterprise, and all hopes of accomplishing my purpose; till, hearing that your Excellency had it in contemplation to send travellers this ensuing summer up the Red River, the Arkansaw, and other tributary streams of the Mississippi, and believing that my services might be of advantage to some of these parties, in promoting your Excellency's design, while the best opportunities would be afforded me of procuring subjects for the work which I have so much at heart; under these impressions I beg leave to offer myself for any of these expeditions, and can be ready, at short notice, to attend to your Excellency's orders.

"Accustomed to the hardships of travelling, without a family, and an enthusiast in the pursuit of natural history, I will devote my whole powers to merit your Excellency's approbation; and ardently wish for an opportunity of testifying the sincerity of my professions, and the deep veneration with which I have the honor to be,

"Sir, your obedient servant,
"ALEXANDER WILSON."

To this application Wilson received no answer, nor was he appointed to take part in the expedition; a result which appears to be highly satisfactory to his Scotch biographer, who exults in it as a proof of the indifference of republics to all scientific interests and claims. It may be doubted, whether, had Wilson written a similar application to the King of Great Britain, unsupported by influence, he would have received an answer by the next mail; but however this may be, if Mr. Jefferson was generally courteous and attentive to such applications, it is more easy to suppose, that Wilson's memorial was mislaid, or that it never reached him, than that it was intentionally neglected. No light can now be thrown upon the subject; but as all the rest of the President's intercourse with Wilson was kind and even flattering, there is no reason to suppose that the naturalist was purposely neglected on this occasion.

Wilson, as has been said, was a devoted admirer of Mr. Jefferson, and of course arranged himself with the prevailing party. But either his experience in Scotland, or his deep interest in his new pursuit, had caused him to reflect, that, while every citizen is bound to do his political duty, he will not be likely to do it any better, for giving up his heart and soul to party. His nephew consulted him upon the subject of politics; having taken charge of a school, and being probably impatient of the inactive life to which it condemned him, Mr. Duncan seems to have thought that he could give an agreeable variety to existence, by taking a more open and vigorous part in political discussion. Wilson answered him, with great good sense, that political ardor had made him so many enemies and done so little good, that he was persuaded, both for himself and his friends, that the less they harangued on that subject, the better. If they attended punctually to the duties of their profession, making their business their pleasure, and aimed, more than any thing else, at the good discipline and instruction of their pupils, they were sure to reach all the respectability and success, to which it was worth while for them to aspire.

These sentiments were highly honorable to his judgment and discretion. There are two classes of men in this country; those who take too much interest in politics, and those who take too little. The former make themselves entire slaves to party, and their minds are in such a state of fiery excitement, that they have not the least power to judge deliberately of measures or men. They deify their own leaders, and libel and slander all other men; and, while in this partial insanity, they are so little capable of discerning between right and wrong, between slavery and freedom, that they exult when some artful demagogue uses them for his own purposes, even if he holds the rein with a hand so tyranical that their bits are covered with blood. The other class are those, who are so disgusted with the atrocious violence of party, that they retreat from all interest in public men and affairs; and, like the disciples of Rousseau, weary of social evils, give up society itself as if the way to remedy evils was to let them alone. By taking this unmanly course they leave the field open to the unprincipled and usurping, and the unhappy result sometimes is, that bad men triumph, not by their own exertions, so much as by the unfaithfulness of good men to their duty.

Wilson, who was seldom wanting in right discernment, adopted the course which alone is honorable and conscientious in a private man; he took sufficient interest in public affairs to be able to know and do his political duty; and, at the same time, refused to surrender his judgment to party dictation, or to suffer party violence to set fire to his heart.

In this same letter, Wilson speaks of his application to Mr. Jefferson, expressing some surprise that the President, who was the friend of Mr. Bartram, should have taken no notice of a memorial which he had presented. "No hurry of business could excuse it." But he was not to be discouraged by this failure ; and as he and his nephew had been gaining something by their schools, he proposed that they should undertake an expedition, by themselves, through the southwestern regions. The close of this letter gives a lively idea of his situation. "I will proceed in the affair as you may think best, notwithstanding my eager wishes and the disagreeableness of my present situation. I write this letter in the schoolhouse, — past ten at night, — L.'s folks all gone to roost, — the flying squirrels rattling in the loft above me, and the cats squalling in the cellar below. Wishing you a continuation of that success in teaching, which has already done you so much credit, I bid you, for the present, good night."

Better days now began to dawn on Wilson ; better, since they placed him in a more favorable position for accomplishing his great design. Mr. Samuel F. Bradford, a publisher in Philadelphia, having undertaken an edition of Rees's Cyclopædia, Wilson was recommended to him, as a person well qualified to superintend the work, and his services were immediately secured. What recompense was offered him, is not stated. In a letter to a friend, he says that it was generous; but he gained by this engagement, what he valued far more than profit, and that was, the prospect of being able to publish his Ornithology, in a manner answering to his imaginations and desires. For, when he explained the nature and object of the work to Mr. Bradford, he readily consented to become the publisher, and to supply the funds necessary for so expensive a publication.

Wilson entered, as usual, with all his heart, upon his new labors. His situation gave him an opportunity of becoming acquainted with scientific men. Among his letters, is one recommending Michaux, the celebrated botanist, to a friend who lived near the Niagara Falls, in which he speaks of the foreigner as his friend, and solicits in his favor the desired attentions. About the same time he writes to Mr. Duncan, that the Ornithology is commenced, and Mr. Lawson is to have one of the plates completely finished on that day, April 8th, 1807. He intends, he says, to set the printer at work to print each bird in its natural colors, that the black ink may not stain the fine tints. Twenty-five hundred copies of the prospectus are to be sent to all parts of the country, and agents to be appointed in every considerable town. All possible means are to be taken to secure the success of the work, and if it brings any harvest, his friend shall share it with him.

That Wilson's new engagements did not interfere with his pursuits as an ornithologist, is sufficiently evident from his own account of himself. He says in a letter, that he went out that morning, at day-break, for the purpose of shooting a nut-hatch, wearing shoes instead of boots, for the sake of more rapid motion. After jumping a hundred fences, he found himself at the junction of the Schuylkill and Delaware, without having overtaken the bird; but not without getting completely wet, while he was flowing with perspiration. Contrary to the maxims of physicians, the prescription. he says, did him good, and he intends to repeat it on the first opportunity. He writes also to Mr. Bartram, whose image is before him, enjoying himself in his Paradise, while spring is casting her leaves, buds, and blossoms, on all around him, the birds lifting up their voices, and the zephyrs shedding fragrance from their wings. With this, he compares his own condition, immured among books, with nothing to look upon but walls and chimneys, and hearing nothing but the city's everlasting din. He concludes with the following characteristic expression; "If I don't launch into the woods and fields oftener than I have done these twelve months, may I be transformed into a street musician."

In the month of August, 1807, he left Philadelphia, and commenced a tour through the state, in which he procured many specimens and much additional information. It is evident, that he had made considerable advances, from his beginning to criticize the nomenclature of American birds, complaining of the specific name "*migratorius*," as not more descriptive of the Robin, than of any other thrush, and the term *Europæa*, as applied to the large nut-hatch, which is quite different from the European. He had thought much on the subject of these names, and was doubtful whether to introduce a new nomenclature, or sanction, by adopting, one which he did not approve.

In the month of September, 1808, the first volume of the AMERICAN ORNITHOLOGY was given to the world. The prospectus had set forth the character of the work, but no one was prepared for so fine a specimen of the arts in this country ; and really, compared with any thing which had gone before it, it might well have caused as much surprise and delight, as the magnificent illustrations of Audubon at the present day. It is matter of great regret, no doubt, but not of wonder, that it met with no greater patronage ; no taste for such luxuries had then been formed in the country ; and those who would have valued it in that light, preferred - luxuries, as expensive perhaps, but less intellectual ; while those who took an interest in the study, were generally persons, who would as soon have thought of paying the national debt, as of raising money for the purchase of such a book.

How would Wilson himself, for example, have been able to buy the work with his slender resources, had it been published by another? Had he lived longer, it would have been considered unfortunate, that he began on so large a scale. His plan was, after his great work was finished, to publish another edition in four volumes octavo, with drawings on wood like Bewick's "British Birds." As this could have been sold at one seventh part of the price of the larger edition, it would have circulated more generally, and would have tended to prepare the way for the more expensive edition; but as the greater work came first, it fell into the hands of many, who were richer in wealth than in taste; and, being thus shut up in the saloons of the affluent or in the libraries of learned institutions, it was a sealed book to most of those, on whom the naturalist must depend, to understand his merits and do justice to his name.

It is melancholy to think, that such a man as Wilson should be compelled to say, as he did in the Preface to the fifth volume, that his only recompense had been the approbation of his countrymen and the pleasure of the pursuit. But still, so far from regarding this as a reproach to his countrymen, it seems honorable to the nation that

he should have been able to publish it at all.
For, as has been said, the expense of the work
far exceeded the means of most of those, whose
taste and feeling would have led them to become
his subscribers ; while a great proportion of those,
who did subscribe, had no fondness for the science, nor even for the display of art which it
afforded ; and, on the contrary, had gathered their
wealth by trade and labor, in which they did not
learn to spend it without what was in their opinion value received.

The probability is, that most of those, who became his patrons, did so, not because they cared
to possess such a work, but because they wished
to encourage an enterprise, which they regarded
as honorable to the American name.   It would
not perhaps be too much to say, that, considering
the increased wealth of the country, the subscription for Wilson's work, was even more liberal,
than that for Audubon's at present ; and yet Wilson had no herald to go before him ; while his
distinguished successor had the benefit of all the
attraction which Wilson had given to the science,
and of many pleasing associations, all tending to
secure him the patronage which his talents and
exertions deserve.

One of the greatest pleasures connected with
the publication of this first volume, was that of
transmitting it to his friends in Europe, of whom

he was never forgetful, either in prosperity or sorrow. His Scotch biographer furnishes a letter, addressed to his father at the time, in which he speaks with great satisfaction of the result of his labors, but seems at a loss to know whether he should lose or gain by the work in a pecuniary point of view. He says, that he has spent all he had in giving existence to the first volume; but he has met with an honorable reception from men whose good opinion he was ambitious to gain, and has collected information to such an amount as will secure to his work *at least* the credit of originality. In the close of the letter, he earnestly desires to be remembered to his old companions, whom he never expects to see again. "I would willingly," he says, "give a hundred dollars to spend a few days with you all in Paisley; but, like a true bird of passage, I would again wing my way across the western waste of waters, to the peaceful and happy regions of America. What has become of David, that I never hear from him? Let me know, my dear father, how you live, and how you enjoy your health at your advanced age. I trust the publication I have now commenced, and which has procured for me reputation and respect, will also enable me to contribute to your independence and comfort, in return for what I owe to you. To my step-mother, sisters, brothers, and friends, I beg to be remembered affectionately."

In the latter part of September, 1808, Wilson set out on a tour to the Eastern States, to exhibit his work, and procure subscribers. He did not undertake the expedition with a very light heart; for he was well aware, that the bearer of a subscription paper is seldom welcomed with rapture, and for a man like him to plead his own cause to the indifferent or the insolent, was a severe and painful trial. Still, as it was necessary, he did not shrink from the undertaking; but he fears lest he shall make the discovery, that he has bestowed a great deal of labor and expense to very little purpose.

One thing consoled him under his darker anticipations; it was, that he should see the glorious face of nature, and gain more familiarity with her admirable productions. He did not mean to sit with folded hands, waiting for circumstances to favor his enterprise; if he could get nothing else by his tour, he could increase his knowledge; and accordingly he tells us, while on his journey, that he has established correspondents, like pickets and outposts, in every corner of the northern regions, so that scarcely a wren or a tit shall be able to pass from York to Canada, without immediate intelligence being conveyed to him. In the patronage which he received, he was certainly disappointed; but, discouraging as it was, he ascribed it to the right cause; and allowed himself to be gratified, as well he might, with the expressions of admiration which he heard in every quarter. These were from men of taste and literature, to whom it was as much matter of regret as to him, that they had nothing but this kind of encouragement to bestow.

The manner, in which he proceeded on these occasions, appears in his account of his visit at Princeton and other places. He put copies of his prospectus in his pocket, took his book under his arm, and went to wait on the doctors of the College. He found Dr. Smith, the President, and Dr. McLean, the Professor of Natural History. In Newark and Elizabethtown, the same process was repeated; and in each he found a few subscribers and many admirers. In New York he received much kind attention from the professors of Columbia College, particularly from one, a Scotchman, whose name was Wilson. He spent his time in traversing the streets from one house to another, till he could perceive gentlemen pointing him out, as he passed with his book under his arm, and he believed that he was as generally known as the town-crier. The business of exhibiting his work to so many who declined subscribing, became very wearisome, and often called forth expressions of impatience in his letters. He never could endure the least appearance of disrespect, while the character in which he appeared, was not likely to secure for him a flattering reception where his merits were not known; and at this time they were of course known to very few.

On the 2d of October, he left New York for New Haven, and after a boisterous passage from morning till night, he saw the red-fronted mountain rising upon his view. In two hours more he landed, and perceived that it was the sabbath by the stillness and desertion of the streets, the confusion of the packet-boat having made him forget the day. He was told by one of the professors of the College, that the wooden spires which rise from the common, were once so infested by woodpeckers, which bored them through in all directions, that it became necessary, in order to save them from destruction, to station men with guns, to shoot the invaders. He gives no information as to his success in New Haven.

After remaining a day and a half in that city, he proceeded to Middletown; and, on entering the town, he had the satisfaction of witnessing a scene, which has now lost its original brightness, and will in a few years, it may be hoped, only survive in description. The streets were filled with troops, and the sides decorated with wagons, carts, and wheelbarrows, filled with roast beef, fowls, bread and cheese, and not wanting in liquors of all descriptions. Some were crying, "Here's the best brandy you ever put into your head!" an uncommonly accurate physiological account of the part to which that fluid goes; others more harmlessly employed, in recommending their "round and sound gingerbread," making up what was wanting in its quality by double vociferation. In one place, a ring was formed, in which many were dancing to the energetic scraping of an old negro, while the spectators looked on with as much gravity, as if they were listening to a sermon; a state of things, which to a British traveller would have proved their entire want of feeling, but to a common observer would have shown that they were not inclined to laugh, except when the jest was good enough to justify such emotion. In Middletown, he became acquainted with a gentlemen, whose tastes were similar to his own, from whom he received a present of several stuffed birds, and letters to gentlemen in Boston.

On reaching Hartford, he received attention from several gentlemen, who gratified him by subscribing for his work. The publisher of a newspaper also gave him aid in his own way, which, Wilson says, would neither buy plates nor pay the printer, but was nevertheless gratifying to the vanity of an author, *when nothing better was to be had*. He was too late in the season, to see the most favorable aspect of nature, and accordingly was not much delighted with his impressions.   His observations in one respect are curiously contrasted with the present state of things ; he saw no coin in New England ; bills, some of so low a denomination as twenty-five cents, were the only currency.   As for the schools, judging from the outside appearance, which is the general rule with travellers, he did not believe that the state of education was very high.

As he came near Boston, he was struck with a visible improvement ; the roads became wider ; the stone fences gave way to posts and rails, and every thing denoted an improved state of civilization.   His enthusiasm was great, as he approached Bunker's Hill ; no pilgrim, he said, ever approached the tomb of his prophet, with more awful enthusiasm, than he felt as he drew near to that sacred ground ; and great was his wrath, to find that a wretched pillar of brick, was the only memorial of those who had shed their blood for their country.   Happily, others, since that time, have felt the same emotions, and the matter is now in a fair way to be amended.

His feeling with respect to Bunker's Hill is too illustrative of his character to be passed over. Hardly had he arrived in Boston, before he ascended a height, in order to see this celebrated hill; and, as soon as it was pointed out to him by a stranger, he began to explore his way to Charlestown. There he was astonished and hurt at the indifference, with which the inhabitants directed him to the spot, without reflecting at the moment on the natural effect of familiarity. He inquired, if there was any one living who had been engaged in the battle, and was directed to Mr. Miller, who had been a Lieutenant in the action. Wilson introduced himself without ceremony, shook hands with him, and told him that he was proud of the honor of meeting with one of the heroes of Bunker's Hill, speaking with warmth and with his eyes suffused with tears. They proceeded together to the place, taking with them another who had also been engaged in the service of that day. With these veterans, he spent three hours upon the field; the most interesting, he says, which he had ever passed in his life. As they pointed out to him the course by which the British came up from the water, the poor defences of the Americans, the place where the action was warmest, and the memorable spot where Warren fell, he felt as if he himself could have encountered an army in the cause of the free. The old soldiers were delighted with his enthusiasm, and, after drinking a glass of wine together, they parted with regret.

He passed on through the Eastern part of Massachusetts and New Hampshire, stopping at every place, where he thought himself likely to meet with any success. He went as far in this direction as Portland, where, the Supreme Court having assembled many visiters, he had the opportunity of gaining information with respect to the eastern birds. While in Portland, he enjoyed a pleasure, to which he was not accustomed; it was that of hearing a prize song, which he had written for the national celebration, read from a newspaper by one of the company, and much applauded by the hearers, who did not know that the author was so near them. From Portland, he proceeded across the country, which he described as wild and savage, with rocks and stones in all directions, grinning horribly through trunks of half-burned trees. At last he reached Dartmouth college, where the officers were extremely obliging and attentive, particularly the president, Dr. Wheelock, who subscribed for the work, as the presidents of all the other colleges had done.

While at New York, Wilson had the curiosity to call on Paine, the author of the "*Rights of Man*," whom he found at Greenwich, at a short distance from the city. He found him in the only tolerable apartment of an indifferent house, sitting in his nightgown, at a table covered with newspapers and materials for writing. Wilson seems to have been struck with the brilliancy of his countenance, which answered to his imagination of Bardolph, even more than with the glow of his conversation. Paine examined his book with great attention, and entered his name as a subscriber. This was in the close of Paine's life; he was then at the age of seventy-two; and the burden of years was rendered ten times heavier by his habits; besides, his attacks upon religion had driven many from his society, and left him in a wretched solitude; he died in the succeeding year, leaving a name and remembrance which few delight to honor.

Wilson's want of success, though it did not discourage him, gave a gloomy tone to his observations while on his journey. After travelling about with his book, as he says, like a beggar with his bantling, from one town to another; after being loaded with kindness and praise, and shaken almost to death in stage-coaches; after telling the same story a thousand times over, he writes to Mr. Lawson from Albany, that for all the compliments which he received, he was indebted to the taste and skill of the engraver. He says, " The book in all its parts so far exceeds the ideas and expectations of the first literary characters in the eastern section of the United

States as to command their admiration and respect. The only objection has been the sum
of one hundred and twenty dollars, which, in innumerable instances, has stood like an evil genius,
between me and my hopes. Yet I doubt not,
but when those copies subscribed for are delivered, and the book a little better known, the
whole number will be disposed of, and perhaps
encouragement given to go on with the rest.
To effect this, to me most desirable object, I
have encountered the fatigue of a long, circuitous,
and expensive journey, with a zeal that has increased with increasing difficulties; and sorry
I am to say, that the whole number of subscribers which I have obtained, amounts only to *forty-
one.*"

His American biographer is severe upon his
countrymen, for not affording more liberal support to this undertaking: It is certainly a misfortune that taste does not always fall to the lot
of those who have wealth to indulge it; but such
is the case, and to most persons then in New
England, the want of one hundred and twenty
dollars, was a difficulty not easily to be overcome,
whether they wished to devote it to this purpose
or any other; and it must be remembered, that
there was no taste for ornithology then existing;
the professor of one of the colleges, from whom
he hoped to receive information in natural histo-

ry, did not know a sparrow from a woodpecker. Wilson was obliged to form the very taste on which he depended for encouragement, and this was a work of time. In the present day, so equally is prosperity diffused, there are ten who would wish, to one who can afford to buy the American Ornithology; in his day the number must have been much less of those, who possessed either the desire or the ability to indulge it.

If his subscription in the Northern States was inconsiderable, his success at the South was not greater. After remaining at home a few days, he commenced a tour in that part of the Union. He writes from Washington, December 24th, 1808, that he was fortunate enough to procure sixteen subscribers in Baltimore. At Annapolis he passed his book through both branches of the legislature then in session; but, after deliberate examination, the *noes* were many, and the *ayes* none. He pursued his way through tobacco fields, sloughs, and swamps, to Washington, a distance of thirty-eight miles; and he has recorded, that he was obliged to open fifty-five gates on the way, each one compelling him to descend into the mud to open it. The negroes were so wretchedly clad, that he was wholly at a loss to know, to what name their garment was entitled; but as often as he made inquiries at their huts, both men and women gathered their rags about them, and came out very civilly to show him his way.

The city of Washington was not in its most palmy state at that time. Wilson says, that the only improvement then going on was the building of one brick house. In this respect there is a change; but in some others the place retains its former character. Wilson remarked, that the taverns and boarding-houses were crowded with placemen, contractors, office-hunters, and adventurers of that description; and, among others, were deputations of Indians, come to receive their last alms from the President, before he retired from public life. He was kindly received by the President, to whom he paid his respects; they conversed much on the subject of Ornithology; and Mr. Jefferson gave him a letter to a person in Virginia, who had spent his life in the study of birds, and from whom he intended to have gathered much information; but his engagements would not permit, and he entrusted the commission to Wilson.

He went from Washington to Norfolk, where he found better success than he expected, but could not sufficiently lament the aspect of the streets; though, according to his own account, they were in a state of improvement, since, not long before, the news-carrier delivered his papers from a boat, which he forced through the mud with a pole; and a party of sailors, having nothing better to do, launched a ship's long-boat in the streets, rowing through the mud with four oars, while one stood at the bow, engaged in heaving the lead. This story would seem to belong to the Apocrypha, or rather to a kind of history, by which the accounts of travellers are sometimes requited, with narratives more amazing than their own.

In his way to Suffolk, he lodged at the house of a planter, who informed him, that almost all his family were attacked every year with bilious fever in the months of August and September, and that, of thirteen children, he had lost all but three. One would suppose that nothing but the hope of following them, could have detained him in such a place of death. Farther on, he came to a place called *Jerusalem*, where he found the river swollen to an extraordinary height. After passing the bridge, he was conveyed in a boat, called a *flat*, nearly two miles through the woods. When he left the boat, he was obliged to wade and swim his horse, breaking the ice as he went on, no luxurious employment for a traveller in the depth of winter.

According to him, the habits of the natives of this region, were not such as to atone for the unkindness of nature. The first operation in the business of the day, was drinking a preparation of brandy, which they said was the only thing that would secure them from the ague. It was often a subject of wonder to those among whom Wilson was thrown, to find how lightly he esteemed the concerns of eating and drinking, particularly the latter. The most vigorous advocate of temperance at the present day, could not make more determined war on ardent spirit in all its forms, than he, though his pursuits were of a kind most likely to betray him into such means to counteract the effects of toil and exposure.

With the accommodation afforded by the public houses Wilson was by no means delighted. Those in this region were desolate and wretched; with bare, bleak, and dirty walls ; one or two old chairs and a bench forming all the furniture. Every thing was conducted by negroes, the white females not deigning to appear. The fragrance of the establishment was such, that it would be wronged by any attempt to describe it, and the meals were so served up, that the appetite of a wolf would have shrunk back in dismay. These hospitable mansions were raised from the ground, on posts, leaving a retreat below for the hogs, which kept up a serenade all night. This country abounded in these animals ; one person would sometimes own five hundred. The leaders were distinguished with bells, and each drove knew its particular call, whether it were the sound of a conch or the bawling of a negro, at the distance of half a mile.

He crossed the river Tar at Washington, in North Carolina, for Newbern, where he found the shad fishery begun, as early as the fifth of February. From Newbern to Wilmington, one hundred miles, he found but one public house open on the whole way, two landlords having been broken up by the fever. The principal features of North Carolina were the dark, solitary pine savanna, through which the road wound among stagnant ponds, swarming with alligators; the sluggish creek with water of the color of brandy, over which is thrown a high wooden bridge without railings, often so crazy and insecure, as to alarm both the horse and the rider, and make it a miraculous escape to go *over*, instead of going *through*; and the immense cypress swamp, the very picture of dreariness and ruin. The leafless limbs of the cypresses were covered with long moss (*Tillandsia usneoides*) from two to ten feet long, and so abundant that fifty men could be concealed under it in the same tree. Nothing seemed more extraordinary, than to see thousands of acres covered with such timber, with its drapery waving in the wind. He attempted to penetrate some of these swamps in search of birds; but, in most instances, he was obliged to give up the attempt in despair. He could, however, explore their borders, in which he found many birds which never spend the winter in Pennsylvania.

It was in vain that he attempted to find an alligator, though he heard many stories of their numbers, and the havoc which they made among the pigs and calves of the farm. He saw a dog at the river Santee, which betrayed no fear of these animals, but would swim across the river whenever he pleased, without consulting their pleasure; if he heard them pursuing him in the water, he would turn and attack them, seizing them by the snout, in a manner which compelled them to retreat in confusion; generally dogs regard them with extreme dread. Mr. Ord was accompanied by a strong spaniel in a tour in East Florida; one day, while wading in a pond with his dog swimming behind him, the dog smelt an alligator, and immediately made for the shore and fled into the woods, whence no persuasions could induce him to return.

Wilson was not much pleased with the inhabitants of this region; and in general it may be said, that he does not see the "happiest attitudes of things;" this was owing doubtless to the business in which he was engaged, that of collecting subscriptions. Till he had explained his own share in the work, those to whom he offered it would naturally have confounded him with the common herd of such adventurers, and perhaps have treated him with very little attention. From Wilmington he rode as before through cypress swamps and pine savannas, sometimes thirty miles without seeing a habitation or a human being, making his course circuitous, in order to visit the planters, who live on their rice plantations among their negro villages. He found their hospitality so great and the roads so bad, that it seemed impossible to get away from a house when he had once entered it.

His horse began to be so exhausted by the continual exertion, that he was obliged to exchange him for another. He proposed to a planter to exchange, giving his horse at least as good a character as he deserved; the planter asked twenty dollars to boot, and Wilson thirty. They could not agree; but Wilson, perceiving that the planter had taken a fancy to his horse, rode on. The planter, as he anticipated, followed him to the sea-beach, under pretence of pointing out the road, and there they came to terms. Wilson found himself in possession of an elegant, powerful horse, that ran away with him at once upon the shore. The least sound of the whip made him spring half a rod, and even the common fare of horses in that region, which was like the rushes with which carpenters sometimes smooth their work, did not produce the least abatement of his fury. Several times the steed came near breaking his new master's neck, and at Georgetown he threw one of the boatmen into the river. But Wilson readily forgave him these offences in consideration of his fleetness.

He accorded more praise to Charleston than was usual with him, though in this case he was extremely sparing; and he intimates that his familiarity with the streets of these cities, through which he walked his unpromising rounds, was one reason of his want of enthusiasm in his applause. The town, he said, was clean and gay in its aspect, with a market, which in neatness far surpassed the boasted one in Philadelphia. The streets crossed each other at right angles, having paved walks at their sides, and a low bed of sand in the middle. They were blackened with negroes, whose quarrels sometimes disturbed the peace of the high-way. In one of the streets was an exhibition, which would have equalled any one on earth for a comic painter, containing female chimney-sweepers, stalls with roasted sweet potatoes for sale, and clubs of blacks, sitting round fires, cooking their victuals, all joyous and light-hearted as if they lived in the golden age.

In the beginning of March, he was pursuing his labors in Savannah, with no very flattering promise of success. When he wrote from this place, he complained that those, who had promised to furnish him in Charleston with lists of persons to whom he should apply, had put him off from day to day, till he was obliged to go forth, and judge as well as he might from the appearance of the houses. Those to whom he had been recommended, did not give him the least aid; but the keeper of the library, a Scotchman, made out a list for him, which considerably abridged his labors. With the exception of this neglect on the part of one or two, he was pleased with the inhabitants of that city. Hearing of General Wilkinson's arrival, Wilson waited on him, and received from him his subscription, his money, and his unbounded praise.

On the way from Charleston to Savannah, he had nearly lost his horse, which, from impatience, threw itself overboard, and was rescued only by the great and dangerous exertions of its master. On this journey, he met with the Ivory-billed Woodpecker, a large and powerful bird. He wounded one slightly in the wing; on being caught, it uttered a constant cry, resembling that of a young child, which so frightened his horse, that it nearly cost him his life. The cry was so distressing, that, as he carried the bird, covered in his chair, through the streets, people hurried to the windows and piazzas, to see whence it proceeded. As he drove up to the tavern, the landlord and bystanders were much disturbed by the sound, nor was their perplexity diminished by Wilson's asking for lodgings for himself and his baby. After amusing himself awhile with their conjectures, he drew out the bird, which was welcomed with a general shout of laughter. He took the woodpecker up stairs, and locked him in a chamber, while he went to give directions concerning his horse. In less than an hour, he returned; and, on opening the chamber, the bird set up the same cry of surprise and sorrow, that he had returned so soon; for it had mounted at the side of the window, and a little below the ceiling, had commenced breaking through. The bed was covered with large pieces of plaster, the lathing was exposed in a space fifteen inches square, and a considerable hole beaten through the lathing, to the weatherboards; so that, had not Wilson returned, it would soon have released itself from bondage. He then tied a string to its leg, that it might not reach the wall, and after fastening it to a mahogany table, left it again to find some suitable food. When he returned, he found that it had turned its rage against the table, which it had entirely ruined, with blows from its powerful bill. While Wilson was drawing it, it cut him in several places, and displayed such an invincible spirit, that he was often tempted to restore it to the woods. It refused all food, and lived but three days after.

Wilson was much disgusted with the indolence, which slavery produces among the whites in the Southern States. The carpenter, bricklayer, and even the blacksmith, he says, stand, with their hands in their pockets, overlooking their negroes. The planter orders his servant, to tell the overseer, to have the stranger's horse taken care of; the overseer sends another negro to tell the driver to send one of his hands to do it. Long before this routine of ceremony is gone through, the traveller, if he cares for his horse, has already given him the requisite attention. He was also displeased with the cold and melancholy reserve, or indolence of manner, which prevailed among the females, almost without exception. Their silence was embarrassing to a stranger, who could not possibly tell whether it proceeded from bashfulness or aversion.

He found it no easy matter, to follow the motions of the higher class of society. At nine, they were in bed, — at ten, breakfasting, — dressing at eleven, — at noon gone out, and not visible again till the next morning. The climate did not please him much better. When in Savannah, though it was so early in the spring, the thermometer, he said, ranged between seventy-five and eighty-two. To him, it was more oppressive than midsummer in Philadelphia. The streets, he said, were beds of burning sand; and, till one learned to traverse them with his eyes and mouth close shut, both were filled at intervals with whirl-winds of drifting sand.   He was fortunate enough, to meet in Savannah with Mr. Abbot, a naturalist, who had published a volume in London, upon the Insects of Georgia.   He had resided in the state more than thirty years, and, being an accurate ob-server, was qualified to afford Wilson that kind of information which he was most desirous to gain.

Whether Wilson's observations were not, in many instances, colored by the state of his feel-ings at the time, may reasonably be doubted. It was so in New England, and probably was so in the Southern States.   What other mortal ever discovered that the Yankees were a lazy people? The sins, with which that much-enduring race have been charged, have always been of precisely the opposite description.   In New England, he saw fields covered with stones, scrubby oaks and pine trees, wretched orchards, scarcely one field of grain in twenty miles, the taverns dir-ty, miserable, and filled with brawling loungers, the people snappish and extortioners, lazy, and two hundred years behind the Pennsylvanians in all agricultural improvements.   There are not many, with the exception perhaps of British travellers, who could recognise, in the elements of this dismal vision, a description of New England. These things, no doubt, may be seen in New England, as well as elsewhere ; but the whole aspect of things is not so melancholy as this, which would almost make the angels weep.

When, at Savannah, he was making arrangements for his return, he summed up the results of his journey, saying that it was the most arduous and fatiguing he ever undertook. He had succeeded in gaining two hundred and fifty subscribers in all, for his ORNITHOLOGY, but they were obtained, he said, at a *price* worth more than five times their amount. In this estimate he includes, of course, his expense of labor and feeling. He now feels as if he had gained his point through a host of difficulties ; and, should the work be continued in a style equal to that of the first volume, he believes that the number of copies may be safely increased to four hundred. He has endeavored to find respectable persons, who will undertake to distribute the work in various towns, receiving as their recompense, only the privilege of first selection ; but the greatest benefit derived from his tour consists in the great mass of information which he has obtained, concerning the birds that winter in the South, and some that never visit the Northern States ; and, as all this information has been collected by himself, he feels that it may be trusted. He says, that he has seen no frost since the 5th of February ; the gardens are green and luxuriant, full of flowering shrubbery, and

orange-trees loaded with fruit ; but, now, he begins to feel the full melody and expression of the
word *home;* more deeply perhaps, on account of
the dangers, hardships, insults, and impositions,
which he had just passed through.   He was
advised to go to Augusta, where he was told that
he could get fifteen subscribers ; but he thought
that this number would not compensate for the
additional expense and trouble ; and, as his means
were running low, and his health was not firm,
he chose rather to take passage by sea for New
York, where he arrived in March, 1809.

Only two hundred copies of the first volume
of the ORNITHOLOGY had been printed ; but it
was thought advisable to strike off three hundred
more.   Meantime the preparation for the second
volume went on vigorously amidst his other labors, and consumed the residue of the year.   On
the 4th of August, he writes to Mr. Bartram, that
it is ready to go to the press, and he is desirous to
know, whether his friend cannot add something to
his information respecting the birds that are to
appear in the number.   He had himself collected
all the particulars which he could possibly gather
by inquiry and personal observation ; but he was
desirous that nothing should be wanting ; and, if
he could secure the approbation as well as aid of
a distinguished naturalist, it would help the success of the publication.   He had received draw-

ings of birds from many parts of the United States, and the presents were accompanied with offers of more ; but, though he was grateful for the attention of those who sent them, they were seldom executed with sufficient accuracy and precision.

Wilson claimed the honor of being a volunteer in the pursuit ; he never had received from it one cent of profit ; and the engraver, Mr. Lawson, was so ready to share in the sacrifice, that his recompense for his labor, such was the time spent in giving finish to the plates, did not exceed fifty cents a day. From the letter just referred to, it appears that Wilson kept up a correspondence with Michaux ; he mentions having just heard from him, that he has not yet received the appointment of inspector of the forests of France, so much was Bonaparte engaged in other undertakings which were more acceptable perhaps, but much less beneficial to his country.

The second volume of the ORNITHOLOGY appeared in January, 1810 ; and hardly had it left the press, before Wilson proceeded to commence a journey to the West. He had been making arrangements, for some time, in preparation for this expedition, endeavoring to ascertain in what manner he could travel to most advantage. He seems to have had some prospect of securing the company of Mr. Bartram ; for we find him offering to proceed, in the way that his friend thinks best. But he was compelled, as usual, to go on his journey alone, without a companion to assist him in his observations, and to relieve the weariness of the way.

From Pittsburg, he wrote to Mr. Lawson, giving him some account of the first stages of his expedition. He tells him, that on arriving at Lancaster, he waited on the governor and other public officers. The former, who seemed to be an unceremonious, plain, and sensible man, praised the volumes and added his name to the list. With the legislators he was much less delighted, finding them, as he says, " a pitiful, squabbling, political mob ; — split up, justling about the forms of legislation, without knowing any thing about its realities." But he was fortunate enough to find in this wilderness some friends to science, by whom he was very kindly treated. In Columbia, he spent one day to no purpose ; after cutting his way through the ice of the Susquehannah, he went to York, where he met with no better success. Not far from this latter place, he saw a singular character, between eighty and ninety years of age, who had subsisted by *trapping* birds and other animals for thirty years. Wilson secured his good graces, by the present of half a pound of snuff, which the old man took by the handful ; and he then exhibited to him the plates of the ORNITHOLOGY, much to the anchorite's amazement and delight. He was acquainted with all the birds of the first volume, and nearly all of the second. Wilson endeavored to secure the particulars of his life, together with a representation of his person; and he doubtless would have made an agreeable figure in a narrative, similar to those which Audubon has so happily introduced into his work.

In Hanover, he encountered one of those persons, whose vulgar insolence he could never endure with the least serenity. A certain judge in that place told him, that such a book as his ought not to be encouraged, because it was not within the reach of the *commonality*, and therefore was inconsistent with republican institutions. Wilson admitted the force of the objection, and proved to him, that he himself was a gross offender, inasmuch as he had built such a large, handsome, three-story house, as was entirely beyond the reach of the *commonality* and therefore outrageously inconsistent with republican institutions. This was placing the subject in a new point of view; but Wilson was not satisfied with imparting a single ray of light to the darkness of such a mind; he talked seriously to the man of law, pointing out to him the importance of science to a rising nation, and with so much effect, that he began to show signs of shame.

On the 11th of February, he left Chambersburg, and soon began to ascend the Allegany mountains, where nothing appeared but prodigious declivities, covered with woods, and where there was silence so profound as to make the scene impressive and sublime. These high ranges continued as far as Greensburg ; thence to Pittsburg he found nothing but steep hills and valleys, descending toward the latter place. He was much struck with the distant view of the town. Within two miles of it, the road suddenly descended a steep hill, and the Allegany River was seen stretching along a rich valley, and bounded by high hills toward the west. While he was yet distant from the town, he saw the cloud of black smoke above it. As they entered, it appeared like a collection of blacksmiths' shops, brew-houses, furnaces, and glass-houses. The ice had just given way in the Monongahela, and was coming down in vast masses ; the river was lined with *arks*, sometimes called Kentucky boats, which were waiting for this movement, in order to descend the stream. He thought that the town, with its vessels, its hills, its rivers, and the pillars of smoke towering in the air, would afford a noble perspective view. He was exceedingly impressed with what he saw, and often regretted that his friends were not with him, to enjoy the spectacle of mountains, of expanded rivers, of deep forests and meadows, which everywhere stood before his eyes.

He succeeded, beyond his expectation, in gaining subscribers in Pittsburg; and after ascertaining that the roads were such as to render a land journey impossible, he bought a small boat, which he named the *Ornithologist*, intending to proceed in it to Cincinnati, a distance of more than five hundred miles. Some advised him not to undertake the journey alone; but he had made up his mind, and only waited, exploring the woods in the interval, till the ice had left the stream.

When Wilson had fairly embarked in this adventure, his account of his journey grows very interesting, and would be more so, could it be given in his own words; but this would interfere with the unbroken narrative, which the character of our undertaking requires. His descriptions can be compared with the same region, as it is described by those who visit it now, and the imagination is almost bewildered at reflecting what a quarter of a century has done.

From Lexington in Kentucky he wrote again to Mr. Lawson on the 4th of April. He says, that the plan of proceeding by water was so convenient for his purpose, that he disregarded what was said by those who advised him against it. Two days before his departure, the river was full of ice, from which he apprehended some interruption. His provisions consisted of some biscuit and cheese, and a bottle of cordial, given him by a gentleman in Pittsburg; one end of the boat was occupied by his trunk, great coat, and gun; he had a small tin vessel, with which to bale his boat, and to drink the water of the Ohio. Thus equipped, he launched into the stream. The weather was calm, and the river like a mirror, except where fragments of ice were floating down. His heart expanded with delight at the novelty and wildness of the scene. The song of the red-bird in the deep forests on the shore, the smoke of the various sugar camps rising gently along the mountains, and the little log-huts, which here and there opened from the woods, gave an appearance of life to a landscape, which would otherwise have been oppressively lonely and still.

He could not consent to wait the motion of the river, which flowed two miles and a half an hour; he therefore stripped himself for the oar, and added three miles and a half to his speed. He passed several *arks*, containing miscellaneous collections of men, women, children, horses, and ploughs, flour and millstones; some of them being provided with counters, from which these amphibious pedlers sold their goods, in the settlements, which they passed through.

So completely have the steam-boats swept the rivers, that these primitive vessels are hardly to be found at the present day, except in description. They were built after the form of the ark of Noah, as it was represented in old Bibles; being a parallelogram, from twelve to fourteen feet wide, and from forty to seventy long, rowed by two oars at the sides, and steered by a long and powerful one behind. They were forced up the stream along the sides, at the rate of twenty miles a day. Vessels of this description poured down the Ohio, from all its tributary streams, such as the Allegany, Monongahela, Muskingum, Scioto, Miami, Wabash, and Kentucky, bound to various parts of the country below.

This scene in 1810 showed a prodigious developement of activity and enterprise since 1804, when, as has been related, a person who descended the Ohio, met but a single voyager, in a small boat, in the whole length of the stream; but even this has been completely eclipsed by the history of succeeding years. In the beginning of 1817, ten steam-boats had been set in motion on the western waters; and in that year, there were public rejoicings on account of a passage, which had been made in twenty-five days, from New Orleans to the Falls of the Ohio. At present, a steam-boat ascends from New Orleans to Cincinnati in ten days. The number of boats in commission amounted, in 1832, to two hundred. This wonderful application of science to the arts of life has caused the western wilderness to rejoice; the work of centuries has been crowded into a few years; the axe rings on the banks of every river; the fire clears a path through the ocean of wood; the village springs up as if by enchantment; and the whole region affords the most striking example that can be found of the power, by which man subdues the earth, and compels it to acknowledge the sovereignty of mind.

Our traveller's lodgings by night were less tolerable than his voyage, as he went down the desolate stream. The first night was passed in a log cabin, fifty-two miles below Pittsburg, where he slept on what seemed to be a heap of cornstalks. Having no temptation to linger in such a bed, he was on his voyage again before the break of day. To him this was a delightful hour, when the landscape on each side lay in deep masses of shade, while the bold, projecting headlands were beautifully reflected in the calm water. Thus, having full leisure for contemplation, exposed to the weather all day and to hard resting-places by night, he persevered, early and inclement as the season was, till he moored his skiff in Bear Grass Creek at the Rapids of the Ohio, after a voyage of seven hundred and twenty miles, in which he spent twenty-one days.

When he was in Marietta, he visited some of the remarkable mounds, which are found in that country. One, called the Big Grave, is three hundred paces round at the base, and seventy feet in height. It is in the form of a cone, and, together with the land around it, was then covered with trees of ancient date. This spot, which abounded in curious remains of unknown antiquity, was the property of a man, whose indifference to the subject was curiously contrasted with the enthusiasm of Wilson. He was earnest to have the mound examined, being persuaded that something would be discovered which would throw light upon its history. As no prospects of this sort had the least attraction for the proprietor, Wilson represented to him that a passage might be cut into it level with the ground, and, by excavation and arching, a noble cellar be formed for turnips and potatoes. But the obstinate utilitarian answered him with the incontestable truth, that all the turnips and potatoes he could raise in a dozen years, would not pay the expense of such a treasury. Wilson left him at last with the firm conviction, that he was poorly endowed by nature with either good sense or feeling.

Near the head of what is called the Long Reach he visited a Mr. Cresap, son of the noted

Colonel of that name, mentioned in the " Notes on Virginia." Wilson inquired of him whether Logan's charge against his father, of having killed all his family, was true. He replied, that Logan believed it, but he had been misinformed. He passed Blannerhasset's Island at night ; but by the light of the clearing-fires, he was able to get a good view both of the house and the Island, which latter, like others in the Ohio, is liable to be overflowed when the river rises in the spring.

When he was about ten miles below the mouth of the Great Scioto, he encountered a storm of rain, which changed to hail and snow, and soon blew down trees in such a manner, that he was obliged to keep his boat in the middle of the stream, which rolled and foamed like the sea. After great exertion, he succeeded in landing near a cabin on the Kentucky shore. There he learned the mysteries of bear-treeing, wolf-trapping, and wildcat-hunting from a veteran professor. This man was one of the people called "squatters," who pitch their tents wherever they please, neither asking nor receiving a welcome. They are the immediate successors of the savages, and, according to Wilson's testimony, are generally very far below them in good sense and good manners. Whatever the skill of this old *trapper* may have been, it did not seem sufficient to secure his property from depredation ; since, by his own confession, the market of the wolves had been supplied with sixty of his pigs in the course of the winter.

Wilson testifies concerning these cabins, that the distant view of them is attractive and romantic, but a nearer approach is apt to break the charm. And yet so universal is human vanity, that the tenants of these dismal sheds boast to the stranger of the richness of their soil, the healthiness of their climate, and the purity of their water; meantime the only bread they have is made of Indian corn, ground in a horse-mill, which leaves half the grains unbroken; their cattle, which look like moving skeletons, are provided with neither stable nor hay; their own houses make a pig-sty a desirable dwelling, and their persons are ragged and filthy, and emaciated to the last degree.

Cincinnati, which is now a large city, was then a town of several hundred houses. He was fortunate enough to find there those who were disposed to exert themselves in his favor. When he reached Big Bone Creek, he left his boat, to visit the Big Bone Lick, five miles distant from the river. He found the place a low valley, surrounded on all sides by high hills. In the centre, by the side of the creek, is a quagmire of an acre in extent; the large bones have been taken from this and a smaller one below. Wilson came near depositing himself among the antediluvian remains. In chasing a duck across the quagmire, he sank in it, and could only relieve himself by desperate exertions. So earnest was he to have the researches in this region followed up with vigor, that he laid strong injunctions on the manager to dig with all his might ; and, as the proprietor was absent, Wilson sat down and wrote him a letter, containing similar exhortations, to be delivered to him when he returned.

It is amusing to see how, while Wilson was sometimes put out of patience by some of the strange characters that he met, it was not unusual to find his good humor restored by the very extravagance of their absurdity. The night before he reached Louisville, after being exposed all day to a storm, from which he could not protect himself, because his great-coat was in request to cover his bird-skins, he reached a cabin, which was decidedly the worst he had ever entered. The owner, a diminutive wretch, boasted of having been one of Washington's life-guards during the revolutionary war, and said that his commander, knowing his skill in sharp-shooting, had sometimes pointed out a British officer, saying "Can't you pepper that there fellow for me ?" on which solicitation, he invariably sent his victim to his long home. Before sitting down to supper he pronounced a long prayer, and immediately after his devotions called out, with a splutter of oaths for pine splinters, that the gentleman might be able to see. Such a combination of oaths and lies, prayers and politeness, though it at first filled Wilson with disgust, soon became an interesting subject of reflection to him, as showing to what unsounded depths of degradation human nature can go.

The next night he reached Louisville, having been detained upon his way by a vain pursuit of wild turkeys so late, that he was alarmed in the evening by hearing the distant sound of the Rapids some time before he reached the town. After sailing cautiously along the shore, lest he should be drawn toward the Falls by the force of the current, he reached Bear Grass Creek, where he landed safely, and, taking his baggage on his shoulders, groped his way to the town. The next day he sold his boat, the *Ornithologist*, for half price, to a man, who was curious to know why he gave the craft "such a droll Indian name," adding, "Some old chief or warrior, I suppose."

Leaving his baggage to be forwarded by a wagon, he proceeded on foot to Lexington, seventy-two miles distant; the walking was uncomfortable; in wet weather it was like travelling on soft soap; the want of bridges was also a serious inconvenience to a wayfarer. In visiting one of those remarkable pigeon-roosts, which are found in Kentucky, he was obliged to wade through a deep creek nine or ten times. He was pleased with the appearance of the country. Though nine-tenths of it was forest, through which the brooks found their way, flowing over loose flags of lime-stone, he saw many immense fields of corn, protected by excellent fences. But nothing fixed his attention so much as the flight of the migratory pigeons. They were moving in a cloud, several strata in depth, and extending on each side farther than the eye could reach. Curious to know how long this overshadowing procession might be, he sat down to observe them; but after the lapse of an hour, so far from seeing the end, he found them crowding on apparently in greater numbers.

He was delighted with the gay appearance of Lexington, which was then a pretty village, ornamented with a small, white spire. To one who had been so long in the solitude of the forest and the river, the aspect of busy streets was very exhilarating; but he seems to have been most struck with the appearance of the Court-house, in which, as he entered, he discerned the judges, like spiders in a window-corner, scarcely distinguishable in the gloom. The building, he

said, though plain and unpretending, had all
the effect of the Gothic; the walls having been
found too weak to sustain the honors of a roof and
steeple, the architect had thrown up from the
floor a number of pillars, with the large end
uppermost, which had a look so threatening as
to fill every spectator with reverential awe.
The religious part of the community seemed
to him the least exclusive of all religionists; since
they neither excluded from the church nor
churchyard any man or any animal whatso-
ever.

But though he took the liberty of amusing
himself with some peculiarities of the place,
he was surprised to see what a vast amount of
industry and improvement had been gathered
there in a few years. It is well known, that a
party of hunters gave the name to the spot,
from having heard, when encamped there, the
news of the battle of Lexington, in the beginning
of the revolution ; and when Wilson was there,
a middle-aged inhabitant remembered when
two log-huts formed the only settlement, surrounded on every side by a deep wilderness,
rendered frightful by the presence of ferocious
Indians.

He was very much surprised at the lateness
of the spring ; but, as he approached Nashville,
the scene rapidly changed.   The blossoms of the

sassafras, red-bud, and dogwood contrasted beautifully with the green of the poplar and buckeye. The song of stranger birds delighted his ear, and the rich verdure of the grain-fields, with the glowing blossoms of the orchard, which surrounded the farm-house, gave a pleasant relief to the eye. On the way he encountered one of the family caravans, which are peculiar to the West. In front was a wagon, drawn by four horses, driven by a negro, and loaded with agricultural implements; next came a heavily loaded wagon, drawn by six horses, attended by two persons; this was followed by a procession of horses, steers, cows, sheep, hogs, and calves, with their bells; next came eight boys, mounted double, and a black girl with a white child before her; then the mother with one child before her, and another at the breast; the rear guard was a party of colts, which moved without regard to order. The sound of the bells, and the shouts of the drivers, repeated by the mountain echoes, made the whole effect very imposing. All this preparation belonged to a single family, removing from Kentucky to Tennessee.

In the course of his journey, Wilson visited some of the remarkable caverns of Kentucky, one of which, on the road from Lexington to Nashville, has been explored to the distance of several miles. The entrance to those caverns is generally found at the bottom of a *sink-hole*, or place formed by the sinking of the soil; these holes, of various size and depth, are very common in this region and are often used as cellars, being cooled by a stream running through them. Great quantities of native Glauber's salts are found in them, and the earth is also strongly impregnated with nitre. One of these caverns belonged to a man who had the reputation, in the country, of being a murderer, and of using the cave to conceal the bodies of his victims. The opportunity of seeing the man was too tempting to be lost; so that Wilson called at his house, which was a tavern, with the express purpose of forming an acquaintance so desirable.

He found the landlord, who was a strong mulatto, with a countenance which might have gone far to establish his general reputation. He invited Wilson to go into his cave, which was entered through a perpendicular rock, behind his house; the offer was accepted, and, when they were in the depth of the gloom alone together, Wilson took occasion to tell him what reputation he and his cavern bore in the surrounding country, advising him to have the cave examined, in order to remove from himself the reproach of such a detestable crime. The advice had no effect, the man treating the subject as if it was a matter of indifference; but the incident serves well to illustrate the character of Wilson, who believed him, judging from his appearance and conversation, to be guilty, and supposed that he wanted nothing but opportunity and temptation to do the same again.

He found the country near Nashville very favorable to his ornithological pursuits. Several of the birds which he shot were entirely new to him. He employed all his leisure time in making drawings, which were transmitted to Mr. Lawson, but unfortunately never reached him. He had thoughts of extending his tour to St. Louis; but, after considering that it would detain him a month, and add four hundred miles to his journey without adding a single subscriber to his list, he gave up the plan, and prepared for a passage through the wilderness toward New Orleans. He was strongly urged not to undertake it, and a thousand alarming representations of hardship and danger were set before him; but, as usual, he gave fears to the winds, and quietly made preparations· for the way. He set out on the 4th of May, on horseback, with a pistol in each pocket and a fowling-piece belted across his shoulder.

Every reader of Wilson's ORNITHOLOGY must recollect the beautiful and affecting passage, in which he speaks of having shed tears over the solitary grave of his friend Lewis in the wilderness. In this journey he had the opportunity of visiting the spot where that enterprising traveller put an end to his own life, at the early age of thirty-six. The cause of this unfortunate act is not thoroughly known ; it is thought, however, that neglect and injury had deeply wounded the mind of the gallant soldier, and that constitutional melancholy bore its part in reducing him to despair. The cabin, at which he died, was seventy-two miles from Nashville, on the borders of the Indian country. The particulars of his death were minutely described to Wilson. It appears that he came to the house, with two servants, and took his lodgings in it for the night, while his men retired to the barn. The woman who kept the house heard him walking about in great agitation for several hours ; when this sound ceased, she heard the report of a pistol, followed by the noise of his fall upon the floor. Another report of a pistol succeeded, and she then heard him crying for water. She was so terrified, that she dared not move ; but, through the crevices of the unplastered wall, she saw him attempt to rise, then stagger and fall. He crept to the bucket, and she heard him scraping it with a gourd for water, but in vain ; and it was not till day-break, that the woman gained courage to call the servants to his relief. When they came he seemed to be in violent agony, and repeatedly entreated them to take his rifle and blow out his brains. He expired, just as the sun was rising above the trees. Wilson paid the proprietor of the soil a sum of money, and received from him a written promise to enclose the grave. He then left the place with a heavy heart, and entered the gloomy wilderness, which he was to traverse alone.

He seems to have enjoyed this journey, though it was exceedingly fatiguing; it was not pleasant to sleep on the ground in the open air, nor was much gained, in point of accommodation, by accepting the hospitality of the Indians. But the woods were full of splendid flowers; birds of rich plumage and sweet song abounded, and the manners of the Indians afforded a subject of interesting observation. But he found that, even with "a lodge in some vast wilderness," he could not be secure from vexation. As he was listening to the song of a Mocking-bird, the first that he had heard in the western country, near the cabin where he intended to pass the night, it was suddenly wounded with an arrow, and fell fluttering to the ground. He hastened to the Indian who had shot the bird, and told him " that it was bad, very bad! that this poor bird had come from a far distant country to sing to him, and, in return, he had murdered it; that the Great Spirit was offended with such cruelty, and for doing so he would lose many a deer." An old Indian, who understood, by an interpreter, what Wilson had said, took pains to explain to him, that these birds deserved no favor, since, when they came singing near a house, somebody would surely die.

He was so much exposed on this journey to the heat of the sun and all the changes of the weather, that he was attacked with dysentery and fever, and became so ill, that it was with difficulty he was able to keep his seat. The remedy which he used, was not one which the faculty would have recommended; he lived wholly on raw eggs for nearly a week, and at length recovered. He was also in danger from a tornado, attended by a drenching rain; trees were broken off or torn up by the roots, and those which resisted were bent to the ground; limbs of vast weight were continually whirled past him, and his life was so exposed, that he declared, he would rather stand in the hottest field of battle, than encounter another such tornado.

He reached Natchez in safety, being uniformly well treated by the Indians, whom he found an inoffensive and friendly race. The boatmen could hardly credit the testimony of their own ears, when they heard that he had accomplished this enterprise without making use of whiskey. When he was suffering with sickness, an Indian recommended the eating of strawberries, which were then in perfection. This specific was probably more effectual in restoring him to health, than the eggs, which were his own prescription. One circumstance deserves to be remembered; thirteen miles from Nashville in Tennessee he passed the night at the house of Isaac Walton, a historical name, which has long been associated with simplicity and kindness of feeling. This landlord was worthy of his name; for, when Wilson was leaving him after breakfast, he said to him, " You seem to be travelling for the good of the world; and I cannot, — I will not charge you any thing. Whenever you come this way, call and stay with me, and you shall be welcome."

The western region of this country is the native soil of hospitality. While Wilson was in Natchez, he received a letter from Mr. William Dunbar, who regretted that he could not wait upon him, being confined by sickness; but invited him to come to his house, and make it his home, so long as he was in that region. The invitation was accepted, and an apartment assigned to the stranger. The house was in the depth of the forest, and afforded Wilson the very position he would have chosen for pursuing his researches, beside giving him the advantage of refined conversation and elegant hospitality. The time passed at this gentleman's house was one of the sunny moments in Wilson's life, which he remembered with the more delight, because they were so few.

He reached New Orleans on the 6th of June; but, as the sickly season was approaching, he did not think it safe to remain there long; and on the 24th he took passage for New York, where he arrived on the 30th of July. He had left home, on the 30th of January, and all his expenses, up to this time, amounted only to four hundred and fifty-five dollars.

He arrived at Philadelphia on the 2nd of August, and immediately applied himself, with unwearied industry, to the preparation of his third volume. He had made several new discoveries in the West, and on the islands near Florida, which he visited on his passage home. In a letter to Michaux, he says, that the number of birds, which he had found, and which had not been noticed by any other naturalist, amounted to forty. The French botanist was then publishing his *American Sylva*, and had transmitted some of the numbers, with colored prints, to Wilson, who immediately made attempts at imitation, in which he succeeded to his own satisfaction.

In 1811, he renewed his correspondence with his nephew, William Duncan, who was engaged in the business of instruction, and had asked some advice of Wilson respecting the general course he should pursue. Nothing can be more judicious than Wilson's reply. After telling him, that he must first determine in his own mind the precise extent of his duty, and then resolve to perform it thoroughly, he gives him the following admirable suggestions. "Devote your whole time, except what is proper for needful exercise, to making yourself completely master of your business; for this purpose, rise by the peep of dawn ; take your regular walk ; and then, commence your stated studies. Be under no anxiety to hear what people think of you or your tutorship ; but study the improvement and watch over the good con- duct of the children consigned to your care, as if they were your own. Mingle respect and affabil- ity with your orders and arrangements. Never show yourself feverish or irritated ; but preserve a firm and dignified, a just and energetic deport- ment, in every emergency. To be completely master of one's business, and ever anxious to dis- charge it with fidelity and honor, is to be great, beloved, respectable, and happy."

At this time, and during the greater part of the interval between his western tour and anoth- er journey to the Northern States in September, 1812, he was an inmate in the family of Mr. Bartram. The retreat of the botanic garden afforded him a good opportunity of observing the habits of birds, and at the same time of improving his health, which had been considerably shaken by his fatigues and sedentary labors. This was, however, only comparative repose; for he went several times to the shores of New Jersey, and made excursions to various places in the vicinity, being determined to leave nothing undone, to make the work as perfect as possible.

His journey to the eastward was undertaken principally for the purpose of visiting his agents and subscribers. No very minute accounts of the tour are preserved. From New York he proceeded up the North River, and contemplated its unrivalled scenery with great delight. From Albany he went to Lake Champlain; and, finding every tavern in that region crowded with officers and soldiers, was obliged to resort to his western habit of sleeping on the floor, which he did with great composure, amidst the wrath of his companions, who would not submit to such prostration, and if they had, could hardly have complimented their slumbers with the name of rest. From Burlington, he crossed to the Connecticut River, and passed some time in the neighborhood of the White Mountains. While he was at Haverhill, in New Hampshire, he visited Moosehillock, a stupendous height, though far inferior to the neighboring ridges. It is singular, that, when he was so near the pass of the White Mountains, he did not take occasion to explore it, with a view to his favorite researches; the whole vicinity abounds in birds, some of which are to be found in no other part of the United States. The only nest of a Snow Bunting, ever found within the pale of civilization, was discovered on the dreary battlements of Mount Washington.

He has recorded one of his adventures, which is sufficiently amusing, and serves to show the feverish excitement of the whole country at the commencement of the last war. The people of Haverhill, observing how closely he was exploring the country, consulted together to determine what he might be ; they came to the conclusion, that he could be no other than a spy from Canada, who was exploring the country with a view to determine the best course, by which a military force could be sent from the British provinces into New England. He was therefore apprehended, and taken before a magistrate with due solemnity and form. That officer, on hearing his explanations, dismissed him with many apologies. Such was the state of the country, that his tour afforded him very little satisfaction. Every gentle sound was drowned by the voice of war; and the charms of nature, he said, were treated with contempt, except when they presented themselves in the form of prize sugars, coffee, or rum.

Before he went on this journey, he had been chosen a member of the Society of Artists of the

United States. In the spring of 1813, he was admitted to the American Philosophical Society in Philadelphia. Meantime he was exerting himself to complete his work, as if he had a presentiment that the sands of his life were running low. In April, of the same year, he writes to Mr. Bartram, that his colorists have all left him, and this circumstance has very much increased his own labors; so that he hardly ever leaves the house, though he longs " to breathe the fresh air of the country, and to gaze once more upon the lovely face of nature."

This was a privilege which he was but once more permitted to enjoy. As soon as the seventh volume of his work had left the press, he went with Mr. Ord to Great Egg-Harbor, where they spent nearly a month, collecting materials for the eighth volume. When they returned, he plunged at once into the midst of those labors, which hurried his life to its close. Those who attempted to assist him, troubled him by their constant failures and errors. Being too proud to suffer any copy of his work to appear in an unworthy form, he took more upon himself than he could possibly perform. He drew largely upon the hours which should have been given to rest, beside spending the day in unceasing exertion; his friends remonstrated with him, and warned him of the inevitable result; but his only reply was, "Life is short, and nothing can be done without exertion."

His Scotch biographer, from the verbal testimony of one of his American friends, explains the immediate cause of the disorder which put an end to his mortal existence. While he was sitting one day conversing with a friend, he caught a glance of a rare bird, which he had long been desirous to see. With his usual ardor, he ran out, swam across a river in pursuit of it, and at last succeeded in killing it; but he took cold from the exposure, which brought on the dysentery, which, after an illness of ten days, brought him to the grave. His brother came to him as soon as he heard of his illness. He says, "I found him speechless; I caught his hand; he seemed to know me, and that was all." He died on the morning of the 23d of August, 1813. He had expressed a wish, more than once, to a friend, when conversing on the subject of death, that, when he died, he might be buried *where the birds might sing over his grave.* But this wish was not known to those who were with him in his last moments; and his remains were deposited, with the respect which his memory deserved, in the cemetery of the Swedish church in Southwark, Philadelphia. A plain marble monument bears the following inscription; —

This Monument
covers the Remains of
Alexander Wilson,
Author of the
AMERICAN ORNITHOLOGY.
He was born in Renfrewshire, Scotland,
on the 6th of July, 1766;
Emigrated to the United States
in the Year 1794;
and died in Philadelphia,
of the Dysentery,
on the 23d of August, 1813,
Aged 47.

The reader, perhaps, has already formed an impression of Wilson's character, from the incidents of his history; but some few particulars remain to be mentioned. In his personal appearance he was tall and handsome, rather slender than athletic in his form. His countenance was expressive and thoughtful, his eye powerful and intelligent. Mr. Ord speaks as if the first impression made by his appearance on a stranger was not very prepossessing. But so far as one might judge from his portrait, taken in his twenty-second year, his face was intellectual and pleasing. The unfavorable impression may have been produced by his manners. He was not accustomed to polished society in his earlier days; and, as he was conscious of possessing powers, greatly superior to those of the laborers with whom he associated, his manner, like that of

Burns, probably became somewhat impatient and overbearing. His conversation was remarkable for quickness and originality ; his whole deportment was that of a man of uncommon intellectual resources, who was perfectly conscious of possessing them.

But if his manners in general were not engaging, and in this he resembled most other men who are deeply concerned in pursuits, which command little sympathy in the world around them, his character was certainly amiable ; he was warm-hearted and generous in his affections ; from first to last he displayed an unfaltering attachment to his friends, after many years of separation ; and there is evidence enough in the preceding narrative to show, that he felt the full weight of obligation, which every relation in life brought with it, and discharged it to the best of his power. Men of great force and energy are not, in general, remarkable for tenderness of feeling ; but in his character there were many fine and beautiful traits, which show that strength and delicacy were united, each in its just measure, in his heart.

There are few examples to be found in literary history of resolution equal to that of Wilson. Though he was made fully aware, both by his friends and his own reflections, of the difficulty of the enterprise in which he engaged, his heart never for a moment failed him. By his agreement with his publisher, he bound himself to furnish the drawings and descriptions for the work, indeed every thing, except the mechanical execution. To procure the materials, he was obliged to encounter heavy expenses; and the money which he received for *coloring the plates*, was the only revenue from which he defrayed them. It is easy to imagine the difficulties which he must have encountered; but his success was complete; and though he did not live to enjoy, he certainly anticipated, what has come to pass; that his work would always be regarded as a subject of pride by his adopted country, and would secure immortal honor for him whose name it bears.

THE

LIFE AND ADVENTURES

OF

CAPTAIN JOHN SMITH;

BY

GEORGE S. HILLARD.

PREFACE.

WHOEVER expects to find much that is new in the following biographical notice of Captain Smith, will probably be disappointed. My aim has been to give a lucid and simple narrative of the events in the life of one of the most remarkable men, "that ever lived in the tide of times;" with the use of materials contained in works, which are familiar to those who have studied the early history of this country. My task has been the humble one of arranging, selecting from, condensing, and transposing these ample though confused materials, so as to form such a narrative as would recommend itself to the popular taste.

Captain Smith's own writings, which have furnished me with nearly all my facts, are not easily accessible to the public at large, and would not be generally read if they were. Their obsolete diction and uncouth spelling would repel any but a professed antiquary. I have endeavored to translate them into a modern style, and to give them a modern garb, though I have permitted

Captain Smith to speak for himself on many occasions.

I have written a Life of Captain Smith, and not a History of the World, or of any considerable portion of it, while he lived in it. Such collateral and contemporaneous facts only have been mentioned, as are necessary to illustrate and elucidate portions of his own biography. It is true, I have given a succinct history of the colony of Virginia, during the two years in which Captain Smith was there; but the reason is, that, from his character and station, such a history is identical with his own life.

In addition to his writings, I have derived assistance from Grahame's " History of the United States," and Stith's accurate and faithful " History of Virginia." I have also been aided by Belknap's well-written Life of Smith, a work of great merit, like every thing which came from his pen, and which, had it been more ample, would have left no room for me or any succeeding writer. I have moreover enjoyed the advantage of an original document, which is of a nature to demand a somewhat extended notice. It is a manuscript Life of Smith, in Latin, the original of which is deposited in the Lambeth Library. By the kindness of the Archbishop of Canterbury, a copy has been obtained for the purpose of being used in compiling the present Memoir. It was written by Henry Wharton, an English clergyman of extraordinary talents and acquisitions, who belonged to the melancholy catalogue of lights too early quenched for their own fame and the interests of literature. He was born November 9th, 1664, at Worstead in Norfolk County, was graduated at the University of Cambridge, and admitted to the order of deacon in 1687. His literary industry was wonderful. He wrote, translated, and edited a variety of works, principally on ecclesiastical antiquities and religious controversies, many of them against the Popish religion. He was warmly patronized by Sancroft, Archbishop of Canterbury, who appointed him one of his chaplains. Many of his works are still in manuscript in the Lambeth Library, having been purchased by Archbishop Tenison. He died at the age of thirty, a victim to immoderate application. Considering the age at which he died, the vast amount of his labors, and the extent of his acquisitions, Henry Wharton may be justly esteemed a prodigy.*

The Life of Smith from his pen is more valuable as a literary curiosity, than as a historical document. It was written in 1685, and is a

* For a full and interesting account of the life and labors of Wharton, see Chalmers's Biographical Dictionary.

compilation from the original sources, to which we now have access, and of course contains not many new or important facts. The greater part of it is devoted to Captain Smith's adventures before going to Virginia; afterwards it is meagre and cursory; and it extends no farther than to his return to England from Jamestown. Its style is not scrupulously classical. Words now and then appear, which would have made "Quinctilian stare and gasp;" but it is full of spirit and vivacity, and the numerous learned and happy allusions in it show the great extent and variety of the author's resources. The name of Smith he latinizes into "Fabricius"; Opechancanough he calls "Opecancanius"; Powhatan, "Poviatanus"; Pocahontas, "Pocaunta"; the Chickahominies, "Cicaminæi." He professes the greatest admiration for his hero, whom he declares to be every way equal to the most renowned heroes of antiquity, and that he would obtain the same amount of fame, if he could meet with a Plutarch, who would record his exploits in a style worthy of them. From the character of its author, and the nature of its subject, this manuscript is a curious and valuable record, and it is fortunate that there is a copy of it on this side of the Atlantic.

GEORGE S. HILLARD.

CAPTAIN JOHN SMITH.

CHAPTER I.

His Birth, early Adventures, and brilliant Achievements in the Turkish Wars.

AMONG the adventurous spirits, whom a restless love of enterprise called from the bosom of repose in England to new scenes and untried perils in our Western wilds, there is no one whose name awakens more romantic associations, than CAPTAIN JOHN SMITH. His life is as brilliant and exciting as a Fairy tale ; and the remarkable adventures he went through served to develope fully his no less remarkable character. It was his good fortune to live in stirring and eventful times, congenial to his bold and roving disposition, and, luckily for posterity, his adventures have been preserved in a characteristic narrative written by himself, from which the principal facts in the following biographical sketch have been drawn.

He was born in Willoughby in the county of Lincolnshire, in the year 1579, and was descended from an ancient family which belonged to the county of Lancashire. His wild spirit of enterprise and dislike to confinement displayed themselves in early boyhood; for, at the age of thirteen, being, as he himself says, " set upon brave adventures," he sold his satchell, books, and whatever other property he had, in order to raise money to furnish him with the means of going privately to sea; but this hopeful enterprise was frustrated by the death of his parents, who left him a competent estate. His guardians put him apprentice, at the age of fifteen, to Mr. Thomas Sendall of Lynn, " the greatest merchant of all those parts;" but the compting-house desk seems to have been as irksome to him as the school-boy's form. He quitted his master's employment, and, with but ten shillings in his pocket, furnished him by his friends (to use his own words) "to get rid of him," he entered into the train of the second son of the famous Lord Willoughby, who was travelling into France.

On arriving at Orleans, he was furnished with funds sufficient to carry him back to England; but such a step was very far from his intention. He went over into the Low Countries, the battle-ground of Europe, where he served for three or four years under the command of Captain Joseph Duxbury. Of the nature of his service he does not inform us;

but he probably belonged to a company of English auxiliaries, who were aiding Prince Maurice in his gallant and successful struggle against the power of Spain, which resulted in the independence of the Netherlands. He met with a Scotch gentleman abroad, whose name was David Hume, who supplied him with money, gave him letters to his friends in Scotland, and assured him of the favor and patronage of King James.

He set sail for Scotland accordingly, and, after having suffered shipwreck and a severe fit of sickness, arrived there, and delivered his letters. By those to whom they were addressed, he was treated with that warmth of hospitality, which seems to have been characteristic of the Scotch nation from the earliest times ; but he found no encouragement to enter upon the career of a courtier. He returned to Willoughby in Lincolnshire ; and, finding himself thrown among those in whose society he took no pleasure, and being perhaps a little soured by disappointment, he built himself a sylvan lodge of boughs in a wood, and studied military history and tactics. He amused himself at the same time with hunting and horsemanship. He was not, however, a genuine and independent man of the woods ; for he kept up an intercourse with the civilized world by means of his servant, who supplied his woodland retreat with all the comforts of artificial life. Rumor soon spread about the country the tale of a young and accomplished hermit, and brought to his "lonely bower" an Italian gentleman in the service of the Earl of Lincoln, of great skill in horsemanship, who insinuated himself into the favor of Smith, and induced him to return with him into the world.

His military ardor soon revived, and he set out a second time upon his travels, intending to fight against the Turks, whom all good Christians in those days looked upon as natural enemies. The first stage of his journey was the Low Countries, where he met with four French adventurers, who, seeing the youth and inexperience of Smith (being at that time but nineteen years old), formed a plan to rob him. One of them pretended to be a nobleman, and the others personated his attendants. They persuaded him to travel with them into France, and they accordingly embarked together on board of a vessel for that purpose. His treacherous friends found in the captain a kindred spirit in villany, and by his assistance their plans were put into execution. In a dark night they arrived at St. Valery in Picardy; and, by the contrivance of the captain, the four Frenchmen were put on shore with the baggage of

Smith, he himself remaining on board, in utter ignorance of the disposition which had been made of his property. The boat with the captain returned the next day towards evening, a delay which he alleged to be in consequence of the high sea, but which was in reality to enable the robbers to escape with their booty. His villany was strongly suspected by the passengers, who, indignant at his baseness and strongly sympathizing with Smith in his misfortune, proposed to him to kill the captain and take possession of the vessel and cargo. This offer, so characteristic of the lawlessness of the times, was rejected by Smith, with a promptness worthy of his honorable and high-minded character.

On his being landed, Smith found himself in such straits as to be compelled to sell his cloak to pay for his passage. One of his fellow passengers generously compassionating his forlorn situation, supplied him with money and brought him to Mortain, the place of residence of the villains who had robbed him. He found it impossible to obtain any satisfaction, however, for the injuries he had received at their hands, the word of a friendless and unknown stranger probably not being deemed sufficient evidence of their guilt; and he could not be aided by his generous fellow passenger, who was an outlawed man and obliged to live in the strictest seclusion.

The rumor of his misfortunes awakened the active sympathy of several noble families in the neighborhood, by whom he was most hospitably entertained and his necessities liberally relieved.

A life of ease did not suit his restless temperament, and his high spirit could not endure his being the constant subject of favors, which he had no means of repaying. He set out upon his wanderings with a light purse, a stout heart, and a good sword. His slender means being soon exhausted, he was reduced to great sufferings, so much so, that one day, in passing through a forest, his strength, worn out by grief and exposure, entirely failed him, and he threw himself down by the edge of a fountain, with little hope of ever rising again. Here he was providentially found by a rich farmer, who acted the part of the good Samaritan towards him, and furnished him with the means of prosecuting his journey.

In rambling from port to port in search of a ship of war, he met, near a town in Brittany, one of the villains who had robbed him. They both drew without exchanging a single word, and the prowess of Smith gave him an easy victory over one, whose arm was paralyzed by the consciousness of a bad cause. He obliged him to make an ample confession of his guilt in the presence of numerous spectators. He obtained nothing, how-

ever, but the barren laurels of victory, and directed his course to the seat of the Earl of Ployer,
whom he had formerly known. By him he was
treated with the utmost kindness and hospitality,
and his purse liberally replenished. Taking leave
of his friendly host, he travelled by a circuitous
route to Marseilles, where he embarked for Italy.

New troubles awaited Smith in this passage.
The author of the manuscript Latin memoir, alluded to in the Preface, remarks, that it is curious
to observe how ingenious Fortune is in contriving
peculiar disasters and perils to try the temper of
heroes and great men, the ordinary mishaps of life
not being sufficient for that purpose; a reflection
naturally enough suggested by the adventures of
his hero. On board the vessel was a great crowd
of Catholic pilgrims of various nations, who were
bound to Rome. They encountered a violent
storm, which obliged them first to put into the
harbor of Toulon, and afterwards to anchor under
the small island of St. Mary, which lies off Nice,
in Savoy. The enlightened devotees, who were
sailing with him, took it into their heads, that the
tempest was sent from heaven, as a manifestation
of its displeasure at the presence of a heretic,
who was, among so many of the true church,
like " a dead fly in the compost of spices."
They at first confined themselves to angry reproaches, directed not only against Smith himself,

but against Queen Elizabeth, an object of especial dread and aversion to all good Catholics. Their displeasure soon displayed itself by more unequivocal signs. The writer above alluded to says, that Smith disdained to stain his sword with the blood of so base a rabble, but that he belabored them soundly with a cudgel; but this probably belongs to that large class of facts, for which historians and biographers are indebted to their own imaginations.

Be that as it may, the result was, that Smith was thrown into the sea, like another Jonah, as a peace-offering to the angry elements. He was so near the island of St. Mary, that he could reach it without any difficulty by swimming. The next day, he was taken on board a French ship, commanded by Captain La Roche, a friend and neighbor of the Earl of Ployer, who, for his sake, treated Smith with great kindness and consideration. They sailed to Alexandria in Egypt, and, delivering their freight, coasted the Levant. In the course of their voyage they met with a Venetian argosy, richly laden. The captain of the French ship desired to speak her, but his motions were misconstrued by the Venetian ship, which fired a broad-side into her, mistaking her probably for a pirate, or supposing, what was probably true in those troubled times, that he could expect none but the treatment of an enemy from those of any other than his own nation. An engagement naturally enough ensued, which resulted in the defeat of the Venetian vessel, after a loss of twenty men, her adversary losing fifteen. Her rich cargo was plundered by the victors, and the most valuable and least bulky portions of it taken on board their own vessel. The valor of Smith had been most signally displayed in this engagement, and he received, as his share of the spoils, five hundred sequins, besides a " little box " (probably of jewels), worth nearly as much more. He was set on shore in Piedmont, at his own request. He made the tour of Italy, and gratified his curiosity by a sight of the interesting objects with which that country is filled. Mindful of his original purpose, he departed from Venice, and travelling through Albania, Dalmatia, and Sclavonia, came to Gratz in Styria, the residence of Ferdinand, Archduke of Austria, afterwards Emperor of Germany.

The war was at that time raging between Rodolph the Second, Emperor of Germany, and Mahomet the Third, the Grand Seignior. Smith's desire to display his prowess against the Turks was soon gratified. He met with two of his countrymen, who introduced him to Lord Eberspaught, Baron Kissell, and the Earl of Meldritch, all of them officers of distinction in the Imperial army.

This was in the latter part of the year 1601. The Turkish army, under the command of Ibrahim Bashaw, had besieged and taken, in the month of October, the strong fortress of Canisia, in Hungary, and were ravaging the neighboring country. They were laying siege to Olympach, with twenty thousand men, and had reduced the garrison, commanded by Eberspaught, to great extremities, having cut off all communication and supplies. Smith served as a volunteer in the army of the Baron Kissell, the general of artillery, who annoyed the besiegers from without. He was desirous of sending a communication to the commander of the garrison, but found no one bold enough to undertake so perilous an enterprise. Smith then communicated to him a plan of telegraphic intercourse, which he had before made known to Lord Eberspaught, anticipating that the chances of war would give rise to an emergency, in which a knowledge of it might be highly useful. By Kissell's order, Smith was conveyed at night to a mountain seven miles distant from the town, and communicated with the commander of the garrison, and conveyed to him the following message. "On Thursday at night, I will charge on the east; at the alarm sally you;" an answer was returned, "I will." The besieged were also aided further by Smith's inventive genius. On the eve of the attack, he had several thousand matches, fastened to strings, extended in a line and fired, so that the report sounded like a discharge of musquetry, and gave to the Turks the impression that there was a large body of men in that quarter, and they consequently marched out to attack them, and at the same moment they found themselves assaulted by Baron Kissell's army and by the garrison of the besieged fortress, who had made the concerted sally. They were in consequence thrown into great confusion and made but a feeble resistance. Many of them were slain, and others driven into the river and drowned. Two thousand men were thrown into the garrison, and the Turks were obliged to abandon the siege. This brilliant and successful exploit obtained for our adventurer the command of a troop of two hundred and fifty horse in the regiment of Count Meldritch. *

---

* Smith's telegraph was by means of torches, each letter from A to L being designated by showing one torch as many times as correspond to the letter's place in the alphabet; each letter from M to Z, in like manner, by showing two torches. It is essentially the same as that described in the tenth book of Polybius and in Rees's Cyclopædia, Art. *Telegraph.* Smith had probably met with it in Polybius, a writer whose military spirit would be congenial to his taste; and the use he thus made of his boyish acquisitions is a proof that a " little learning " may be a very good thing, even to a soldier.

In the year 1601, the campaign began with great spirit and vast preparations. The Emperor raised three armies, one commanded by Gonzago, Governor of Hungary, one by Ferdinand, Archduke of Styria, and the third by the Archduke Matthias, the Emperor's brother, whose lieutenant was Duke Mercury, who raised with him an army of thirty thousand men, and under whom Smith served. He laid siege to Alba Regalis, a strongly fortified town in Hungary. Smith's talents as an engineer were here called into exercise; for he contrived a sort of bomb or grenade, to be discharged from a sling, which greatly annoyed the Turks in their sallies, and two or three times set the suburbs of the place on fire. The city was finally taken by an ingeniously contrived and boldly executed military manœuvre; a loss so great to the Turks, that it is related that the Bashaw of Buda, who was a prisoner in Vienna, on hearing of it, abstained from eating a whole day, prostrate upon his face, praying to Mohammed, who, as he said, had been all that year angry with the Turks.

The Sultan had raised an army of sixty thousand men, under the command of Hassan Bashaw, for the purpose of relieving Alba Regalis. He, having heard of its capture, still continued his march, in the hope of taking it by surprise. Duke Mercury, though far inferior in numbers, marched out to meet him, and encountered him in a desperate battle on the plains of Girke, which resulted in the defeat of the Turks, with the loss of six thousand men. In this action Smith behaved with great valor, was severely wounded, and had a horse shot under him.

Duke Mercury, after this, divided his forces into three parts, one of which, under the command of Count Meldritch, was sent into Transylvania, which was the seat of a triple war. Sigismund Bathor, the native prince, was contending for his crown with the Emperor of Germany, and, at the same time, waging war against the Turks, who were also the foes of the Emperor; so that each party had their attention distracted and their forces thinned by a common enemy. Meldritch had been ordered to join the army of the Emperor, which was acting against Sigismund. But Meldritch was himself a Transylvanian and little inclined to oppose himself to his countrymen, to whom he probably wished success in his heart. He and his officers were most of them soldiers of fortune, bound by slack allegiance to the Emperor, and ready, like Captain Dugald Dalgetty, to enlist under that leader, who could give them the highest pay and the best chance for gaining booty; and the Emperor, it seems, was not a very prompt paymaster. He therefore offered his services to Sigismund, by whom they were cordially accepted ; and from him he obtained permission to turn his arms against the Turks, an enterprise to which he was stimulated by personal feeling, for they had possession of that part of Transylvania in which his own family estates were situated.

In the course of the desultory and partisan warfare, which he carried on, he laid siege to Regal, a frontier town in the mountainous parts of Transylvania, so strong by nature and art as to be deemed impregnable, and garrisoned by a motley assemblage of Turks, Tartars, renegades, and robbers. Count Meldritch had with him eight thousand men, and he was afterwards joined by Prince Moyses with nine thousand more, to whom he surrendered the chief command.

The siege was long and obstinate, owing to the great strength of the place ; and frequent and bloody, but undecisive skirmishes took place. The Turks grew insolent at the ill success of the Christians, and laughed to scorn their slow and ineffectual movements. One of their number, the Lord Turbashaw by name, a man of rank and military renown, sent a challenge to any captain of the Christian army, to fight with him in single combat, giving a reason characteristic of the times for this message, that it was to delight the ladies of Regal, " who did long to see some court-like pastime." So many were ready to accept this challenge, that their conflicting claims were settled by lot, and the choice fell upon Smith, who had burned for the privilege of meeting the haughty Turk.

On the day appointed for the combat, the ramparts of the town were lined with ladies and soldiers. The Lord Turbashaw entered the lists in a splendid suit of armor, blazing with gold and jewels, and " on his shoulders were fixed a pair of great wings, compacted of eagle's feathers, within a ridge of silver, richly garnished with gold and precious stones." He was attended by three Janizaries, one of whom bore his lance, and two walked by the side of his horse. Smith soon followed, attended by a single page bearing his lance, and rode by his antagonist, courteously saluting him as he passed. At the sound of the trumpet, they met in mid career, and the well-directed lance of Smith pierced through the visor into the brain of the Turk, and he fell dead from his horse, without having shed a drop of his adversary's blood. His head was cut off and borne in triumph to the Christian army, and his body given up to his friends.

The death of the Lord Turbashaw was heavily borne by the garrison ; and a friend of his, by name Grualgo, burning to avenge him and to pluck the fresh laurels from Smith's brow, sent him a particular challenge, which was readily accepted, and the battle took place the next day

after receiving it.   At their first encounter, their
lances were ineffectually shivered, though the
Turk was nearly unhorsed.   They then discharged their pistols, by which Smith was slightly wounded and his antagonist severely in the
left arm.   Being thus rendered unable to manage
his horse, he offered a faint resistance and was
easily slain ; and his horse and armor, by previous agreement, became the property of the vic-
tor.

   The siege was slowly protracted in the meanwhile, and Smith found but few opportunities for
signalizing his valor.   His high spirit, flushed
with success, could not brook the rust of repose ;
and he obtained leave of his general to send a
message into the town, that he should be happy
to furnish the ladies with further entertainment,
and to give to any Turkish knight the opportunity
of redeeming the heads of his slain friends, and
carry off his own besides, if he could win it.
The challenge was accepted by a stout champion,
to whom the Fates had given the unharmonious
name of Bonny Mulgro.   Having the privilege
of choosing his own weapons, he avoided the
lance, having had proof of Smith's dexterity
in the use of it, and selected pistols, battle-
axes, and swords.   In the encounter, they discharged their pistols without effect, and then
fought with their battle-axes.   Smith seems to

have been inferior to his adversary in the use of this weapon, for he received so heavy a blow, that the axe dropped from his hands and he nearly fell from his horse ; and the Turks, seeing his mishap from the walls, set up a loud shout, as if the victory were already won. But Smith quickly recovered himself, and by his skilful horsemanship not only escaped the heavy blows aimed at him by the ponderous battle-axe, but ran his foe through the body with his sword. The ladies of Regal were certainly well entertained by our adventurer, and they could not complain of disappointment when he was master of the feast.

For these brilliant exploits Smith was rewarded by suitable honors. He was conducted to his general's tent by a military procession, consisting of six thousand men, three led horses, and, before each, the head of one of the Turks he had slain, borne on a lance. The general received him with much honor, embraced him, and presented him with a horse superbly caparisoned, and a scimitar and belt worth three hundred ducats ; and his colonel, Count Meldritch, made him major of his regiment.

The siege was prosecuted with renewed vigor ; and the place was finally taken, and its brave garrison put to the sword, in retaliation of the same inhuman barbarity, which they had shown to the Christian garrison, from whom they took it. The prince of Transylvania, hearing of the valor of Smith, gave him his picture set in gold and a pension of three hundred ducats per annum. He also bestowed upon him a patent of nobility and a coat of arms bearing three Turks' heads in a shield, with the motto "Vincere est vivere." * This patent was afterwards admitted and recorded in the Heralds' College in England by Sir William Segar, Garter King at Arms.

CHAPTER II.

His Captivity, Escape, and Return to England.

THE summer heaven of Smith's fortunes was soon to be overcast; and fate had trials in store for him, far exceeding any he had before known. Sigismund, the prince of Transylvania, found that he could no longer maintain a war against the Emperor and the Turks at the same time, the resources of his flourishing principality being utterly exhausted by his long-continued and unequal struggle. He accordingly acknowledged the Emperor's authority, gave up his station as an independent prince, and passed the remainder

* The date of this patent is December 3d, 1603, which was not until after Smith's return from his captivity.

of his days in the more obscure, but probably happier rank of a private nobleman in Prague, in the enjoyment of a munificent pension, which he had received in exchange for the uneasy splendor of a crown.

By this arrangement the armies of Sigismund were thrown out of employment, and transferred their allegiance to the Emperor. His generals were somewhat embarrassed by the presence of so many well disciplined and veteran troops, who were well known to be devotedly attached to their old master and not very fond of their new one; and they were anxious to keep them constantly employed, well knowing that idleness is the mother of mutiny. An opportunity soon occurred; for there was seldom peace in those days on the frontiers of Christendom and "Heathenesse."

The inhabitants of Wallachia, at that time a Turkish province, unable to endure the tyranny of their Waywode, or prince, revolted and applied to the Emperor for assistance, who gladly afforded it; and the Earl of Meldritch, accompanied by numerous officers, and Smith among the rest, and by an army of thirty thousand men, who had served under Sigismund, went to support the claims of the new Waywode, Lord Rodoll. The former one, whose name was Jeremy, had raised an army of forty thousand Tartars, Moldavians, and Turks, to maintain his pretensions.   A bloody battle was fought between them, in which the Turkish army was totally defeated with the loss of twenty-five thousand men, and Wallachia became subject to the Emperor.

The deposed Waywode collected together some troops, and assumed a dangerous attitude in the neighboring province of Moldavia; and the Earl of Meldritch was sent to reduce him.   He was successful in several skirmishes, in one of which he was materially assisted by Smith's ingenuity in the construction of fire-works, a gift which seems to have been peculiar to him. Pressing on too eagerly and incautiously, he was decoyed into an ambuscade, in a mountainous pass near the town of Rottenton, and attacked by an army of forty thousand men.   The Christians made a gallant and desperate resistance, but could avail nothing against such immense odds; and they were all slain or cut to pieces, except about thirteen hundred, who, with the Earl of Meldritch, escaped by swimming a river.

In this unhappy battle were slain many gallant noblemen and gentlemen, the flower of Sigismund's army and his most devoted friends, and, among the rest, nine Englishmen, whose names Smith affectionately preserves, who, for the sake of sustaining the cross and humbling the crescent, had exposed themselves to peril and death in an obscure war, and in a remote corner of Europe. Such is the soldier's unequal lot. Some are proudly slain on famous fields; "honor decks the turf that wraps their clay," and their names become in after-times watch-words and rallying cries; while others, with arms as strong, hearts as brave, hopes as warm, and souls as aspiring, fall in petty skirmishes, the very spot of which soon becomes uncertain, and tradition itself preserves not a record of their names.

Smith was severely wounded and left for dead upon the field. Some sparks of life were found in him, and the Turks, judging him to be a man of distinction by the richness of his armor, healed his wounds in order to secure a large ransom. As soon as he was recovered, he was taken to Axiopolis with many other prisoners, and there they were all sold, "like beasts in a market-place." Smith was sold to the Bashaw Bogall, who sent him to Constantinople as a present to his mistress, the young Charatza Tragabigzanda (a name not very manageable in a sonnet), telling her that he was a Bohemian nobleman, whom he had captured in war.

This young lady viewed with compassion the afflicted condition of her captive, who was at that time in the flower of his youth, and adorned with those manly graces, which make valor more attractive, and affliction more pitiable. Not having her time so much occupied as modern young ladies, she would often contrive an excuse for asking a question of the interesting captive who dwelt so much in her thoughts, as she had a slight knowledge of Italian. To her surprise she learnt, that the story told by her lover was a sheer fabrication, that Smith was an English gentleman, who had never seen the Bashaw till he had been bought by him in the market-place of Axiopolis. The tender feeling, with which she had, perhaps unconsciously to herself, begun to regard Smith, was probably increased by the indignation, with which she heard of the deception that had been practised upon her. She drew from him the whole story of his adventures, to which she did, like Desdemona, "seriously incline," and, like Desdemona, "she loved him for the dangers he had passed," as well as for his graceful manners, fascinating conversation, and that noble and dignified bearing, which the weeds of a captive could not conceal. She mitigated the pains of his captivity by all the means in her power; and, apprehensive lest her mother (who probably suspected the dangerous progress he was making in her daughter's affections) should sell him in order to remove him from her sight, she resolved to send him, with a letter to her brother Timour, Bashaw of Nalbritz, in the country of Cambia, and province of Tartary, who resided near the borders of the sea of Azof.

In this letter she enjoined it upon her brother to treat Smith with the greatest kindness, and, to make " assurance doubly sure," she frankly told him of the state of her feelings towards him, which disclosure had, however, upon the haughty Tartar an effect very different from what she anticipated. Highly incensed that his sister should have disgraced herself by an attachment to a Christian slave, he vented his displeasure upon its unfortunate object. He ordered his head to be shaved, his body to be stripped and clothed with a rough tunic of hair-cloth, and a large ring of iron to be fastened around his neck. He found many companions in misfortune, and, being the last comer, he was, as he says, " slave of slaves to them all ; " though, he continues, " there was no great choice, for the best was so bad, that a dog could hardly have lived to endure."

Smith does not inform us of the length of his captivity, nor have we any data for ascertaining it, but it could not have been many months ; for the battle, in which he was taken, was fought in 1602, and we hear of his return from slavery, to Transylvania in December, 1603. He has left an account of the manners and customs, religion and government, of the " Crym-Tartars," as he calls them, which does credit to his powers of observation, and the retentiveness of his memory, but which would be neither new nor interesting to the reader. Of their offensive and comfortless style of living he speaks with the energy of personal disgust, but makes honorable mention of their justice and integrity. For their military equipments, knowledge, and discipline he expresses the contempt natural to a thorough master of the art of war, but does justice to their bravery, their skill in horsemanship, and their powers of endurance. The brave spirit of Smith could not be conquered even by the galling chains of bondage, which were rendered heavier by his despair of being ever able to throw them off; for he says, that "all the hope he had ever to be delivered from this thraldom was only the love of Tragabigzanda, who surely was ignorant of his bad usage; for, although he had often debated the matter with some Christians, that had been there a long time slaves, they could not find how to make an escape by any reason or possibility; but God, beyond man's expectation or imagination, helpeth his servants, when they least think of help, as it happened to him." He was employed to thresh corn in a country-house belonging to Timour, which was a league distant from his residence. His cruel master, who felt a particular ill-will towards him, never passed him without displaying it by gross abuse, and even personal violence. His ill-treatment, on one occasion, was so outrageous, that Smith, maddened and transported beyond the bounds of reason by a sense of insult, and reckless of consequences, knowing that, happen what might, his miserable condition could not be changed for the worse, rose against him and beat out his brains with his threshing-flail. The instinct of self-preservation is fertile in expedients. He clothed himself in the rich attire of the slain Timour, hid his body under the straw, filled a knapsack with corn, mounted his horse, and galloped off to the desert.

Save the exulting sense of freedom, his condition was but little improved, however, and he could hardly hope for any thing but a death more or less speedy, according as he was recaptured or not. He was in the midst of a wild, vast, and uncultivated desert, dreading to meet any human beings, who might recognise him as a runaway slave by the iron collar which he still wore about his neck, and again reduce him to bondage. He wandered about two or three days without any end or purpose, and in utter loneliness and despair; but Providence, who had brought him out of captivity, befriended him still further, and directed his random steps to the main road, which leads from Tartary into Russia.

After a fatiguing and perilous journey of sixteen days, he arrived at Ecopolis, upon the river

Don, a garrison of the Russians; where, he says, "the governor, after a due examination of those his hard events, took off his irons, and so kindly used him, he thought himself new risen from death, and the good lady Calamata largely supplied his wants." This last clause is characteristic of Smith. His gentlemanly courtesy prompts him to acknowledge the kind attentions of a lady, while his modesty forbids him to mention any of the reasons which induced her to take an interest in him, still less to exaggerate that interest into a warmer feeling.

Being furnished by the friendly governor with letters of recommendation, he travelled, under the protection of convoys, to Hermandstadt in Transylvania. His journey through these desolate regions was made delightful by the kind attentions which he constantly received. He says, "in all his life, he seldom met with more respect, mirth, content, and entertainment, and not any governor, where he came, but gave him somewhat as a present, beside his charges." Their own exposed situation on the frontiers made them constantly liable to be carried into slavery by the Tartars, and they could sympathize with one who had just escaped a fate of which they were continually apprehensive.

On his arrival in Transylvania, where he found many of his old friends and companions in arms, and where his brilliant exploits had made him generally known and popular, he was received with enthusiasm, as one risen from the grave, and overwhelmed with honors and attentions. He says, that "he was glutted with content, and near drowned with joy," and that he never would have left these kind friends, but for his strong desire to "rejoice himself" in his own native country, after all his toils and perils. At Leipsic he met with his old Colonel, the Earl of Meldritch, and Prince Sigismund, who gave him a diploma, confirming the title of nobility he had previously conferred upon him, and fifteen ducats to repair his losses. From thence he travelled through Germany, France, and Spain, visiting the places most worthy of note in each.

Hearing that a civil war had broken out in Barbary, eager to gain new honors and encounter new perils, he sailed in a French ship of war to the African coast, and went to the city of Morocco; but, finding that the contending parties were equally treacherous and unworthy, he refused to throw his sword into either scale. He describes some of the objects most worthy of note in the cities of Morocco and Fez, and gives a slight sketch of the conquests and discoveries of the Portuguese in the southern portions of Africa. He departed from Morocco in the same vessel in which he had come, and which, on the voyage, sustained a desperate fight against two Spanish men-of-war, and succeeded in beating them off. He returned to his own country about the year 1604.

CHAPTER III.

State of public Feeling in England in regard to Colonizing the Coast of America.— Smith becomes interested in the Subject. — Establishment of the Virginia and Plymouth Companies. — An Expedition sets Sail from England. — Dissensions on the Voyage. — Arrival in Virginia.

THE times, of which we are writing, were fruitful alike in great enterprises and in great men. The brilliant discoveries of the Portuguese in the East, and of Columbus and Sebastian Cabot in the West, had startled the civilized world like the sound of a trumpet, and given to the human mind that spring and impulse, which are always produced by remarkable events. The fiery and adventurous spirits of Europe found the bounds of the old world too narrow for them, and panted for the untried spheres of our new and broader continents.

The wealth and fertility of the newly discovered lands, of course, lost nothing in the narratives of the few, who had by chance visited them, and returned home to astonish their admiring and less fortunate friends with tales of what they had seen and heard. They had seen climes which were the favorites of the sun, and his burning glances filled the earth, the air, and the sea with strange beauty. There were birds of gorgeous plumage, dazzling the eye with their motions and colors, flowers of the richest hues and most delicate odors, and aromatic forests that made the air faint with perfume, and "old Ocean smile for many a league." But the most extravagant accounts were given of the mineral treasures of the new countries. Gold and silver were so plentiful, that the most common utensils were made of them; and every one had some story to tell of "the Eldorado, where" (in the words of Mike Lambourne in "Kenilworth") "urchins play at cherry-pit with diamonds, and country wenches thread rubies for necklaces instead of rowan-tree berries; where the pantiles are made of pure gold, and the paving-stones of virgin silver." The good and bad passions of men were alike stimulated. There were savages to be civilized and heathen to be converted; there were worlds to be conquered and laurels to be won; avarice was allured by dreams of untold wealth, and enterprise by prospects of boundless adventure.

England was strongly infected by the general feeling, and the genius and accomplishments of Sir Walter Raleigh kindled in all ranks a strong passion for foreign adventures. Several attempts had been made in the reign of Elizabeth, under the auspices of that remarkable man, to plant a colony in North America, the earliest settlement having been made, in 1585, on the island of Roanoke, in Albemarle Sound, on the coast of North Carolina; but no one had taken firm root. The history of these short-lived colonies, and an examination of the causes which led to their failure, would be out of place here. *

At the time of Smith's arrival in England there was not any English colony on the continent of North America; but the public attention had been strongly awakened to the subject by the animated representations of Captain Bartholomew Gosnold, who, in 1602, had made a prosperous voyage to the coast of New England, and had, on his return, spoken in the warmest terms of its fertility and the salubrity of its climate, and strongly urged upon his coun-

---

* The reader will find a minute and accurate account of their fortunes in Stith's *History of Virginia*, and a succinct and well-written one in Grahame's *History of the United States*.

trymen the importance of colonizing it. He and Captain Smith seem to have been drawn towards each other by that kind of instinct, which brings together kindred spirits, and Smith entered into his plans with characteristic ardor. It was indeed precisely the enterprise to be embraced by a man like Smith, who panted for action, who dreaded nothing so much as repose, who sighed for perils, adventures, "hair-breadth 'scapes," and "moving accidents by flood and field."

The statements of Gosnold having been amply confirmed by subsequent voyagers, and King James, who was well-inclined to any plan, which would give employment to his frivolous and restless mind, and increase his power and consequence, encouraging the plan of establishing a colony, an association was formed for that purpose. Letters patent, bearing date April 10th, 1606, were issued to Sir Thomas Gates, Sir George Somers, Richard Hackluyt, and their associates, granting to them the territories in America, lying on the seacoast between the thirty-fourth and forty-fifth degrees of north latitude, together with all islands situated within a hundred miles of their shores. The associates were divided into two companies, one consisting of London adventurers, to whom the northern part was assigned, and under whose auspices New England was afterwards settled. It was provided, that there should be at least one hundred miles' distance between the two colonies. The terms of this charter were strongly expressive of the King's arbitrary character, and of that jealous regard for his prerogatives, which, in after times, proved so fatal to his race. The most important provision was, that the supreme government was vested in a council resident in England, to be nominated by the crown, and the local jurisdiction was confided to a colonial council, appointed and removable at the pleasure of the crown, who were to be governed by royal instructions and ordinances from time to time promulgated.

The royal favor was yet more abundantly vouchsafed to them. The King busied himself in the employment, highly agreeable to his meddling and insatiable vanity, of drawing up a code of laws for the colonies that were about to be planted; which, among other things, provided, that the legislative and executive powers should be vested in the colonial council, with these important qualifications, however, that their laws were not to touch life or limb, that they should conform to the laws of England, and should continue in force only till modified or repealed by the King or the supreme council in England.

It was not until the 19th day of the following December, that an expedition set sail from

England. This delay arose from a variety of causes, and especially a want of funds. On that day a hundred and five colonists embarked from London in a squadron of three small vessels, the largest of which did not exceed a hundred tons in burden. Among the leading adventurers were Captains Gosnold and Smith, George Percy, brother of the Earl of Northumberland, Edward M. Wingfield, a London merchant, and Mr. Robert Hunt, a clergyman. The transportation of the colony was entrusted to Captain Christopher Newport, who was esteemed a mariner of skill and ability on the American coast. Orders for government were given to them, sealed in a box, which was not to be opened till their arrival in Virginia.

They went by the old and circuitous route of the Canary Islands and the West Indies. Being detained by contrary winds for six weeks upon the coast of England, troubles and dissensions sprang up among them, as often occurs in those expeditions, in which unanimity and harmony of feeling are of the most vital importance. Peace was with difficulty restored by the mild and judicious counsels of Mr. Hunt, who, though afflicted with a severe illness and the object of special dislike to some of the leading men, (who, as we are told, were "little better than Atheists,") devoted himself with unshaken firmness to his duty, and preferred the service of God and his country in a perilous and irksome enterprise, to the comforts and security of his own home, which was but twenty miles distant from the spot where the wind-bound fleet was lying.

On their arrival at the Canaries the flames of discord broke out with renewed fury, and Captain Smith became the victim of unjust suspicions and groundless enmity. His high reputation and frank, manly bearing had made him popular with the majority of the colonists, and his influence over them had excited the envy and dislike of some of the leaders ; while his pride of character and conscious innocence prevented him probably from making any exertions to conciliate them. He was accused by Wingfield and others of entering into a conspiracy to murder the council, usurp the government, and make himself king of Virginia. Upon these ridiculous charges he was kept a prisoner during the remainder of the voyage.

From the Canaries they steered to the West Indies, where they traded with the natives, and spent three weeks in recruiting. They then set sail for the Island of Roanoke, their original destination, but a violent storm providentially overtook them on the coast and carried them to the mouth of the Chesapeake Bay. They discovered land on the 26th of April, 1607, which they named

Cape Henry, in honor of the Prince of Wales. They sailed into the James River, and explored it for the space of forty miles from its mouth. The appearance of the country on each side filled them with delight. It was fertile and well watered, the landscape picturesquely varied with hills, valleys, and plains, and newly decked with the green mantle of spring. To the sea-worn voyagers, the scene was like enchantment, and this spot seemed to be pointed out by the finger of Heaven, as their resting-place and home.

They were employed seventeen days in pitching upon a convenient spot for their settlement. Upon the very first day of their arrival they went on shore, and were attacked by some Indians, who came "creeping upon all fours, from the hills, like bears," and who wounded some of the party with their arrows, but were forced to retire by a discharge of muskets. They found, in one of the shallow rivers, abundance of oysters, "which lay on the ground as thick as stones," and in many of them there were pearls. Going on shore, says the writer,* " we past through excellent ground, full of flowers of divers kinds and colors, and as goodly trees as I have seen, as cedar, cypress, and other kinds ; going a little further we came to a little plat of ground, full of

---

* See note on page 214.

fine and beautiful strawberries, four times bigger and better than ours in England." The northern point at the entrance of Chesapeake Bay they named Point Comfort, because they found there deep water for anchorage, "which put them in good comfort." Landing on this point on the fourth day after their arrival, they saw five Indians, who were at first alarmed at the sight of the English, "until they saw the captain lay his hand upon his heart," upon which they came boldly up and invited them to Kecoughtan, their town. This invitation they accepted; and on arriving at the village they were kindly entertained by the Indians, who gave them corn-bread, tobacco, and pipes, and expressed their welcome by a dance. Four days afterwards, they were kindly entertained by the chief of the Pashiphay tribe, and received an invitation from the chief of the Rappahannas to come and visit him. He sent them a messenger to guide them to his habitation, and stood on the banks of the river to meet them as they landed, "with all his train," (says the writer,) "as goodly men as any I have seen of savages or Christians, the Werowance * coming before them, playing on a flute made of a reed, with a crown of deer's hair, colored red, in fashion of a rose, fasten-

---

* A name by which the chiefs of tribes in Virginia and its neighborhood were designated.

ed about his knot of hair, and a great plate of copper on the other side of his head, with two long feathers in fashion of a pair of horns placed in the midst of his crown. His body was painted all with crimson, with a chain of beads about his neck ; his face painted blue, besprinkled with silver ore, as we thought; his ears all behung with bracelets of pearl, and in either ear a bird's claw through it, beset with fine copper or gold. He entertained us in so modest a proud fashion, as though he had been a prince of civil government, holding his countenance without laughter or any such ill behavior. He caused his mat to be spread on the ground, where he sat down with a great majesty, taking a pipe of tobacco, the rest of his company standing about him. After he had rested a while, he rose and made signs to us to come to his town. He went foremost, and all the rest of his people and ourselves followed him up a steep hill, where his palace was settled. We passed through the woods in fine paths, having most pleasant springs which issued from the mountains. We also went through the goodliest corn-fields that ever were seen in any country. When we came to Rappahanna town, he entertained us in good humanity."

On the 8th day of May they went farther up the river. They went on shore in the country belonging to the tribe of Apamatica, where they were met by a large body of Indians armed " with bows and arrows in a most warlike manner, with the swords at their backs beset with sharp stones and pieces of iron, able to cleave a man in sunder." But, on making signs of peace, they were suffered to land without molestation. On the 13th day of May, they pitched upon the place of their settlement, which was a peninsula on the north side of James River, about forty miles from the mouth, to which they gave the name of Jamestown. The shore was so bold, that their ship could be in six fathoms of water, and be moored to the trees on the land. *

From this date the history of the United States of America begins, after a lapse of one hundred and ten years from the discovery of the continent by Sebastian Cabot, and twenty two years after the first attempt to colonize it by Sir Walter Raleigh. Who can look back and compare the past with the present without reflections of the most serious and interesting cast? In this little

---

* This slight sketch of their proceedings, after their arrival in James River, and before they settled in James-town, is taken from a Narrative in Purchas (Vol. IV. p. 1685), written by George Percy, the brother of the Earl of Northumberland, one of the early settlers, and as distinguished for high character as for high birth. He succeeded Captain Smith as governor. His Narrative is comprised in six folio pages, and is very interesting.

handful of men, occupying a strip of land in the
southeastern corner of Virginia, surrounded by
pathless woods and savage men, we behold the
" seminal principle " of a mighty people, destined
to subdue the vast continent to the mild sway of
civilization, letters, and Christianity, and to con-
nect two oceans by a living and unbroken chain.
Owing their political existence to the charter of
a tyrant, which deprived them of some of the
most valuable privileges of Englishmen, the colonists laid the foundations of a state, in which the
sternest and fiercest spirit of liberty was to be
developed, and which was destined to break out,
in little more than a century and a half, in deadly
opposition to that mother-country, to whose ample robe they had so long clung for support ; not
so much to obtain redress for actual oppressions,
as in denial of the right to oppress, and in defence
of those principles of truth, freedom, political
equality, and natural justice, which descended
to them with their Saxon blood and Saxon speech.
The tree of liberty was first planted in the soil of
America by despotic hands. The results which
followed the settlement of this country were such,
as the most sagacious wisdom could not have
foreseen, nor the most visionary enthusiasm have
hoped. History, no less than revelation, teaches
us our dependence upon a higher Power, whose
wise and good plans we can as little comprehend

as oppose, who is ever bringing real good out of seeming evil, and who, in the discipline with which he tries both men and nations, is ever making misfortune, discouragement, and struggle, the elements of unbounded growth, progress, and prosperity.

CHAPTER IV.

Early Struggles of the Colony. — Active Exertions of Captain Smith in Providing Food and Suppressing Insubordination.

BEFORE going any further it will be proper to give the reader a short account of the original inhabitants of the soil, as their history becomes almost immediately blended with that of the colony. At the time of the first settlement by the Europeans, it has been estimated that there were not more than twenty thousand Indians within the limits of the state of Virginia. Within a circuit of sixty miles from Jamestown, Captain Smith says, there were about five thousand souls, and of these scarce fifteen hundred were warriors. The whole territory between the mountains and the sea was occupied by more than forty tribes, thirty of whom were united in a confederacy under

Powhatan, whose dominions, hereditary and acquired by conquest, comprised the whole country between the rivers James and Potomac, and extended into the interior as far as the falls of the principal rivers.

Campbell, in his "History of Virginia," states the number of Powhatan's subjects to have been eight thousand. Powhatan was a remarkable man; a sort of savage Napoleon, who, by the force of his character and the superiority of his talents, had raised himself from the rank of a petty chieftain to something of imperial dignity and power. He had two places of abode, one called Powhatan, where Richmond now stands, and the other at Werowocomoco, on the north side of York River, within the present county of Gloucester. He lived in something of barbaric state and splendor. He had a guard of forty warriors in constant attendance, and four sentinels kept watch during the night around his dwelling. His power was absolute over his people, by whom he was looked up to with something of religious veneration. His feelings towards the whites were those of implacable enmity, and his energy and abilities made him a formidable foe to the infant colony.

Besides the large confederacy of which Powhatan was the chief, there were two others, with which that was often at war. One of these, called the Mannahoacs, consisted of eight tribes, and occupied the country between the Rappahannoc and York rivers; the other, consisting of five tribes, was called the Monacans, and was settled between York and James rivers, above the Falls. There were also, in addition to these, many scattering and independent tribes.

Captain Smith describes at considerable length their manners and customs, dress, appearance, government, and religion. They did not differ materially, in any of these respects, from the northern tribes. They had the straight black hair, the tall, erect, and graceful forms, and the copper complexion. Their characters displayed the same virtues and vices, which those, who are in any degree familiar with the early history of our country, recognise as peculiar to the Indian race. They were equally removed from the romantic *beau-idéal*, which modern writers of fiction have painted, and the monstrous caricature, drawn by those, who, from interested motives, have represented them, as " all compact " of cruelty, treachery, indolence, and cowardice.

As soon as the colony had landed, the box containing their orders was opened; and it was found that Edward M. Wingfield, Bartholomew Gosnold, John Smith, Christopher Newport, John Ratcliffe, John Martin, and George Kendall were appointed a council. They were to choose a President from among their own number, who was to hold his office a year, with the privilege of having two votes. The council made choice of Mr. Wingfield as President.

It is curious that almost the first act of the council should have been one of disobedience to their superior power; for, though Captain Smith had been expressly named one of the council, they excluded him, and gave their reasons for so doing in a speech made probably by the President, to the whole colony. However dissatisfied they might have been, the time was too precious to be spent in brawls and wrangling. All hands set themselves diligently to work. The council planned a fort, others cut down trees to clear a place to pitch their tents, while others were employed in making nets and preparing spots for gardens. The "overweening jealousy" of the President would not permit any military exercises or any fortifications to be erected, except a barrier of the boughs of trees in the shape of a half-moon. Soon after, an expedition was sent to discover the head of James River, consisting of twenty men, under the command of Newport and Smith, whose noble nature did not suffer him for a moment to abate any thing of his zeal for the good of the colony, under the influence of personal pique or disappointment. They passed by several habitations, and on the sixth day arrived at the Falls, and erecting a cross, took possession of the country in the name of King James.   Here they visited Powhatan, whose town consisted of but twelve houses pleasantly situated on a hill.   He received them with seeming kindness, and gratefully accepted a hatchet which Captain Newport presented to him. Their further progress up the river was obstructed by the Rapids or Falls.   They were kindly and hospitably treated by the natives, whom they encountered in their excursion.

On their return they found, that the colony had in their absence suffered from the carelessness of the President in leaving them without military defences; for the Indians had attacked them, wounded seventeen men, and killed one boy.   The writer of the narrative contained in Smith's History says, that had not a cross-bar shot from the ship, struck off a bough from a tree in the midst of the Indians and caused them to retire in affright, the colonists would have been entirely cut off, they being securely at work and unarmed.   The President, made wiser by experience, ordered the fort to be palisadoed, the ordnance to be mounted, and the men to be armed and exercised.   They were frequently attacked by the savages, whose numbers and activity generally gave them the advantage, notwithstanding the superiority of the whites in arms.

At the end of six weeks, Captain Newport, who had been engaged merely to transport the colony, made preparations for returning to England. The enemies of Captain Smith pretended, out of compassion to him, a desire to refer him to the council in England to be reprimanded by them, rather than expose him to the publicity of a legal trial, which might injure his reputation and endanger his life. But he was not a man to be bullied or cajoled. He was strong, not only in the consciousness of innocence, but in the affections and respect of a large majority of the colonists. He loudly demanded a trial, the result of which was highly honorable to him. The arts of his enemies were revealed, and those who had been suborned to accuse him betrayed their employers. He was acquitted by acclamation, and the President condemned to pay a fine of two hundred pounds, which Smith generously added to the public property of the colony. Many other difficulties had arisen, which were amicably adjusted, by the "good doctrine and exhortation" of Mr. Hunt, who seems to have richly deserved the blessing promised to the peace-makers, and, by his influence, Captain Smith was admitted a member of council. On the next Sunday, they all partook of the communion, as a bond of Christian harmony, and a pledge that their recent reconciliation was sincere. On the following day, the Indians in the neighborhood voluntarily sued for peace. Captain Newport sailed for England, on the 15th of June, leaving one hundred and four persons behind, and promising to return again in twenty weeks with fresh supplies.

The colony, owing to gross mismanagement and improvidence in the council in England, were very inadequately furnished with provisions. While the ships remained, they did not suffer from want, as they could always, either for " love or money," obtain a portion of the sailors' stores, of which they had great abundance. But this resource was cut off by the departure of the squadron, and they were reduced to a daily allowance of a half-pint of barley and the same quantity of wheat, both of the worst quality, and, from their long remaining in the ship's hold, alive with insects. Their historian says, with melancholy mirth, that " had they been as free from all sins as gluttony and drunkenness, they might have been canonized for saints; " for this wretched fare, with some sturgeon and shell-fish from the river, was all they had to subsist upon till the month of September. Disease and death made frightful havoc among them; for, besides their scanty and unhealthy food, their constitutions were weakened by extreme toil in the heat of the summer, by imperfect shelter, and by the sudden change from the habits and comforts of civilized life to constant labor and exposure. Before September, fifty of their number had died, including Captain Gosnold, the first projector of the expedition.

The President, Wingfield, by embezzling the public stores and converting them to his own use, had escaped the general famine and sickness,* but had thereby much increased the dislike, which had always been felt towards him. In the beginning of the Autumn he laid a plan to escape to England in the colony's bark, which treacherous conduct (to borrow the language of the historian) "so moved our dead spirits, that we deposed him." Captain John Ratcliffe was elected in his place. Kendall, who was concerned with him in the plot, was expelled from the council, so that it was now reduced to three members, the President, Martin, and Smith. After the discovery of this conspiracy, the sufferings of the colonists reached their utmost extent. Their provisions were consumed, no prospect of relief appeared, and they were in hourly expectation of an attack

* This charge seems hardly credible; but it is positively asserted by Smith, whose honesty and integrity are beyond suspicion, and not contradicted by any writer, to my knowledge.

from the Indians, to whom they could have offered no effectual resistance, in their present enfeebled condition. But they, so far from doing them any violence, supplied them liberally with provisions; a treatment so welcome and unexpected, that the grateful piety of Smith ascribes it to a special interposition of divine Providence.*

Smith's eminent abilities and high character, it was evident from the beginning, would sooner or later give him the first place in the colony, whatever might be his nominal rank. In times of peril and adversity, men, by a kind of unerring instinct, discover who is the ruling spirit, and put the helm into his hands as the only pilot that can weather the storm. Such times had

---

* The writer in Smith's History acquits the council in England of all blame in respect to their scanty provisions, and sums up the causes, which led to their difficulties, in the following terms.

"And now where some affirmed it was ill done of the council to send forth men so badly provided, this incontradictable reason will show them plainly they are too ill advised to nourish such ill conceits; first, the fault of our going was our own; what could be thought fitting or necessary we had, but what we should find or want, or where we should be, we were all ignorant; and, supposing to make our passage in two months with victual to live and the advantage of the Spring to work, we were at sea five months, which we both

now come upon the infant settlement, and they turned their eyes upon Smith, as the only man who could rescue them from the difficulties in which they were involved. The new President and Martin were neither able nor popular, and the official rank of the former was but dust in the balance, when weighed against Smith's native superiority. From this time the chief management of affairs devolved upon him.

He entered upon his duties with characteristic ardor and energy. He set about the building of Jamestown, and by kind words and encouraging promises, and, more than all, by his own example, taking upon himself the most laborious and fatiguing duties, he pushed on the work with so

---

spent our victual in passing and lost the opportunity of the time and season to plant, by the unskilful presumption of our ignorant transporters, that understood not at all what they undertook. Such actions have ever since the world's beginning been subject to such accidents, and every thing of worth is found full of difficulties, but nothing so difficult as to establish a commonwealth so far remote from men and means, and where men's minds are so untoward as neither to do well themselves nor suffer others." Stith, on the other hand, an accurate and painstaking writer, accuses the council and especially Sir Thomas Smith, their treasurer, of want of care and thoughtfulness, and says that the same mismanagement and carelessness marked the whole of that gentleman's administration of the affairs of the colony.

much diligence, that he had in a short time provided most of them with lodgings, neglecting any for himself. Their stock of provisions being well nigh exhausted, he resolved to make search for a fresh supply. His ignorance of the language of the natives, and his want of men and equipments, were great impediments to the expedition, but no discouragement to his adventurous spirit. Attended by only five or six men, he went down the river in a boat, to Kecoughtan, where Hampton now stands. The natives, who were aware of their condition, treated them with contempt as poor, starved creatures, and, when invited to traffic, would scoffingly give them a handful of corn or a piece of bread in exchange for their swords, muskets, and clothing.

Finding that kind looks and courteous treatment produced only insult and contumely, Smith felt himself constrained by necessity to adopt a different course, though he frankly acknowledges that he thereby exceeded the terms of his commission. He discharged his muskets among them and ran his boat ashore, the affrighted Indians betaking themselves to the shelter of the woods. Marching to their houses he found them abounding with corn; but he would not permit his men to touch it, expecting that the Indians would return in large numbers to attack him, in which expectation he was not disappointed. Sixty or seventy of them soon appeared, some painted black, some red, some white, and some party-colored, in a square column, singing and dancing, with their *Okee* borne before them. This was an idol made of skins, stuffed with moss, painted, and ornamented with copper chains. They were armed with clubs, shields, bows, and arrows, and boldly advanced upon the English, who received them with a volley of musketry, which brought many of them to the ground, and with them their idol. The rest fled in dismay to the woods. They sent a priest with a proposition to make peace and restore their idol. Smith told them, that, if six of them would come unarmed and load his boat with corn, he would not only return them their idol, but give them beads, copper, and hatchets besides, and be their friend. These terms were accepted and the stipulations performed. They brought ample supplies, not only of corn, but of turkeys, venison, and wild fowl, and continued, until the English departed, singing and dancing in token of friendship.

The success of this expedition induced Captain Smith to repeat his excursions, both by land and water, in the course of one of which he discovered the people of Chiokahominy, who lived upon the banks of the river of that name. The provisions, however, which he so carefully and toilsomely provided, the colonists improvidently wasted,

Whenever Smith was out of sight, owing to the President's imbecility and Martin's ill health, every thing was in tumultuous confusion, like a school in the absence of its teacher. Wingfield and Kendall, who were smarting under their recent disgrace, took advantage of one of these seasons of insubordination to conspire with some disorderly malcontents, to escape to England in the bark, which by Smith's direction had been fitted up for a trading voyage to be undertaken the next year. Smith's unexpected return nipped their project in the bud, which was not done, however, without recourse to arms, and in the action Captain Kendall was slain. Soon afterwards the President and Captain Archer intended to abandon the country, which purpose was also frustrated by Smith, a circumstance which puts in the strongest light his power and influence. We are told, " that the Spaniard never more greedily desired gold than he victual, nor his soldiers more to abandon the country than he to keep it." Having found plenty of corn in the neighborhood of Chickahominy River, he made an excursion there, where he found hundreds of Indians awaiting his approach with loaded baskets in their hands. At the approach of winter too, the rivers were covered with swans, geese, and ducks, which, with corn, beans, and pumpkins supplied by the Indians, furnished their tables amply and luxuriously. This abundance of good cheer had its natural effect in producing good-humor and curing home-sickness, "none of our Tuftaffety humorists" (to borrow a curious expression of the historian) desiring to return to England. A craving stomach has in all ages been the fruitful source of discontent and mutiny; and Captain Smith showed his knowledge of human nature, in taking so much pains to address it with the only arguments whose force it is capable of acknowledging.

CHAPTER V.

Captain Smith's Captivity among the Indians. — His Life is saved by Pocahontas. — His Return to Jamestown.

CAPTAIN SMITH's gleams of prosperity and repose were, like the "uncertain glories of an April day," broken by constant interruptions of clouds and misfortune. He was murmured against by some cross-grained spirits, and even rebuked by the council, for his dilatoriness in not penetrating to the source of Chickahominy river, a charge, one would think, the most unreasonable that could be brought against such a man. Stung by these unmerited complaints, he immediately set out upon a new expedition.   He proceeded as far as his barge could float, reaching that point with great labor, and having been obliged to cut a way through the trees which had fallen into the river.   Having left the barge securely moored, with strict orders to his men not to leave it till his return, and taking with him two Englishmen and two Indians as guides, he went higher up in a canoe.   This he left in charge of the Englishmen and went up twenty miles further to the meadows at the head of the river, where he occupied himself in shooting game.   The disorderly and ill-disciplined crew, whom he had left in charge of the barge, had disobeyed his injunctions and gone straggling into the woods.   They were suddenly attacked by a party of three hundred bowmen commanded by Opechancanough, King of Pamunkey and brother to Powhatan, and one of their number, George Cassen by name, was taken prisoner.   The rest, with great difficulty, regained their barge.   The Indians extorted from their prisoner information of the place where Captain Smith was, and then put him to death in the most barbarous manner.   In their pursuit of Captain Smith, they came upon the two men, by name Robinson and Emry, who had been left with the canoe and who were sleeping by a fire, and discharged their arrows at them with fatal effect.

Having discovered Smith, they wounded him in the thigh with an arrow. Finding himself beset with numbers, he bound one of his Indian guides to his left arm with his garters as a buckler, and defended himself so skilfully with his gun, that he killed three and wounded many others. His enemies retreating out of gun-shot, he attempted to reach his canoe, but paying more heed to his foes than to his own footsteps, he sunk, with his guide, up to the middle in a treacherous morass. Helpless as he was, his bravery had inspired such terror, that they dared not approach him, until, being almost dead with cold, he threw away his arms and surrendered himself. They drew him out, and led him to the fire, by which his slain companions had been sleeping, and diligently chafed his benumbed limbs.

Though in expectation of an immediate and cruel death, his presence of mind did not forsake him, and his inexhaustible resources were not found wanting in that trying hour, when he was an unarmed captive in the hands of merciless savages. Without asking for his life, which would only have lowered the respect with which his bravery had inspired them, he demanded to speak with their chief. When he was presented to him, he showed to him a pocket compass which he happened to have with him. The tremulous vibrations of the needle, which they could see, but not touch, on account of the glass, amused and surprised the Indians ; and when Captain Smith, partly by language, he having acquired some knowledge of their tongue, and partly by signs, proceeded to explain to them the nature and properties of this wonderful instrument, and the discoveries to which it had led, and also described to them the courses of the heavenly bodies, the spherical shape of the earth, the alternations of day and night, the extent of the continents, oceans, and seas, the variety of nations and their relative position, which made some of them antipodes to others, they were filled with wonder and amazement.*

Notwithstanding this, within an hour they tied him to a tree and prepared to shoot him with their arrows.   But when the chief held up the compass, they threw down their arms, and led him in a sort of triumphal procession, to Orapax,

---

* The above is the account contained in Smith's History, and, of course, came originally from Smith himself. It is impossible to believe, that the ignorant Indians could have comprehended such abstruse matters.   They probably regarded the compass as the Englishman's god, a "great medicine," like the wig of the officer, which came off when grasped by his swarthy foe, and cheated him of a scalp to his inexpressible amazement.   A wig and a mariner's compass would be equally mysterious, and entitled to equal reverence, in the eyes of these untutored children of nature.   "*Omne ignotum pro magnifico.*"

a village situated a few miles northeast of where Richmond now stands. They marched in single file, their chief being in the midst, with the English swords and muskets borne before him. After him came Captain Smith held by three stout men, and on each side six archers. When they arrived at the village, the women and children flocked round to behold their pale-faced captive. The warriors who conducted him, after some military manœuvres, placing Smith and their chief in the midst, performed a war-dance around them with frightful yells and strange contortions of their limbs and features. After this dance had been thrice performed, they conducted him to a "long house," where he was guarded by forty men. He was served so liberally with provisions, that he supposed their intention was to fatten and eat him, a reflection which did not at all tend to sharpen his appetite.

At this time one of those little incidents occurred which show that even barbarous manners, fierce hostility, and familiarity with scenes of bloodshed and cruelty, cannot turn the heart wholly into stone, or quench the natural instinct of compassion. An Indian to whom Smith, upon his first arrival in Virginia, had given some beads and trinkets, brought him a garment of furs, which was a most acceptable present, as he was well nigh perishing with the cold, which in

that year (1607) was very great both in Europe
and America. The name of this grateful and
benevolent savage was Maocassater. I take
pleasure in recording it, as well as the anecdote,
which has made it so deserving of being preserved, and is so delightful an exception to the
acts of cruelty, treachery, and oppression, that
generally mark the conduct of both whites and
Indians towards each other.

Two days after this, he was attacked, and, but
for his guard, would have been killed by an
old Indian, whose son was lying at the point of
death. Whether this was a natural sickness,
which the father supposed was occasioned by the
sorceries of Smith, and was therefore provoked
to seek revenge, or whether he had been wounded
by Smith before his capture, we do not learn ;
probably the latter. They brought him to the
dying man's side, in hopes that he might recover
him. Smith told them that he had a medicine
at Jamestown which would restore him. But
they would not permit him to go after it. .

The Indians were making great preparations
to attack Jamestown, and desired to secure
Smith's aid and coöperation. They promised
him in return for his services, not only life and
liberty, but as much land and as many women
as he could wish. He endeavored to dissuade
them from their attempt, and pointed out the

formidable dangers to which they would be exposed from the springing of mines, the cannons, and warlike engines; to which they listened with alarmed attention. In order that his statements might be confirmed, he proposed to send messengers to the colony, to which they assented. He wrote a note, in which he informed his countrymen of the plans in agitation against them, desired them to send him certain enumerated articles, and to give the messengers a wholesome fright, at the same time informing these last of all that would happen to them. These men started off in a season of extreme cold and arrived at Jamestown. Seeing men come out to meet them, as Smith had told them would be the case, they fled in dismay, leaving their note behind them. Coming again in the evenning, they found the articles mentioned in the note, in the very spot where Smith told them to look for them. They returned in three days and related their adventures to the great amazement of all, who supposed, that " he could either divine, or the paper speak."

This incident, which confirmed their suspicion of Smith's supernatural powers, induced them to lay aside all thoughts of attacking Jamestown. They then carried him about in triumph through the country, showing him to the various tribes which dwelt on the Rappahannoc, and Potowmac rivers, and finally brought him to Pamunkéy, the residence of Opechancanough, which was situated near the fork of York River. Here they performed a strange ceremony, the object of which was, as they told him, to ascertain whether his intentions towards them were friendly or not. The following was the order of performances. Early in the morning, a great fire was made in a long house, and a mat spread on each side, on one of which he was seated, and then his guard retired. "Presently came skipping in a great, grim fellow, all painted over with coal, mingled with oil, and many snakes' and weasels' skins stuffed with moss, and all their tails tied together, so as they met on the crown of his head in a tassel; and round about the tassel was a coronet of feathers, the skins hanging round about his head, back, and shoulders, and in a manner covered his face; with a hellish voice and a rattle in his hand." This personage, who was a priest, commenced his invocation by a variety of wild gestures and grimaces, and concluded by surrounding the fire with a circle of meal. This being done, "three more such like devils came rushing in with the like antique tricks," whose bodies were painted half black and half red, and their faces daubed with red and white streaks to resemble mustachios. These three danced about for some time, "and then came in three more as ugly as the rest," with their eyes painted red and with white streaks upon their black faces. Finally, they all seated themselves opposite to the prisoner, three on the right hand of the priest and three on his left. They then began a song, accompanying it with their rattles; and when this was done, the chief priest laid down five grains of corn, and after a short oration, attended with violent muscular exertion, laid down three more. After that they began their song again, and then another oration, laying down as many grains of corn as before, till they had twice encircled the fire. Then, continuing the incantation, they laid sticks between the divisions of the corn. The whole day was spent in these ceremonies, during which time neither Smith nor the performers tasted food, but at night they feasted abundantly on the best provisions they had. These rites were continued for three successive days. They told him that the circle of meal signified their own country, the circles of corn the bounds of the sea, and the sticks his country. They imagined the world to be flat and round like a trencher, and themselves to be placed in the middle of it.

They afterwards showed him a bag of gunpowder, which they had taken from him or his companions, and which they carefully preserved till the next spring to plant, as they did their corn, supposing it to be a grain. He was afterwards invited by Opitchapan, the second brother of Powhatan, to his house, and sumptuously entertained ; but here, as on all other occasions, none of the Indians would eat with him, though they would partake of the portions which he left unconsumed.

At last they brought him to Werowocomoco, the residence of Powhatan, which was situated on the north side of York River, in Gloucester County, about twenty-five miles below the fork of the river. It was at that time Powhatan's principal place of residence, though afterwards, not being pleased with its proximity to the English, he removed to Orapax. Upon Smith's arrival in the village, he was detained, until the Indian emperor and his court could make suitable preparations to receive their captive in proper state. In the meanwhile more than two hundred of his "grim courtiers" came to gaze at him, as if he had been a monster. Powhatan, who was at that time about sixty years old, is described as having been, in outward appearance, "every inch a king." His figure was noble, his stature majestic, and his countenance full of the severity and haughtiness of a ruler, whose will was supreme and whose nod was law.

He received Captain Smith with imposing, though rude ceremony. He was seated on a kind of throne, elevated above the floor of a large hut, in the midst of which was a fire. He was clothed with a robe of racoon skins. Two young women, his daughters, sat one on his right and the other on his left; and on each side of the hut there were two rows of men in front, and the same number of women behind. These all had their heads and shoulders painted red. Many had their hair ornamented with the white down of birds. Some had chains of white beads around their necks, and all had more or less of ornament. When Smith was brought home, they all set up a great shout.

Soon after his entrance, a female of rank was directed to bring him water to wash his hands, and another brought a bunch of feathers instead of a towel to dry them with. They then feasted him in the best manner they could, and held a long and solemn consultation to determine his fate. The decision was against him. Two large stones were brought in and placed before Powhatan, and Smith was dragged up to them and his head was placed upon them, that his brains might be beaten out with clubs. The fatal weapons were already raised and the stern executioners looked for the signal, which should bid them descend upon the victim's defenceless head. But the protecting shield of divine Providence was over him, and the arm of violence was arrested. Pocahontas, the King's favorite daughter, — at that time a child of twelve or thirteen years of age, — finding that her piteous entreaties to save the life of Smith were unavailing, rushed forward, clasped his head in her arms, and laid her own upon it, determined either to save his life, or share his fate. Her generous and heroic conduct touched her father's iron heart, and the life of the captive was spared, to be employed in making hatchets for himself, and bells and beads for his daughter.

The account of this beautiful and most touching scene, familiar as it is to every one, can hardly be read with unmoistened eyes. The incident is so dramatic and startling, that it seems to preserve the freshness of novelty amidst a thousand repetitions. We could almost as reasonably expect an angel to have come down from heaven, and rescued the captive, as that his deliverer should have sprung from the bosom of Powhatan's family. The universal sympathies of mankind and the best feelings of the human heart have redeemed this scene from the obscurity which, in the progress of time, gathers over all, but the most important events. It has pointed a thousand morals and adorned a thousand tales. Innumerable bosoms have throbbed and are yet to throb with generous admiration for this daughter of a people, whom we have been too ready to underrate. Had we known nothing of her, but what is related of her in this incident, she would deserve the eternal gratitude of the inhabitants of this country; for the fate of the colony may be said to have hung upon the arms of Smith's executioners. He was its life and soul, and, without the magic influence of his personal qualities, it would have abandoned, in despair, the project of permanently settling the country, and sailed to England by the first opportunity.

The generosity of Powhatan was not content with merely sparing his prisoner's life. He detained him but two days longer. At the end of that time, he conducted him to a large house in the woods, and there left him alone upon a mat by the fire. In a short time, from behind another mat that divided the house, "was made the most dolefullest noise he ever heard; then Powhatan, more like a devil than a man, with some two hundred more, as black as himself," came in and told him, that they were now friends, and that he should return to Jamestown; and that, if he would send him two pieces of cannon and a grindstone, he would give him the country of Capahowsic, and esteem him as his own son. He was faithful to his word, and despatched him immediately, with twelve guides. That night they quartered in the woods; and during the whole journey Captain Smith expected every moment to be put to death, notwithstanding Powhatan's fair words. But, as the narrative of his adventures has it, " Almighty God, by his divine Providence, had mollified the hearts of those stern barbarians with compassion." Smith reached Jamestown in safety, after an absence of seven weeks, and treated his savage guides with great hospitality and kindness. He showed them two demi-culverins and a millstone, which they proposed to carry to Powhatan, but found them too heavy. He ordered the culverins to be loaded with stones and discharged among the boughs of a tree covered with icicles, in order to magnify to them the effects of these formidable engines. When they heard the report and saw the ice and the branches come rattling down, they were greatly terrified. A few trinkets restored their confidence, and they were dismissed with a variety of presents for Powhatan and his family.

The generous conduct of Powhatan, in restoring a prisoner who had given such fatal proofs of courage and prowess, is worthy of the highest admiration. There is hardly any thing in history, that can afford a parallel to it. He was stimulated to take the prisoner's life, not only by revenge, a passion strongest in savage breasts, but by policy and that regard to his own interests, which Christian and civilized monarchs are justified in observing. He seems to have acted from some religious feeling, regarding Smith, either as a supernatural being, or as under the special protection of a higher power. How far this may have actuated him, or how far he may have been influenced by affection for his daughter, it is impossible to say; but, supposing both to have operated, we only elevate his conduct by elevating his motives. He must have been a noble being indeed, in whom religion or domestic affection could overcome the strong impulses of passion, revenge, and interest.

CHAPTER VI.

Arrival of Newport from England. — His Visit to Powhatan. — His Return.

SMITH's absence from Jamestown seems to have been always attended with evil consequences to the colony. The moment his back was turned, the unruly spirits, whom he alone could curb, broke out into disaffection and mutiny. He found "all in combustion" on his return. The colony was split into two factions, the stronger of which was preparing to quit the country in the bark. Captain Smith, at the hazard of his life, defeated this project, bringing his cannon to bear upon the bark, and threatening to sink her if they did not stay. In revenge for this, a conspiracy was formed by several, and among them the President, to put him to death, for the lives of Robinson and Emry, whom they said, he had led to their death, and he was consequently guilty of their murder. Such cobweb meshes as these could not hold a man like Smith; for "he quickly took such order with such lawyers, that he laid them by the heels, till he sent some of them prisoners to England." His relation of the plenty he had witnessed in the Indian territory, and of the power and liberality of Powhatan, cheered their drooping spirits, which were revived and sustained by the kindness of Pocahontas; whose deliverance of Smith was not a transient impulse, but consistent with her whole character, and who, with her attendants, every four or five days brought them abundance of provisions, thereby saving the lives of many that must otherwise have perished with hunger. The savages also came in great numbers, bringing presents continually to Captain Smith, and offering commodities for sale, at the prices which he himself set. His influence over them was unbounded, and they were ready, at his nod, to do any thing he required. They knew that he worshipped one supreme God, the Creator and Preserver of all things, whom they would call, in conversation, the God of Captain Smith.

This high opinion was much confirmed by the arrival of Captain Newport, at the time at which Smith had predicted to them it would happen, being in the latter part of the year 1607. Two ships had sailed from England, one commanded by Newport, and the other by Captain Nelson, the latter of which was dismasted on the coast of America, and blown off to the West Indies. Newport brought with him a reinforcement of men and provisions, and all things necessary. His arrival was a source of great joy to the colonists, but was in the end productive of some embarrassments. The President and council (Ratcliffe and Martin, Smith himself being the third), who had been always jealous of Smith's influence over the natives, endeavored to raise their credit and authority over them higher than his, by giving them four times as much for their goods as he had appointed. To gratify the mariners also, they gave them liberty to trade as much as they pleased; and the consequence was in a short time, that the market was so glutted, that a pound of copper could not procure what was formerly obtained for an ounce, the laws of political economy operating, before the science was heard of. Their trade was also injured by Captain Newport, who lavished his presents with the profuseness of a true sailor. They served, however, to impress Powhatan with a high idea of Newport's greatness, and made him very desirous of seeing him.

Accordingly the bark was prepared for a visit to Powhatan. Captain Newport was attended by Smith and Mr. Matthew Scrivener, a gentleman of sense and discretion, who had come over with Newport, and been admitted a member of the council, and by a guard of thirty or forty men. When they came to Werowocomoco, Newport began to entertain suspicions of treachery. They were obliged to cross many creeks and streams on bridges loosely made of poles and bark, and so frail that he imagined them to be traps set by the Indians. But Smith assured him there was nothing to fear, and with twenty men, leaving the bark, undertook to go forward and accomplish the journey alone. He went on, and was met by two or three hundred Indians, who conducted him and his companions into the town. He was received with shouts of welcome on all sides. Powhatan exerted himself to the utmost to set before him the most sumptuous and plentiful banquet he could provide. Four or five hundred men attended as a guard, and proclamation was made, that no one should do any harm to the English on pain of death.

The next day Newport came on shore, and was likewise warmly and hospitably received. An English boy, named Thomas Savage, was given by him to Powhatan, and he received in exchange, an intelligent and faithful Indian, named Namontack. Three or four days they spent in feasting, dancing, and trading, during which time the old chief behaved with such dignity, discretion, and propriety, as impressed his English visitors with the highest opinion of his natural capacity. His shrewdness in driving a bargain was displayed in a manner, which, but for Smith's superior tact, would have resulted in the great pecuniary loss of the English.

He would not condescend to haggle and barter for specific articles, as his subjects did, and told Captain Newport that it was not agreeable to his greatness "to trade for trifles in this peddling manner," and that, as they were both great and powerful men, their mutual transactions ought to be conducted on a scale of proportionate magnitude. He proposed to him, that Newport should lay down his commodities in a lump, and that he should select from them what he wanted, and give in return what he considered an equivalent.

The proposal was interpreted to Newport by Smith, who, at the same time, told him that all these fine words meant merely that Powhatan intended to cheat him if he could, and warned him not to accept his terms. Newport, however, who was a vain, ostentatious man, expecting to dazzle the chief with his greatness, or charm him with his liberality, accepted them, in the hope of having any request, he might make, readily granted. The result proved that Smith was right; for Powhatan, in selecting the articles that he wished and giving others in return, valued his corn at such a rate, that, as the writer of the narrative says, it might have been bought cheaper in old Spain, for they hardly received four bushels where they counted upon twenty hogsheads.

Smith was much provoked at Newport's being so palpably overreached; but, dissembling his chagrin so as to avoid suspicion, he determined to obtain an equivalent advantage over the wily savage. He took out, as if accidentally, a variety of toys and gewgaws, and contrived to let Powhatan observe some blue beads. His eyes sparkled with pleasure at the sight, and he eagerly desired to obtain them. Smith, however, was reluctant to part with them, they being, as he said, composed of a very rare substance, of the color of the skies, and fit to be worn only by the greatest kings in the world. Powhatan's ardor was inflamed by opposition, and he resolved to have the precious jewels at any price. A bargain was finally struck to the satisfaction of all parties, by which Smith exchanged a pound or two of blue beads for two or three hundred bushels of corn. A similar negotiation was entered into with Opechancanough at Pamunkey. These blue beads were held in such estimation among the Indians, that none but their principal chiefs and the members of their families were allowed to wear them.

They returned with their treasures to Jamestown, where, shortly after, a fire broke out, which burnt several of their houses (they being thatched with reeds, which rendered them very combustible), and occasioned them a considerable loss in arms, bedding, wearing-apparel, and provision. Among the principal sufferers, was their good clergyman, Mr. Hunt, who lost all he had, including his books, which must have been a most severe affliction to a scholar in that lone wilderness. Yet we are told, that no one ever heard him repine on account of his loss. Notwithstanding this misfortune, their remaining stock of oat-meal, meal, and corn would have been sufficient for their wants, had not the ship loitered in the country fourteen weeks, when she might have sailed in fourteen days, and thereby greatly increased the number of mouths to be fed. They were also obliged, on the departure of the ship, to furnish to the crew abundant provisions without any equivalent, as they had neither money, goods, nor credit. All this was to be done cheerfully, that the report of it might induce others to come, and gain " golden opinions " for them from the council at home. " Such," says Stith, " was their necessity and misfortune, to be under the lash of those vile commanders, and to buy their own provisions at fifteen times their value; suffering them to feast at their charge, whilst themselves were obliged to fast, and yet dare not repine, lest they should incur the censure of being factious and seditious persons." Their stock of provisions was so contracted by these means and by their unlucky fire, that they were reduced to great extremity. The loss of their houses exposed many, with very imperfect shelter, to the severity of a most bitter winter; and not a few died before spring, from the combined effects of cold and hunger.

The delay of Newport's ship was occasioned by one of those gold-fevers which break out so frequently among men, to the great prejudice of their reason and common sense. As it is well known, the most extravagant notions were entertained in Europe of the riches of the New World; and it is not going too far to say, that it was thought impossible to thrust a shovel into American soil, without bringing up a lump of gold. As a proof that Virginia formed no exception to this general rule, among those who left England with Captains Newport and Nelson, were two goldsmiths, two refiners, and one jeweller, artificers, one would think, in very little demand in a new colony, where most men would, like Æsop's cock, prefer a grain of barley to the most precious gem in the world.*

---

* There appears to have been a great want of judgment shown in the selection of the colonists. Of eighty-two persons, whose names are preserved, that first came over to Jamestown, forty-eight were designated gentlemen, four were carpenters, twelve were laborers, and the others boys and mechanics. Of seventy-four names of those who came out with Newport and Nelson (one hundred and twenty in all,) thirty-two were gentlemen, twenty-three were laborers, six were tailors, and two apothecaries. These "gentlemen" were probably dissolute, broken-down adventurers, bankrupts in character as well as fortune, needy and extravagant younger sons of good families, whom their friends were happy to be quit of on any terms; incapable alike of industry and subordination, indolent, mutinous, and reckless. These are the men, who so constantly tried the patience of Smith, a saving grace, which, as the reader may have perceived, he had not in great abundance; and who provoked him to write in the following terms; "Being for the most part of such tender educations and small experience in martial accidents, because they found not English cities, nor such fair houses, nor at their own wishes any of

In a small rivulet near Jamestown was found a glittering, yellowish sand, (its lustre probably derived from particles of mica,) which their excitable imaginations immediately believed to be gold. This became the all-absorbing topic of thought and discourse, and " there was no talk, no hope, no work, but dig gold, wash gold, refine gold, load gold." The unskilful refiners, whom Newport had brought over with him, pronounced this shining sand to be very valuable ore, forgetting that " all that glisters is not gold." This, of course, carried the frenzy to its height, and, confirmed by the testimony of men of supposed skill and experience, every one indulged in the most magnificent

---

their accustomed dainties, with feather beds and down pillows, taverns and ale-houses in every breathing-place, neither such plenty of gold [and silver and dissolute liberty, as they expected, they had little or no care of any thing, but to pamper their bellies, to fly away with our pinnaces, or procure their means to return for England. For the country was to them a misery, a ruin, a death, a hell, and their reports here and their actions there according." Another writer, describing the character of the colonists at the time of Smith's departure for England, observes, after enumerating a few useful mechanics, " All the rest were poor gentlemen, tradesmen, serving-men, libertines, and such like, ten times more fit to spoil a commonwealth, than either begin one, or but help to maintain one." — *Smith's Virginia, (Richmond Edition,)* Vol. I. p. 241.

visions of wealth and aggrandizement. Nothing would content Newport, but the freighting of his ship with this worthless trash, to the great mortification and chagrin of Captain Smith, who was no believer in golden dreams, and foresaw the evil consequences of neglecting duties of the most important nature, to chase phantoms and bubbles. The writer of this portion of the History of the colony says, "Never did any thing more torment him, than to see all necessary business neglected, to fraught such a drunken ship with so much gilded dirt." Wingfield and Captain Archer returned with Newport to England, which afforded to Smith a slight balm of consolation for his troubles and vexations.

As soon as the spring opened, Smith and Scrivener (who had been admitted a member of the council) set themselves diligently to work to rebuild Jamestown, to repair the church, storehouse, and fortifications, and to cut down trees and plant corn for the ensuing season. While they were thus occupied, Captain Nelson arrived in the Phœnix, from the West Indies, where he had remained during the winter. He was received with great joy, as he had long been given up for lost. He brought an ample stock of provisions, enough to relieve the colony from all apprehensions of want for the next half-year. His generous and manly conduct endeared him to the settlers, and his presence seemed to diffuse a general activity and spirit of enterprise among them. Even the President was roused from his usual sluggishness and imbecility ; for, says the writer of this portion of the History, "to re-lade this ship with some good tidings, the President (not holding it stood with the dignity of his place to leave the fort) gave order to Captain Smith to discover and search the commodities of the Monacans' country beyond the Falls." Sixty men were allotted to him for this expedition, which he was prevented from undertaking, by troubles near at hand.

At Captain Newport's departure, Powhatan, who perceived the superiority of the English weapons over the rude ones of his own people, made him a present of twenty turkeys, as a token of his regard, desiring him to send in return twenty swords, which request was inconsiderately granted.   He afterwards made a similar present to Captain Smith, expecting a like return ; but, finding himself disappointed, he ordered his people to hover round Jamestown, and take possession of the Englishmen's weapons, whenever they had an opportunity, either by stratagem or force. These orders were faithfully executed, and were productive of great annoyance and inconvenience to the colonists.   No notice was taken of their depredations for a time, because they had strict orders from England to keep on the best possible terms with Powhatan and his people. " This charitable humor prevailed till well it chanced they meddled with Captain Smith," who then took the matter into his own hands, and acted with such promptness and energy, punishing so severely the offenders whom he detected, that Powhatan found he was playing a losing game; so " he sent his messengers and his dearest daughter Pocahontas with presents, to excuse him of the injuries done by some rash untoward captains, his subjects, desiring their liberties for this time with the assurance of his love for ever." * Smith dismissed his prisoners, after giving them " what correction he saw fit," pretending to be thus merciful only for the sake of Pocahontas. His conduct was too resolute and spirited to meet the approbation of his colleagues in the council; though it had struck such terror into the Indians, and that too without any bloodshed, that they no longer molested the colonists, whereas before they " had sometime peace and war twice in a day, and very seldom a week but they had some treacherous villany or other."

The Phœnix was sent home in June, 1608,

---

* How consistent is tyranny! Powhatan's disavowal of his express orders is worthy of King John or Louis the Eleventh.

with a load of cedar, by Captain Smith's influence ; though Martin was very anxious that she also should be loaded with golden sand.   He was "willingly admitted" to return with her to England, being a sickly and inefficient man, and having his head so full of golden dreams, as to make him useless, whatever might have been his natural capacity.

CHAPTER VII.

Captain Smith explores the Chesapeake in two Expeditions. — He is chosen President of the Colony.

THE enterprising character of Captain Smith prompted him to an arduous undertaking, namely, the examination and survey of Chesapeake Bay, to ascertain more completely the resources of the country and to open a friendly communication with its native inhabitants.   He set out in an open barge of about three tons' burthen, accompanied by Dr. Russell and thirteen others.   They left Jamestown on the 2d of June, 1608, in company with the Phœnix, and parted with her at Cape Henry.   They then crossed the bay to the eastern shore and fell in with a cluster of islands east of Cape Charles, to which they gave the name of Smith's Isles, in honor of their commander, an appellation still retained.

They were directed by two Indians, whom they saw, to Accomac, the habitation of their chief, situated in the southwestern part of Northampton county. He received them with kindness, and is spoken of by them as the most affable and good-looking savage they had ever seen. He spoke the language of Powhatan, and told them that his people had been afflicted with a heavy pestilence, which had carried them almost all off. They then coasted along the eastern shore of the bay, searching every inlet that seemed proper for habitations or harbors, and landing frequently, sometimes upon the main land, sometimes upon the islands, which they called Russell's Islands, since called Tangier Islands. They discovered and sailed up the River Pocomoke in search of fresh water, for want of which they suffered a good deal, that which they obtained being very muddy.

Leaving this river, they directed their course to certain other islands, and when they were among them, their sail and mast were blown overboard by a sudden squall, and for two days the weather was so stormy, that they had great difficulty in keeping their boat from sinking. They named these islands Limbo, in commemoration of their toils and sufferings, a name which has since been changed to Watts's Islands.

Departing from these islands, they came to the River Wicomico, on the Eastern Shore of Maryland, where the natives were at first disposed to resist them, but were conciliated and made friendly by some toys left in their huts, after they had been a little frightened by discharges of fire-arms. These Indians were the wealthiest and most given to commerce and manufactures of any they had ever seen. Finding the eastern coast lined with low, irregular islands, and for the most part without fresh water, they directed their course westward to the mouth of Patuxent River. They sailed thirty leagues further to the north without finding any inhabitants, the coast being well watered but mountainous and barren, except the valleys, which were fertile, well wooded, and abounding in wolves, bears, deer, and other animals. They passed by many coves and small streams, and came to a large river, which they named Bolus, and which was probably that now called Patapsco. At this place, discontent broke out among Smith's crew, who were most of them unaccustomed to a life of such toil and hardship. They had spent twelve or fourteen days in an open boat, toiling at the oar, and their bread was damaged with the rain ; yet, as we are told, "so good were their stomachs that they could digest it." Captain Smith addressed them in terms of mingled authority and persuasiveness; told them how disgraceful it would be for them to return, while they had such abundance of provision, and before they had accomplished any thing of importance; and assured them of his readiness to share every danger and labor, and to take the worst upon himself whenever there was any choice. Their reluctance to proceed any further was much increased by adverse weather, and, three or four of them falling sick, their piteous entreaties induced Captain Smith to return.

On the 16th of June they fell in with the mouth of the Potomac. The sight of this majestic river revived their drooping spirits, and, their invalids having recovered, they readily consented to explore it. For thirty miles, they found no inhabitants, but were afterwards conducted by two of the natives up a little creek, where they found themselves surrounded by three or four thousand Indians, lying in ambuscade, " so strangely painted, grimed, and disguised, shouting, yelling, and crying, as so many spirits from hell could not have showed more terrible." Their demeanor was very menacing; but Smith prepared to receive them with great coolness, and commanding the muskets to be discharged, the grazing of the bullets upon the water, and the report, which the woods multiplied into a thousand echoes, filled them with alarm. They threw down their arms, and made professions of peace, which was ratified by an exchange of hostages. They now treated the English with great kindness, and frankly told them that they had been commanded to lie in wait for them, and cut them off, by Powhatan, who had been informed of the expedition, and incited to take this step, by some discontented spirits at Jamestown, because Captain Smith obliged them to stay in the country against their will. This fact alone will give the reader some notion of the infamy and worthlessness of some of the colonists.

They were conducted by Japazaws, the chief of the Indians in that part, to a mine, of which they had heard a good deal, upon one of the tributary streams of the Potomac. It produced a substance like antimony, which the Indians, after having washed it and put it up in bags, used to paint themselves and their idols with. It made " them look like Blackamoores dusted over with silver." Newport had carried some of these bags to England, and reported that the substance they contained was half silver. They reached the mine, and brought back as much of its product as they could carry, which proved in the end to be of no value. No mineral treasures at all were found, but they collected some furs. The Indians, whom they met, generously supplied them with the flesh of animals. They frequently found the waters alive with innumerable fish, and not having any net, as their bark was sailing among them, they attempted to catch them with a frying-pan, " but," the narrative gravely adds, " we found it a bad instrument to catch fish with."

They explored the Potomac as far as their bark would go, and then returned. Though they frequently were exposed to danger from the open or treacherous assaults of the savages, Captain Smith's resolute conduct always averted it. He invariably met them with great boldness; and, if they were desirous of peace, he would demand their weapons and some of their children, as sureties for their good faith, and by their refusal or compliance he learned in what light to consider them and what measures to take with them.

Desiring before his return to visit the Indians whom he had known in his captivity, he entered the mouth of the River Rappahannoc, where, at low tide, their boat ran aground. While they were waiting for the flood, they occupied themselves in sticking with the points of their swords the fishes, which were left upon the flats in such numbers, that they took in this way more in an hour than they could eat in a day. Captain Smith, in taking from the point of his sword a *stingray*, (which is described in the narrative as "being much in the fashion of a thornback," but with "a long tail like a riding-rod, whereon the midst is a most poisoned sting, of two or three inches long, bearded like a saw on each side,") was wounded by its sharp thorn, to the depth of an inch and a half, in the wrist. The wound, though it drew no blood, became extremely painful; and in a few hours his arm and shoulder were so much swollen, that his companions concluded his death was at hand, and were so confident of it, that with heavy hearts they dug his grave in an island hard by. But by the timely application of a "precious oil" by Dr. Russell, after the wound had been probed, he recovered from the ill effects of it so quickly, that he was able to take his revenge upon the fish by eating a piece of it for his supper. The place, where this accident occurred, was named in consequence of it Stingray Point, as it is still called.

They returned to Jamestown on the 21st of July. By way of frolic, they disguised their boat with painted streamers in such a way, that they were mistaken by the colonists for a Spanish frigate, to their no small consternation. Smith found that his absence had been attended with its usual ill consequences. All those who had lately come over were sick; and the whole company were spiritless, discontented, and full of indignation against their selfish and inefficient President ; who, instead of actively mingling in the interests of the colonists, and sharing their toils and privations, had been living in abundance upon the public stores, and was building for himself a pleasant retreat in the woods, where his ear might not be pained by murmurs and complaints.

They were somewhat comforted by the accounts of the expedition, and (what now cannot be read without a smile) by " the good hope we had by the savages' relation, that our bay had stretched into the South Sea or somewhat near it." They would not hear, however, of Ratcliffe's continuing in the office of President, but insisted upon his being deposed, which was accordingly done, and Smith chosen in his place ; by which he was invested with the title and badges of a station, the substantial authority of which he had long enjoyed. Being about to depart upon another expedition, he appointed Mr. Scrivener, his deputy, who at that time was sick with a fever. This deputy distributed impartially the public stores which Ratcliffe had engrossed, and made such arrangements as would enable the colonists to interrupt their labors during the extreme heat of the summer, and thus recruit their wasted strength.

Captain Smith remained at home but three days, and on the 24th of July set out on another exploring expedition accompanied by twelve men. They were detained two or three days at Kecoughtan (Hampton) by contrary winds, where they were hospitably entertained by the Indians. At night they discharged a few rockets into the air, which greatly alarmed their simple hosts. The first night of their voyage they anchored at Stingray Point, and the next day, crossing the Potomac at its mouth, they hastened on to the River Bolus (Patapsco.) They proceeded onwards to the head of the bay, which ended in four streams, all of which they explored as far as their boat would carry them. Two of them they found with inhabitants on their banks, namely the Susquesahanoc (Susquehanna) and Tockwogh, since called Sassafras. In crossing the bay they met seven or eight canoes full of Massawomecs. These were a great and powerful nation dwelling far to the north, of whom Captain Smith had heard a great deal among Powhatan's people. They were a great terror to the tribes living on the Chesapeake Bay, with whom they were almost constantly at war. *

---

* The Massawomecs are supposed to have been the great Northern Confederacy, called by the French the

They prepared at first to assault the English, which might have been attended with fatal consequences to the whole company, as they had but six men who could stand upon their feet, the rest being disabled by sickness. By putting upon sticks the hats of the sick and stationing between every two sticks a man with two muskets, they contrived to multiply their apparent strength, so that the Indians paddled swiftly to the shore. They were followed, and with some difficulty persuaded to go on board the barge, where presents were interchanged. By signs they intimated that they were at war with the Indians dwelling on the river Tockwogh; and the fresh and bleeding wounds upon some of them showed that there had been a recent battle.

The next day, on entering the river Tockwogh, they were surrounded with a fleet of canoes filled with armed men. On seeing the weapons of the Massawomecs in the hands of the English, (which they had received as presents, but which, sacrificing truth to policy, they gave the Indians to understand had been taken in battle,)

Iroquois, and by the English, The Five Nations, and afterwards, The Six Nations; whose seat was in the State of New York, but whose conquests were extended so far, that they have been called the Romans of America. — *Stith*, p. 67; *Encyclopædia Americana*, Art. *Iroquois*.

they led them in triumph to their village and entertained them hospitably. They saw among this people hatchets, knives, and pieces of iron and brass, which, they said, were obtained from the Susquesahanocs, a mighty nation, who dwelt upon the river of the same name, two days' journey above the Falls, and who were mortal enemies of the Massawomecs. Captain Smith prevailed upon them to send an embassy to this people inviting them to come and see him ; which was accordingly done, and, in three or four days, sixty of them came down with presents of various kinds.

Captain Smith has spoken of these Susquesahanocs in terms which would lead one to suppose that he borrowed more from imagination than memory in his description, and that his romantic fancy and ardent temperament made him, perhaps unconsciously, exaggerate the sober truth. He speaks of them as a race of giants, " and, for their language, it may well beseem their proportions, sounding from them as a voice in a vault." Their clothing was the skins of bears and wolves, with the paws, the ears, and the head disposed in such a way, as to make it at once more picturesque and terrible. " One had the head of a wolf hanging in a chain for a jewel, his tobacco-pipe three quarters of a yard long, prettily carved with a bird, a deer, or some such device at the great end, sufficient to beat out one's brains; with bows, arrows, and clubs, suitable to their greatness." To those who have since seen this gigantic people, with the unassisted eye of reason, they have dwindled to the common proportions of mankind.

Their tribe was a numerous one, mustering six hundred fighting men. They dwelt in palisadoed towns to defend themselves against the Massawomecs, their deadly foes. In their manners they were mild and simple, and knew nothing of Powhatan or his people except by name. They informed the English, that their hatchets and other commodities came from the French in Canada. They looked upon the English as beings of an order superior to men, and for Captain Smith their veneration was unbounded. An incident is related by the narrator of the progress of this expedition, which shows at once the piety of Captain Smith, and that natural instinct of religion which dwells alike in the breast of the heathen and the Christian, the savage and the civilized man. "Our order was daily to have prayer with a psalm, at which solemnities the poor savages much wondered; our prayers being done, a while they were busied with a consultation till they had contrived their business. Then they began in a most passionate manner to hold up their hands to the sun, with a most fearful song;

then embracing our Captain, they began to adore him in like manner; though he rebuked them, yet they proceeded till their song was finished." They afterwards invested him with the office of a chief, loaded him with presents, and invited him to come and aid them against the Massawomecs.

Leaving these kind and friendly strangers, they returned down the bay, to the Rappahannoc, exploring every inlet and river of any consequence, and giving to the various capes and headlands the names of members of the company or of their friends. At the extreme points to which they explored the several rivers, they cut crosses in the bark of trees, and in some places bored holes in them, wherein they deposited notes, and, in some cases, brazen crosses, to signify that the English had been there.

In passing up the river Rappahannoc, they were kindly entertained by a tribe of Indians called the Moraughtacunds. They met there an Indian named Mosco, who is styled an "old friend," though we hear of him now for the first time. They had probably seen him on their former expedition. They supposed him to be the son of some Frenchman, because, unlike every other Indian whom they had seen, he had a bushy black beard. He was not a little proud of this distinction, and called the Englishmen "his countrymen." He devoted himself to them with great assiduity and uniform kindness. He advised them not to visit the Rappahannocs, who lived higher up the river, as they would endeavor to kill them for being the friends of the Moraughtacunds, who had lately stolen three of their chief's women.

Captain Smith, thinking that this was merely an artifice to secure a profitable trade to his own friends, disregarded his counsels ; but the event proved that he was right. Under pretence of trade, the English were decoyed by them into a creek, where an ambuscade was prepared for them. A skirmish took place in which the Rappahannocs had many killed and wounded, but none of the English were hurt. They took three or four canoes, which they presented to Mosco in requital of his kindness.

Before proceeding any further, they employed themselves in surrounding their boat with a sort of bulwark, made of the targets, which they had received from the Massawomecs, and which they had found a great protection against the arrows of the Rappahannocs. They were made of small twigs, woven together with strings of wild hemp and silk-grass, so firmly and compactly as to make them perfectly arrow-proof. Their virtue was soon put to the test ; for on the next day they received a volley, while they were in a narrow part of the river, from thirty or forty Rappahannocs, who

" had so accommodated themselves with branches," that they were mistaken for bushes growing
along the shore. Their arrows however, striking
against the targets, fell harmless into the river.

They were kindly treated by the rest of the
nations as far as the Falls. While they were
upon the river, they lost one of their number, Mr.
Richard Fetherstone, by death. He had borne an
unexceptionable character from the first, behaving
himself " honestly, valiantly, and industriously."
His remains were buried, with appropriate honors,
on the shore of a small bay, which they called
by his name. The other members of the expedition, who had almost all of them been more or
less sick, had now recovered their health.

Having sailed up the Rappahannoc as far as
their bark would carry them, they set up crosses
and carved their names upon the bark of trees,
as usual. While they were rambling about the
Falls, they were suddenly attacked by about a
hundred Indians, who, in their irregular mode of
warfare, kept darting about from tree to tree, continually discharging arrows, but with no effect.
In about half an hour they retreated as suddenly as they approached. As the English returned
from pursuing them they found one of their number lying upon the ground, having been wounded
in the knee with a bullet. Mosco, who had behaved with great courage in the skirmish, showed,

at the sight of him, the unrelenting cruelty of his race ; for, says the narrative, with more force than elegance, " never was dog more furious against a bear, than Mosco was to have beat out his brains." But he was rescued from this violence ; and, his wounds having been dressed by the surgeon, he was in an hour so far recovered as to be able to eat and speak. By the aid of Mosco, they learned from him that he was the brother of the chief of the tribe of Hassininga, one of the four which made up the nation of the Mannahocs. When asked why his people attacked the English, who came to them with both the intentions and the appearance of friends, he said, that they had heard that the English were a nation come from under the world to take their world from them. Being further asked how many worlds he knew, he answered, that he knew of none but that which was under the sky that covered him, whose sole inhabitants were, besides his own nation, the Powhatans, the Monacans, and the Massawomecs. To the inquiry, what there was beyond the mountains, he replied, the sun. They made him many presents and persuaded him to accompany them.

At night they set sail and proceeded down the river. They were presently followed by the Mannahocs on the banks, who kept discharging arrows at the boat and yelling and shrieking so loud, as to render it impossible for their countryman in the boat, whose name was Amorolec, to make his voice audible to them. But in the calm of the morning they anchored in a quiet and broad bay, and their captive was able to address his countrymen and inform them, how kindly the English had treated him ; that he had been promised his liberty if they would be friendly ; and that as to injuring the strangers at all with their inferior weapons, it was quite out of the question. Encouraged by these statements, they hung their bows and arrows upon the trees, and two of them, without suspicion, swam to the bark, bringing the one a bow and the other a quiver of arrows, which they presented to Captain Smith in token of submission. He received them very kindly, and told them that, if the chiefs of their four tribes would submit to him, that the great King, whose subject he was, would be their friend. This was immediately assented to ; and, on going ashore on a low, jutting point of land, the four chiefs came and received their countryman, Amorolec. They wondered at every thing belonging to the English, and mistook their pistols for pipes. After giving and receiving many presents, the English took their departure, leaving four or five hundred Indians singing, dancing, and making merry.

On their return, they visited their friends the Moraughtacunds, who were desirous that Captain Smith should make peace with the Rappahannocs, as he had done with the Mannahocs. This pacific counsel, so foreign to the Indian character, was probably given, that they themselves might be more secure, as they were generally understood to be the friends and allies of the English. Captain Smith told them that he was ready to make peace, but that, as the Rappahannocs had twice assaulted him without any provocation, and when he came with the most friendly intentions, he should exact certain conditions from them. These were, that they should present him with the bow and arrows of their chief, in token of submission, that they should never come armed into his presence, that they should make peace with the Moraughtacunds and give up their chief's son, to be a hostage and a security for the performance of the stipulated terms.

A message was sent to the chief of the Rappahannocs, who accepted all the conditions except the last, saying that he had but one son and could not live without him, a strong instance of affection, in one of a race, which has generally been supposed to be peculiarly devoid of the finer sensibilities of the heart. He offered, instead of his son, to give up the three women whom the Moraughtacunds had stolen from him, which proposition was accepted. The women being brought before Captain Smith, he presented each of them with a chain of beads. He then permitted the chief of the Rappahannocs to choose, from the three, the one whom he preferred; to the chief of the Moraughtacunds he gave the next choice; and the remaining woman he gave to Mosco; an arrangement which was satisfactory to all parties. The triple peace was concluded with great rejoicings of men, women, and children, of whom no less than six or seven hundred were assembled. Mosco, to express his love for the English, changed his name to Uttasantough, which means *stranger*, the word by which they were called.

On departing from the Rappahannoc, they explored the Piankatank as far as it was navigable, and steered for home. While they were in the bay, a few miles south of York River, they were surprised in the night with so violent a storm of rain, attended with thunder and lightning, that they gave themselves up for lost, but were enabled finally to reach Point Comfort. As they had discovered so many nations at a distance, they thought it would be hardly consistent for them to return home, without visiting their neighbors, the Chesapeakes and Nansemonds, of whom as yet they had only heard. Therefore they set sail for the southern shore, and went up a narrow river, then called the Chesapeake but since Elizabeth, on which Norfolk stands. They sailed six or seven miles, but seeing no living beings, though they observed signs of habitation, they returned. Having coasted along the shore to the mouth of the Nansemond, they perceived there six or seven Indians mending their weirs for fishing, who fled at the sight of the English. They went on shore and left some toys in the place, where the Indians had been working, and returned to their boat. They had not gone far, before the Indians returned, and began to sing and dance and call them back. One of them came into the boat of his own accord, and invited them to his house, which was a few miles up the river. This invitation they accepted and sailed six or seven miles, the other Indians accompanying them, running on the banks. They saw on the western shore large corn-fields, and in the midst of the river an island, upon which was situated the house of the Indian who was with them, and which was also thickly covered with corn. The Indian treated them kindly, and showed them his wife and children, to whom they made suitable presents. The other Indians invited them further up the river to their houses, and accompanied them for some distance in a canoe.

Some suspicious circumstances in their deportment led the English to apprehend that all was

not right, and to provide for the worst, especially
when they perceived that they were followed by
seven or eight canoes full of armed men.   They
were not long left in suspense, for they were suddenly attacked by two or three hundred men,
from each side of the river, who discharged arrows at them as fast as they could draw their
bows.   Those in the canoes also shot at them;
but they returned so galling a fire from their
muskets, that most of them leaped overboard, and
swam to the shore.   The English soon fell down
the stream, till they reached a position, where the
arrows of the Indians could not touch them, but
which was within musket-shot of their foes, and
a few discharges made them retire behind the
trees.   The English then seized upon their deserted canoes, and moored them in the stream.
Though they had received more than a hundred
arrows in their targets, and about the boat, no
one was hurt.   They determined to punish the
treacherous Indians, by burning every thing upon
the island at night, and in the mean time began
to demolish their canoes.   At the sight of this,
those on shore threw down their arms and sued
for peace; which was granted on condition that
they would bring their chief's bow and arrows
and a chain of pearl, and four hundred baskets of
corn, otherwise their canoes should be destroyed
and their houses burnt.   These conditions they

assented to, and loaded the boat with corn as full as it would hold, with which the English departed, and arrived at Jamestown without any further adventure, on the 7th of September, 1608.

In these two expeditions Captain Smith was absent a little over three months, excepting an interval of three days which was spent at Jamestown ; and he had sailed, upon his own computation, about three thousand miles. It was an enterprise of great difficulty and considerable hazard, and its complete success is to be ascribed to his remarkable personal qualities. His intercourse with the natives required the exercise of the greatest firmness, address, and self-command ; while, in the management of his own company, authority and persuasive influence were to be mingled with the nicest tact. He was obliged to overawe the refractory, to encourage the sick and drooping, to enliven the desponding, and to infuse his own adventurous and enterprising spirit into the indolent and timid. He explored the whole of the Chesapeake Bay, and of the country lying upon its banks, and constructed a map of it, which is very accurate, taking all circumstances into consideration.

CHAPTER VIII.

Second Arrival of Newport. — Abortive Expedition to explore the Interior. — Injudicious Conduct of the Council in England. — Their Letter to Captain Smith. — His Reply.

ON their arrival at Jamestown they found that many had died during their absence and many were still sick ; but that some, whom they had left sick, Mr. Scrivener among the rest, were restored to health. This gentleman had performed well the duties of deputy-governor, and had provided for the gathering and storing of the harvest. Ratcliffe, their late President, was a prisoner for mutiny. On the 10th of September, Captain Smith was formally inducted into the office of President, and entered upon the administration of its duties with his usual spirit and activity. The church and store-house were repaired, and a new building was erected for the supplies, which were expected from England. The fort was put in order, a watch duly set, and the whole company was drilled in military exercises, every Saturday, on a plain towards the west, where the Indians would often gather round them in great numbers, to witness the execution done by their bullets upon the bark of a tree, which they used as a target.

As it was about the time of the Indian harvest, an expedition set out under the command of Lieutenant Percy to trade with the Indians; but, meeting Captain Newport in the bay, they came back with him. He had brought over about seventy individuals, some of whom were persons of distinction, and two of whom, Captain Peter Wynne and Captain Richard Waldo, were appointed members of the council. In this ship there came the first Englishwomen, that ever were in Virginia, Mrs. Forrest and her maid Anne Burras. The company had also, with singular want of judgment, sent out eight Germans to make pitch, tar, glass, and potash, who would have been welcome to a populous and thriving country, but who were useless incumbrances in an infant colony, which was struggling for existence, and all the energies of which were directed to the procuring of daily bread.

The instructions which Captain Newport had brought out with him, and the authority with which he had been clothed, are a monument of the folly of the council in England, in dictating the measures and course of policy to be pursued in a colony, three thousand miles distant, and of whose interests and condition they showed themselves so thoroughly ignorant. Stith, in his homely fashion, says of Newport himself, that he was " an empty, idle, interested man, very fearful and suspicious in times of danger and difficulty, but a very great and important person in his own talk and conceit." He had a mean jealousy of Captain Smith on account of his brilliant qualities and the estimation in which he was held by the colonists; and his influence with the council and company in England induced them to give him such peculiar powers as would enable him at once to gratify his own conceit, and, as he thought, to vex and mortify his rival. He obtained from them a special commission, by which he was authorized to act, in certain cases, independently. of the council, and in which three objects were laid down as essential. He was not to return without either discovering the South Sea, or bringing back a lump of gold or some one of the lost company, which had been sent out by Sir Walter Raleigh.*

It is difficult to believe that such preposterous requisitions could have been made by men in their senses; but their madness was deliberate, as its "method" will show. A barge had been constructed and brought over, which was capable of being taken to pieces and put together again, and

---

* This refers to a colony of one hundred persons, who had been left on the island of Roanoke in North Carolina, by Captain White, under the guidance and direction of Sir Walter Raleigh, in 1587, and were never afterwards heard of, being probably cut off by the Indians.

in which they were to make a voyage to the head of the river. It was then to be carried across the mountains and launched upon the streams, which were supposed to run westerly and flow into the South Sea. As they must pass through Powhatan's territory, it was proper to make extraordinary exertions to secure his favor; and for this purpose a royal present was brought over for him, consisting of a bason and ewer, a bed and furniture, a chair of state, a suit of scarlet clothes, a cloak, and a crown.

Newport soon opened his budget, and unfolded to the council his strange powers and wild schemes. Captain Smith, whose strong good sense and knowledge of the country enabled him to perceive, at a glance, their impolicy and even impracticability, opposed their execution most strenuously. He said, that it was sheer madness to employ the precious time of the colonists, which ought to be fully occupied in providing for the winter, in the visionary scheme of a search for the South Sea, through an unknown country, full of merciless enemies; and that, worn out with fatigue and sickness as they were, it would be impossible for them to carry the boat over the mountains. As to the sumptuous presents brought over for Powhatan, he was opposed to their being presented, because he said that he could always be sure of his good-will by a piece of copper or a few beads, but that this "stately kind of soliciting" would make him insolent and contemptuous beyond all endurance. These arguments, convincing in themselves and strongly recommended by the character and experience of their supporter, were however overruled in council principally by means of Newport's sanguine promises and assurances. He was ungenerous enough to insinuate that Smith's opposition to his expedition arose from a wish to monopolize the glory of the discovery himself, and that the only obstacle to its success would be the desire of the Indians to take vengeance upon the English for the cruelties which he had formerly inflicted upon them.

This decision afforded to Captain Smith an opportunity to show the real greatness and magnanimity of his character. Though he was President, no sooner did he find the majority of the council against him, than, without any further opposition or sullen obstinacy, he lent his most vigorous efforts to the prosecution of the plans they had decided upon. To show how unfounded were Newport's charges of cruelty and how little he himself had to fear from the Indians, he volunteered to go with four others and invite Powhatan to Jamestown to receive his presents. He travelled by land twelve miles and crossed York River in a canoe to Werowocomoco, where he expected to find Powhatan. But he was thirty miles distant, and was immediately sent for. Pocahontas and her women did their utmost to entertain their guests.

As they were seated around the fire, they suddenly heard a hideous noise in the woods. The English, supposing that they were betrayed, seized upon two or three old men who sat near, as hostages for their safety. But Pocahontas came running up to them, and assured them that no harm was intended to them, and that, if any happened, she would willingly give up the lives of herself and her women to atone for it. Her assurances removed their suspicions, and enabled them to attend to the pageant, which was prepared for their entertainment. Thirty young women sallied from the woods, variously painted, clothed only with a girdle of leaves, and ornamented with sundry devices. The writer of the narrative describes their dance, in the following rather ungallant terms; "These fiends with most hellish shouts and cries, rushing from among the trees, cast themselves in a ring about the fire, singing and dancing with most excellent ill variety, oft falling into their infernal passions, and solemnly again to sing and dance; having spent near an hour in this mascarado, as they entered, in like manner they departed." This dance was followed by a feast, at which the good Captain was much annoyed by the officious caresses of the above mentioned masquerading damsels. The Englishmen were then conducted to their lodgings, with firebrands carried before them instead of torches.

The next day Powhatan arrived, and Captain Smith delivered to him his message, desiring him to come to Jamestown, to receive the presents from the hands of his father, Captain Newport, and concert with him plans for taking revenge upon his enemies the Monacans. The reply of the savage monarch is strikingly characteristic of his haughtiness, self-respect, and knowledge of human nature. "If your King," said he, " have sent me presents, I also am a King and this is my land ; eight days I will stay to receive them. Your father is to come to me, not I to him, nor yet to your fort, neither will I bite at such a bait ; as for the Monacans, I can revenge my own injuries ; for any salt water beyond the mountains, the relations you have had from my people are false." At the same time, he drew upon the ground a rude chart of the countries of which he spoke. After some complimentary discourses, Captain Smith took leave of him, and carried his answer to Jamestown.

Whereupon the presents were sent round by water, and Captains Smith and Newport went across by land, with a guard of fifty armed men. All having met at Werowocomoco, the next day was appointed for Powhatan's coronation. Then his presents were brought to him, and the bason, ewer, bed, and furniture were set up. His scarlet cloak and suit were put on, but not until he had been persuaded by Namontack (the Indian youth whom he had formerly presented to Newport, and who had been to England with him), that there was nothing dangerous in them. They had great trouble in inducing him to kneel in order to receive his crown. He understood nothing of the " majesty or meaning "(as the narrative has it) of a crown, nor of the ceremony of bending the knee ; which obliged them to use so many arguments and so much persuasion, that their patience was entirely worn out. They succeeded at last in making him stoop a little by leaning hard upon his shoulders ; and, as soon as the crown was put upon his head, a volley was fired from the boats, at which he started up in great affright, till he was informed what it meant. What would this sylvan monarch have said, if he had witnessed the cumbrous splendor of a modern coronation ?

By way of making a proper acknowledgment
of the honors which had been shown to him,
he generously presented Captain Newport with
his mantle and old shoes. He endeavored to
dissuade the English from their wild scheme
of exploring the inland country, and refused to
give them men or guides for that object, except
Namontack. After many civil speeches had
been exchanged, he gave Newport a heap of
ears of corn containing seven or eight bushels,
and about as much more was purchased in the
village, with which they returned to Jamestown.

Immediately after this, Captain Newport set
out upon his expedition of discovery, with a hundred and twenty chosen men, leaving Captain
Smith at Jamestown with eighty or ninety weak
and sickly ones, to load the ship. The enterprise proved a total failure, and its history may
be told in a very few words. They proceeded in
their boat to the Falls of James River, and then
went by land about forty miles, through a fertile
and well-watered country. They discovered two
villages of the Monacans on the south side of the
river, the inhabitants of which used them neither
well nor ill, but, by way of security, they took
one of their petty chiefs and led him bound in order to guide them. A journey of two days and a
half sufficed to cool their spirit of adventure and to

weary their delicate limbs so much, that they turned about and resumed their march homeward, taking with them some quantity of a certain earth, from which their refiner pretended to have extracted silver. They arrived at Jamestown "half sick, all complaining, and tired with toil, famine, and discontent;" having gained nothing but experience. Every thing had turned out exactly as Captain Smith had foretold, which, of course, sharpened the sting of disappointment.

Captain Smith who would allow no man to be idle, immediately set them all at work; some in making glass; others, tar, pitch, and potash. These he left under the care of the council at Jamestown, and he himself took thirty men about five miles down the river, and employed them in cutting timber and making clapboards. Among these were several young gentlemen, who had not been used to felling trees and sleeping on the ground; but, as there was something exciting in the employment, and their President shared all their toils and hardships, they soon became reconciled to their situation, "making it their delight to hear the trees thunder as they fell." But the axe frequently blistered their tender fingers, so that "many times every third blow had a loud oath to drown the echo." To correct this evil habit, the President contrived an ingenious and effectual remedy, which operated without any loss of good humor on the part of the offenders. He had a register kept of the number of oaths every man uttered in the course of the day, and at night, he ordered the same number of cans of water to be poured down his sleeve. The consequence was, that there was hardly an oath to be heard in a week. The writer of the narrative says, that though these thirty gentlemen, who worked with spirit and from choice, would accomplish more than a hundred who must be driven to it, yet twenty good stout workmen would do more than all.

Captain Smith, on his return to Jamestown, finding that much time had been unprofitably spent, and that their provisions were running low, resolved to go in search of corn among the Indians. He went up the river Chickahominy, in two barges with eighteen men, leaving orders for Lieutenant Percy to follow him. He found the Indians surly and disobliging, who, though they knew his wants, refused to trade, with many contemptuous expressions. Immediately changing his tone, and appearing no longer in the attitude of a petitioner for food, he told them that his purpose was to avenge his own imprisonment, and the death of his countrymen whom they had slain. He then landed his men and drew them up in military order. This spirited conduct produced a sudden change of opinion in the Indians, who sent ambassadors to make their peace, with presents of corn, fish, and wildfowl. They told him that their harvest had not been abundant that year, and that they had hardly enough to supply their own wants; but they furnished him with two hundred bushels of corn, which was a most welcome gift to the colony.

Captain Smith's enemies seem to have turned his most praiseworthy and successful efforts into accusations; for we read, " that though this much contented the company, (that feared nothing more than starving,) yet some so envied his good success, that they rather desired to hazard a starving, than his pains should prove so much more effectual than theirs." A plot was even formed by Newport and Ratcliffe to depose him, because, being President, he had left his place and the fort without their consent; but " their horns were so much too short to effect it, as they themselves more narrowly escaped a greater mischief."

While the ship remained, a brisk trade was carried on between the sailors and the Indians, to the great gain of the former, but to the prejudice of the colony. They would even pilfer articles from the public stores in order to exchange them for furs and other valuable commodities. And these very men, after having enriched themselves in this manner at the expense of the colonists, would grossly misrepresent them to the council in

England, and report that they had great abundance of every thing; so that they took no pains to supply them with stores, and would send over crowds of hungry adventurers to eat up their hard-earned substance.   Captain Smith was so provoked with Newport's conduct, that he threatened to send the ship home without him and detain him a year in the colony, that he might have the benefit of a full experience of their sufferings; but, upon his making proper submission, he consented to let him go.   He carried with him, in his ship, specimens of pitch, tar, frankincense, potash, clapboards, and wainscot, also a quantity of *pocones*, a red root used in dyeing.

The council in England had not been satisfied with the proceedings of the colony.   They had listened to misrepresentations and calumnies from interested or offended individuals, and had taken little pains themselves to ascertain the true state of affairs.   They were disappointed in not receiving any gold and silver from Virginia; and under the influence of these irritated feelings, and probably instigated by Newport, they had written by him an angry letter to Captain Smith.   They complained of the vain hopes with which they had been entertained, and the disappointments in which these had ended; they reproved the colonists for their dissensions, and spoke of a project for dividing the country, about which the former President had written a letter to the Earl of Salisbury; and threatened them, that, unless the expenses of the present voyage, amounting to two thousand pounds, were defrayed by the ship's return, the colony would be deserted and left to shift for themselves.

To this tirade, Captain Smith sent a reply by Newport, combining the dignity proper to his office with a soldier-like frankness and spirit. He denies indignantly the charge of awakening hopes which have never been realized; and, as to the plot for dividing the country, he says he never heard nor dreamed of such a thing. He says, that their directions sent by Newport had all been strictly followed, though he was opposed to them himself, and that all had been taught by experience to confess that he was right. For the two thousand pounds, which the voyage had cost, the colony had not received the benefit of a hundred. He tells them of the great preparations, which Newport had made for his expedition, and its utter failure; and says, "As for the quartered boat to be borne by the soldiers over the Falls, if he had burnt her to ashes, one might have carried her in a bag; but, as she is, five hundred cannot, to a navigable place above the Falls." He takes them to task for their folly in sending the Germans to make pitch, tar, and glass; and in his remarks shows great good sense, and even considerable knowledge of political economy. He tells them, that they could buy, in a single week, as great a quantity of these articles as would freight a ship, in Russia or Sweden, countries peculiarly adapted by nature to the manufucture of them ; but that it was most impolitic and unprofitable to devote to such occupations any part of the energies of a young colony, in which they all had as much as they could do to provide subsistence and defend themselves against the Indians.

He complains of Newport, of his vain projects, and his indolence, and contrasts the luxury and plenty, in which he and his sailors lived, with the coarse and scanty fare of the colonists. He says, that Archer and Ratcliffe were the authors of all their factions and disturbances ; and that the latter is an impostor, whose real name is Sicklemore ; and he sends him home to save his throat from being cut by the colonists, by whom he is detested. He entreats them to send out carpenters, husbandmen, gardeners, fishermen, blacksmiths, and masons, thirty of whom would be worth more than a thousand idle gentlemen, and to provide for their support and subsistence for the present, and leave all projects of gain for the future. At the same time, he sent them two barrels of stones, which he conjectured to be iron ore, with labels, designating the places in which he found them. To convince them that he could make as ample a discovery as Newport, and at a less expense than he had incurred at every meal, he transmitted to them a map of Chesapeake Bay and its rivers, which he had explored, together with a description of the same.*

CHAPTER IX.

Difficulties in Procuring Provision. — Captain Smith's Unsuccessful Attempt to obtain Possession of Powhatan's Person.

UPON the departure of the ship, the colonists began to be in apprehension that they should

---

* This was sent by Captain Nelson, who left Jamestown early in June, 1608, and it contains a narrative of events up to that date. It was printed the same year in London, and does not differ materially from the accounts subsequently published in the *History*. The original pamphlet is rare and curious, being in black letter and of the quarto size. There is a copy of it in the Library of Harvard College, but the title-page is wanting. In Mr. Rich's *Catalogue of American Books*, the title is printed as follows; " True Relation of such Occurrences and Accidents of Noate, as hath happened in Virginia since the Planting of the Colony." There is also a copy of the same work in Colonel Aspinwall's invaluable collection of books relating to America. It was written in the form of a letter and addressed to an individual ; probably to the Secretary of the London Company.

suffer from want of food, their supply being but
scanty. In order to obtain corn, Captain
Smith, with Captain Wynne and Mr. Scrivener set out for Nansamond, where, upon his
arrival, the Indians not only refused to give
him the four hundred bushels, which they had
promised, but would not trade with him at all;
saying that their stock was almost consumed,
and that they had been commanded by Powhatan to keep what was left, and not permit
the English to enter their river. Captain Smith,
finding that persuasion did no good, was constrained to employ force. At the first discharge
of the muskets, the Indians fled without shooting an arrow. The English marched towards their
houses, and set fire to the first one they came
to. Upon the sight of the flames, the Indians
came forward and offered to give them half
the corn they had, if they would desist from
further violence.

They loaded the three boats, with which
the English returned to their place of encamp-
ment, four miles down the river. This was
an open plain, sheltered by a hill, and at that
time the ground was frozen hard and covered
with snow. They were accustomed to dig away
the snow, and make a large fire; and, when the
ground was thoroughly warmed, they would
remove the fire and ashes, spread their mats

upon the spot and lie down, using another mat as a screen against the wind. When the ground grew cold, they shifted their fire again. Many cold winter nights they passed in this manner; and those, who were thus exposed to the elements in these expeditions, were always stouter and healthier than those, who remained at home and slept in warm beds.

Soon after their return to Jamestown, the first marriage which took place in Virginia, was celebrated between John Laydon and Anne Burras.

Captain Smith, indefatigable in securing the settlers against even the apprehension of want, remained but a short time at Jamestown, but, accompanied by Captain Waldo, went up the bay in two barges. The Indians, on all sides, fled at the sight of them, till they discovered the river and people of Appomatox. These had but little corn; but that little they divided with the English, and received in exchange bits of copper and other trifles, with which they were well contented.

The supplies procured in this manner were, however, temporary and precarious; and Captain Smith, who was determined that no one should be in fear of starvation, while he was President, resolved upon the bold and questionable measure of surprising Powhatan, and taking possession of all his store. In this project he was seconded by Captain Waldo, but opposed by Captain Wynne and Mr. Scrivener, which latter gentleman had become an enemy to him.   As if to favor his purposes, he was requested by Powhatan to come and see him, with a promise, that he would load his ship with corn, if Smith would build him a house, give him a grindstone, fifty swords, some muskets, a cock and a hen, and a large quantity of beads and copper. Captain Smith determined to improve the opportunity thus fortunately presented, although he suspected that the crafty old savage had some ulterior design in his specious offers. He accordingly sent two Englishmen and four Germans to build him a house, giving them instructions as to their conduct, and unluckily informing them of his plans. He soon after set out himself in the bark and two barges, accompanied by Captain Waldo and forty-six men. As this was an enterprise of great danger, he took with him only those who volunteered to go. He left the government in the hands of Mr. Scrivener.

On the 29th of December, they departed from Jamestown, carrying with them provisions for only three or four days. They lodged that night at Warraskoyac, an Indian village, a few miles from Jamestown, where they made additions to their stores.

The chief of the tribe treated them with great kindness, and endeavored to dissuade Captain Smith from going to see Powhatan ; but, finding him resolved, he warned him to be on his guard, for that Powhatan, notwithstanding all his seeming kindness, had sent for them merely for the purpose of cutting their throats. The Captain thanked him for his caution, and requested him to furnish guides to the nation of the Chawonocs, who dwelt between the rivers Nottaway and Meherrin, in North Carolina, to which he readily consented. Mr. Michael Sicklemore, a valiant and honest soldier, was sent upon this enterprise, the object of which was to obtain silk-grass and to inquire after Sir Walter Raleigh's lost colony.

The next night they lodged at Kecoughtan (Hampton), where they were detained several days by violent storms. This obliged them to keep their Christmas among the Indians.* But we are told that they had a very merry one, warmed by blazing fires, and their tables amply spread with fish, flesh, oysters, and wildfowl. After various accidents, they arrived on the 12th

---

* The narrative states, that they left Jamestown on the 29th of December, and yet that they afterwards kept Christmas among the savages. Of course, both statements cannot be correct. The matter is fortunately of little consequence, as there are no means of ascertaining which is right.

of January at Werowocomoco, where they found
the river frozen to nearly half a mile from the
shore.   They broke the ice to make a passage
for the barge, till she was grounded by the ebbing
of the tide, when they leaped out and waded to
the shore through the ice and mud.

They quartered in the first cabins which they
found, and sent for provisions to Powhatan, who
supplied them with bread, turkeys, and venison.
The next day, after having given them an entertainment, he very inhospitably inquired of them
when they purposed to go away, saying, that he
had never invited them to come, and that neither he nor his people had any corn to spare.
Captain Smith then confronted him with the men
who had brought his invitation, and quietly asked
him how he came to be so forgetful ; "thereat
the King concluded the matter with a merry
laugh," and asked for his commodities.   Nothing
suited him, however, but guns and swords, and
he valued a basket of corn at a higher rate than
a basket of copper.   Captain Smith, perceiving
that the wily savage was trifling with him, said to
him with some sternness, that he had confidently
relied upon his promises to supply the colony
with provisions, and had neglected to procure any
from other sources, which he might have done ;
and, to testify his regard to him, he had sent mechanics to construct buildings for him, while his

own were standing unfinished. He charged him with having monopolized his people's corn and forbidden them to trade with the English, in hopes, by starvation, to bring them to his own terms. As to guns and swords, he had none to spare, as he had told him long before ; but they would contrive to keep from starving by the aid of those which they had, though they would do him no wrong nor violence, nor break the friendship which existed between them, unless constrained to do so by ill usage.

Powhatan listened attentively to this discourse and promised that both he and his people would supply the English with as much corn as could be spared, and that they should receive it within two days. "But," he added, "I have some doubts about the reason of your coming here. I am informed by many, that you come, not to trade, but to invade my people, and to possess my country. This makes me less ready to relieve you, and frightens my people from bringing in their corn. And therefore to ease them of that fear, leave your arms aboard, since they are needless here, where we are all friends."

Powhatan's doubts were very reasonable, and his wary conduct perfectly justifiable ; for Smith's whole plot had been revealed to him by the Germans, who had been sent to build a house for him. These men, seeing Powhatan's wealth and plenty, and the wretched condition of the colony, and supposing that he must finally extirpate them, had, in order to secure his favor, basely betrayed the purposes of the English. Their treachery was the more odious, because one of them had been honored with particular marks of confidence by Captain Smith on account of his intelligence and supposed integrity, and had been sent on this errand to act as a spy upon Powhatan. Captain Smith was entirely unsuspicious of the fact at the time, and did not hear of it till six months afterwards; so it is easy to see what an advantage the savage monarch had over him, which he did not fail to improve to the utmost.

A contest of ingenuity ensued between Captain Smith and Powhatan, reminding us of the efforts of two skilful boxers, to find an opening to plant the first blow. The savage chieftain was very anxious that the English should lay aside their arms, of which he and his people had a most wholesome terror; and he made use of arguments of the following tenor. "Captain Smith," said he, "I am a very old man, having seen the death of three of the generations of my people, and know well the difference between peace and war. I must soon die, and my brothers must succeed me. I wish to live quietly with you, and I wish the same for them. But the rumors, which have reached us, disturb us, and alarm my people so that they dare not visit you. What advantage will it be to you to destroy us, who supply you with food ? What can you gain by war, if we escape to the woods and hide our provisions there ? Why are you so suspicious of us ? You see we are unarmed, and are ready to supply your wants. Do you think I am so simple as not to prefer eating good meat, sleeping quietly with my wives and children, laughing and making merry with you, having copper, hatchets, and every thing else, as your friend, to flying from you, as your enemy, lying cold in the woods, living upon acorns, roots, and such trash, being so hunted by you that we can neither rest, eat, nor sleep in peace, but if a twig break, my men will cry out, ‘ Here comes Captain Smith.’ In this miserable manner, I must come to a miserable end, and you likewise, sooner or later. Be assured of our friendship then, and we will readily and abundantly supply you with corn. Lay aside your guns and swords, and do not come armed as into an enemy's country."

To these sentimental speeches Captain Smith replied after the following fashion. "As you will not understand our words, we must make our deeds speak for us. We have scrupulously adhered to the terms of the treaty of peace concluded between us, which your men have constantly violated ; and, though we have had ample opportunities for avenging ourselves, we have refrained out of our regard to you. And you know enough of us to know, that, if we had intended you any injury, we could long ago have succeeded in doing it. It is our custom to wear arms in the same manner as clothes, and we can by no means part with them. Your people come frequently to Jamestown with bows and arrows, and are entertained without suspicion or remark. As to your flying into the woods and hiding your provisions out of our reach, you need not think that will trouble us. We have a way of discovering hidden things, unknown to you."

Many other discourses, of the same tenor, passed between them. Powhatan, seeing that his wishes were not received as law by the English, and that they would not lay aside their arms or omit any of their usual precautions, gave utterance to these sentiments, with a heavy sigh. " Captain Smith, I have never treated any chief with so much kindness as I have you ; but I have never in return received any at your hands. Captain Newport gave me swords, copper, clothes, and every thing else I desired, taking, in exchange, whatever I offered him. He would at any time send away his guns at my request. No one refuses to gratify my wishes, but you. You will give me nothing, to which you attach any value; and yet you insist upon having every-thing from me, which you desire. You call Captain Newport father, and so you do me; but I see, in spite of us both, you will have your own way, and we must study to please you. If your intentions are as friendly as you profess them to be, send away your arms, and I will be-lieve you."

Captain Smith, seeing that Powhatan was mere-ly wasting the time in idle speeches, in order to gain an opportunity to attack them and put them to death, resolved to strike a decisive blow. He gave directions to the Indians to break a passage through the ice, that his boat might come to the shore, and ordered some more of his men to land, to aid him in surprising Powhatan. In order to keep him free from suspicion, till the proper hour came, he entertained him with "much specious and fallacious discourse,* telling him, that he was his friend and not his subject, and promising the next day to give up his arms, and to show him, that he honored him as a father, by trusting im-plicitly to his words. The wily chieftain, when he heard that they were breaking a passage through the ice, suspected that all was not right, and suddenly fled with his women, children, and luggage. To avoid suspicion, he left two or

---

* Stith, p. 88.

three women to talk with Captain Smith, while he secretly made his escape ; and in the mean time his warriors beset the house, in which they were conversing. When this was told to Captain Smith, he boldly sallied out armed with sword, pistol, and target, with which, as we are told, "he made such a passage among these naked devils, that, at his first shot, they next him tumbled one over another, and the rest quickly fled, some one way, some another." He reached the main body of his men without any injury.

The Indians, seeing that he had escaped unharmed and was guarded by eighteen resolute, well armed men, endeavored to put a fair construction upon their unequivocal doings ; and Powhatan, to excuse his flight and the sudden gathering of his warriors, sent an "ancient orator," who, like more civilized diplomatists, sought to gain a favorable hearing by a present of a great bracelet and a chain of pearls, and addressed Captain Smith, as follows ; " Captain Smith, our king is fled, fearing your guns, and knowing that, when the ice was broken, more men would come. He sent the warriors, whom you assaulted, to guard your corn, which might be stolen without your knowledge. Though some have been injured in consequence of your mistake, Powhatan is still your friend, and will ever continue so. Now, since the ice is broken, he would have you send away your corn; and, if you would have his company, your guns also, which so affright his people, that they dare not come to you, as he has promised they should." The corn referred to in the Indian ambassador's speech consisted of a quantity amounting to eighty bushels, which had been purchased of Powhatan for a copper kettle.

The English were immediately oppressed with attentions. Baskets were provided for them to carry the corn to the boat, and the Indians kindly offered their services to guard their arms, that none might steal them. This favor was, with suitable acknowedgments, declined. To show the dread which they had of fire-arms, we are told, that "a great many they were of goodly, well proportioned fellows, as grim as devils; yet the very sight of cocking our matches and being to let fly, a few words caused them to leave their bows and arrows to our guard, and bear down our corn upon their backs; we needed not importune them to make despatch." The English were under the necessity of waiting for the next tide before they could depart, and the day was spent in feasting and merry sports.

Powhatan, who burned to get possession of Smith's head, had prepared his forces to make an attack upon the English at night, which would probably have been fatal to them all, had they not been warned of it by Pocahontas, on this, as on all occasions, the guardian angel of the whites. It is better to relate the incident in the unvarnished language of the original narrative, than to ornament it with any rhetorical embellishments of my own. After mentioning that a plot had been formed by Powhatan, it states that, " Notwithstanding, the eternal, all-seeing God did prevent him, and by a strange means. For Pocahontas, his dearest jewel and daughter, in that dark night, came through the irksome woods, and told our Captain great cheer should be sent us by and by; but Powhatan, and all the power he could make, would after come kill us all, if they that brought it could not kill us with our own weapons, when we were at supper. Therefore, if we would live, she wished us presently to be gone. Such things as she delighted in he would have given her; but, with the tears running down her cheeks, she said she durst not be seen to have any; for, if Powhatan should know it, she were but dead; and so she ran away by herself, as she came." This simple and beautiful picture of disinterested attachment and heroic self-forgetfulness needs not the " foreign aid of ornament " to recommend it to the heart, which has a throb left for generous deeds and noble qualities.

Pocahontas had been gone less than an hour, when there came eight or ten stout fellows, with large platters of venison and other articles of food, who invited them to sit down and eat, and were very importunate for them to put out their matches, the smoke of which, as they said, made them sick. But Captain Smith made them taste of every dish (probably to ascertain whether it was poisoned or not), and sent some of them back to Powhatan, bidding him make haste for he was ready to receive him, telling him that he knew upon what deadly errand his first messengers were sent, but that he could guard against that as well as all his other intended villanies. Messengers came from Powhatan from time to time, to learn the position of things; but the English passed the night in such watchful preparation, that no blow was struck. They departed at high water, and left behind them the Germans, whose good faith was entirely unsuspected, and (what seems a little strange, after these events) one of their own number, Edward Brynton by name, to kill birds for Powhatan.

The conduct of Captain Smith in attempting to seize the person of Powhatan cannot be justified, and no one can feel sorry that he did not succeed. The principle of gratitude should alone have prevented him from dealing so treacherously with a man who had spared his life, when he had him in his power. His only excuse is to be found in the strong necessity of the case, of the extent of which, however, we have no means of forming a conception. The opinions of the age, in all that relates to the rights of men and nations, were characterized, not even by a nice sense of honor, much less by a feeling of Christian brotherhood. The manner in which his conspiracy was betrayed to Powhatan, enforces the lesson taught by all the great plots and intrigues of the world, that he who aims at treacherous designs is never sure of his instruments. When a man has once consented to become a spy and act a borrowed part, it is easy for him to go a step further and betray his employer by a double treachery. He, who has once deserted the path of moral rectitude, has never a firm footing, and is continually liable to slide into deeper and more inextricable guilt.

CHAPTER X.

Captain Smith's Adventures with Opechanca-
nough, Chief of Pamunkey. — His Return to
Jamestown.

No sooner had the English set sail, than Powhatan sent two of the Germans to Jamestown. These imposed upon Captain Wynne with a plausible story, that every thing was going on well, and that Captain Smith had need of some weapons, ammunition, and clothing, all of which were unsuspectingly delivered to them. While they were there, by their artful speeches and by working upon the hopes of the selfish and the fears of the timid, they prevailed upon six or seven to leave the colony and join them with Powhatan.

These apostates, among their other accomplishments, had a peculiar dexterity in stealing, which they exerted so successfully, that they filched from the colonists a great number of swords, pikeheads, and muskets, with large quantities of powder and shot. There were always Indians prowling around in the neighborhood to carry them off. By these means, and by the labors of one of the Germans, who had remained behind and who seems to have been a blacksmith, the armory of Powhatan was very materially increased.

Captain Smith and his party in the mean while had arrived at Pamunkey, the seat of Opechancanough, the brother of Powhatan, who received them kindly and entertained them many days in his most hospitable style. A day was appointed for traffic, upon which Captain Smith with fifteen others went up to the village where the chief resided, about a quarter of a mile from the river. They found no human being there, except a lame man and a boy, and the houses were abandoned and stripped of every thing. Soon, however, the chief arrived with many warriors, armed with bows and arrows; but their commodities were so trifling and offered at so exorbitant a price, that Captain Smith remonstrated with him in the following manner; "Opechancanough, you profess, with your words, great love to me, but your actions are inconsistent with your professions. Last year, you kindly freighted our ship, but now you have invited us here that you might see us starve with hunger. You know my wants and I know your plenty, of which I will, by some means, have a share. Remember that it becomes kings to keep their promises. I offer you my goods; you may take your choice, and the rest I will apportion justly among your people." The chieftain accepted his offer seemingly with a good grace, persuaded, probably, more by the muskets, than by the intrinsic force of the suggestions themselves. He sold them what they wanted, at their own prices, promising the next day to meet them with more people and more commodities.

On the next day, Captain Smith and his party marched up to his house, where they found four or five Indians newly arrived, each furnished with a great basket. The chief himself soon after arrived, and with a "strained cheerfulness" magnified the pains he had been at in keeping his promise. While they were discoursing, Mr. Russell, one of the party came suddenly in and with a face of alarm, told Captain Smith that they were all lost, for seven hundred armed men had environed the house and were swarming round about in the fields.

Captain Smith seeing dismay painted in the countenances of his followers at these tidings, addressed to them a few words of encouragement. He told them that he felt far less concern at the number of the enemy than for the malicious misrepresentations, which the council would make in England, of his readiness to break the peace and expose their lives; that they had nothing to fear, for that he alone had been once assaulted by three hundred, and but for an accident, would have made good his way through them; that they were sixteen in number, and the Indians not more than seven hundred, and that the very smoke of their pieces would be enough to disperse them. At any rate, he exhorted them to fight like men, and not tamely die like sheep; and if they would resolutely follow his example, he doubted not that he should be able, with the blessing of God, to extricate them from their present perilous situation.

They all resolutely promised to second him in whatever he attempted, though it should cost them their lives. Whereupon he addressed Opechancanough to the following effect; "I see that

you have entered into a plot to murder me, but I
have no fears as to the result. Let us decide
the matter by single combat. The island in the
river is a fit place, and you may have any weapons you please. Let your men bring each a basket of corn and I will stake their value in copper,
and the conqueror shall have all and be ruler
over all our men."

This proposal was declined by the chief, who
had no chivalrous notions of honor, and could not
conceive of any one's voluntarily giving up any
advantage, which he could gain by treachery or
other means over an enemy. He artfully endeavored to quiet Smith's suspicions, and invited
him outside of the door to receive a present,
where he had stationed two hundred men, with
their arrows on the string, ready to shoot at him
the moment he appeared. Captain Smith, who
had discovered, or at least strongly suspected his
perfidious purpose, no longer restrained his indignation, but seizing him by his long lock of hair,
and clapping his pistol to his breast, led him out
trembling into the midst of his people. They
were petrified with horror, that any one should
dare to lay violent hands on the sacred person
of their chief, and were amazingly frightened besides. He readily gave up his vambrace,* bow,

---

* Vambrace, armor for the arm. *Avant-bras*, Fr.
— *Bailey.*

and arrows in token of submission, and his subjects followed his example.

Captain Smith, still retaining his grasp upon him, addressed his subjects as follows; " I perceive, ye Pamunkeys, the desire you have to kill me, and that my longsuffering has brought you to this pitch of insolence. The reason I have forborne to punish you is the promise which I formerly made to you, that I would be your friend till you gave me just cause to be your enemy. If I keep this vow, my God will keep me and you cannot hurt me ; but if I break it, he will destroy me. But if you now shoot one arrow to shed a drop of blood, or steal any of these beads, or of this copper, I will take such a revenge, as that you shall not hear the last of me while there is a Pamunkey alive who will not deny the name. I am not now half-drowned in the mire of a swamp, as I was when you took me prisoner. If I be the mark you aim at, shoot, if you dare. You promised to load my vessel with corn, and if you do not, I will load her with your carcasses. But, if you will trade with me like friends, I once more promise that I will not trouble you, unless you provoke me, and your chief shall be my friend, and go free ; for I did not come to hurt him or any of you."

This speech had an effect like magic. The savages threw down their bows and arrows, and thronged round Captain Smith with their commodities, in such numbers, for the space of two or three hours, that he became absolutely weary of receiving them. He accordingly retired, and, overcome with his toils and excitements, fell asleep. The Indians seeing him in this condition, and his guard rather carelessly dispersed, went into the house in great numbers armed with clubs or English swords, and with intentions by no means friendly. The noise they made aroused him from his slumbers, which we may suppose were not very deep; and, though surprised and confused at seeing so many grim forms around him, he seized his sword and target, and, being seconded by some of his countrymen, drove out the intruders more rapidly than they came in. Opechancanough made a long speech to excuse the rude conduct of his subjects. The rest of the day, was spent in kindness and good-will, the Indians renewing their presents and feasting the English with their best provisions.

Captain Smith here received the news of a most melancholy accident which took place at Jamestown during his absence. Mr. Scrivener had received some letters from England, which gave him extravagant notions of his own importance, and made him feel very coldly towards Captain Smith, who still regarded him with the affection of a brother. He took it into his head to visit an island in the vicinity of Jamestown, called Hog Island, on a very cold and stormy day, when it seemed little short of madness to tempt the angry elements. Notwithstanding the most earnest remonstrances he persisted in going, and persuaded Captain Waldo with nine others to accompany him. The skiff would have hardly floated with so large a freight, in calm weather; but, as it was, she sunk immediately, and all who were in her were drowned. Their dead bodies were found by the Indians, which encouraged them in their projected enterprises against the colony.

No one, for some time, would undertake to inform Captain Smith of this heavy news, till finally Mr. Richard Wiffin volunteered. His journey was full of dangers and difficulties. He at first went to Werowocomoco, where he found that all were engaged in warlike preparations, which boded no good to his countrymen. He seems to have narrowly escaped with his life here; for we are told, that " Pocahontas hid him for a time, and sent them who pursued him the clean contrary way to seek him." He finally reached Captain Smith after travelling three days, and communicated his sad message to him; who charged him to keep it a secret from his followers, and, dissembling his grief as much as he could, at night-fall he went on board the boat, leaving Opechancanough at liberty and unmolested according to his promise.

Captain Smith cherished a hope, that he might be able, on his return, to entrap Powhatan, an intention which he had never abandoned. Powhatan, on his part, had commanded his subjects, on pain of death, to kill Captain Smith by some means or other. The consequence was, that on their second meeting, as at their first, both parties were on their guard; and, though many stratagems were practised on both sides, nothing decisive took place. Such a terror was Captain Smith to the Indians, that not even the commands of Powhatan could induce them to attack him in battle, notwithstanding their immense superiority in numbers; and they were ready to propitiate him by loads of provision, if they had any reason to suspect hostile intentions on his part towards them. We are told, however, that they attempted to take his life by poison, a mode more characteristic of civilized malice, than of savage hatred. The particulars are not related; it is said that Captain Smith, Mr. West, and others were taken sick, and thus threw off from the stomach some poisonous substance which would have been fatal, had it been left to its natural operation. It was probably not prepared with great skill by these untutored chemists. No other notice was taken of the outrage, except that the Indian who brought the poisoned articles was soundly beaten by Captain Smith's own hand, which, we have every reason to believe, was a very heavy one. He finally returned to James-town after an enterprise full of perils and difficulty, bringing with him two hundred pounds of deer suet, and four hundred and seventy-nine bushels of corn.

CHAPTER XI.

Troubles with the Indians. — Scarcity of Pro-visions. — Mutinous and Treacherous Disposi-tion of Some of the Colonists. — Arrival of Captain Argall.

CAPTAIN SMITH, on his arrival, found as usual that nothing had been done during his absence. Their provisions had been much injured by the rain, and many of their tools and weapons had been stolen by or secretly conveyed to the Indians. The stock of food which remained, increased by that which had been procured from the Indians, was, however, found on compu-tation to be sufficient to last them a year; and consequently their apprehensions of starving were for the present laid aside. They were divided into companies of ten or fifteen, as occasion required, and six hours of each day were spent in labor and the rest in amusement and exhilarating exercises.

The majority of them, unaccustomed to discipline or regular employment, showed symptoms of stubborn resistance to his authority, which provoked him to reprove them in sharp terms. He told them, that their recent sufferings ought to have worked a change in their conduct, and that they must not think that either his labors or the purses of the adventurers would for ever maintain them in idleness. He did not mean that his reproaches should apply to all, for many deserved more honor and reward than they could ever receive; but the majority of them must be more industrious or starve. That it was not reasonable that the labors of thirty or forty honest and industrious men should be devoted to the support of a hundred and fifty idle loiterers, and that, therefore, whoever would not work must not eat. That they had often been screened in their disobedience to his commands by the authority of the council; but that now the power, in effect, rested wholly in him. That they were mistaken in their opinion, that his authority was but a shadow, and that he could not touch the lives of any without peril of his own. That the letters patent would show them the contrary, which he would have read to them every week, and that they might be assured that every one, who deserved punishment, should receive it.

He also made a register, in which he recorded their merits and demerits, "to encourage the good, and with shame to spur on the rest to amendment;" a simple device, one would think, for those who had long left school, but which, owing probably to the President's great personal influence, proved of considerable efficacy. They missed from time to time powder, shot, arms, and tools, without knowing what had become of them, but found afterwards that they were secretly conveyed to the Germans, who were with Powhatan, by their countrymen and confederates at Jamestown. Four or five of these latter, according to a previous agreement, had deserted from Jamestown, a short time before, to join the former; but, meeting in the woods some of Captain Smith's party on their return, to avoid suspicion they came back. Their countrymen sent one of their number, disguised as an Indian, to learn the reason of their delay. He came as far as the glass-house, which was about a mile from Jamestown, and was the scene of all their plots and machinations, and their common place of rendezvous.

At the same time and near the same place, forty Indians were lying in ambush for Captain Smith. He was immediately informed of the German's arrival (how or by whom we are not told), and, taking twenty men, marched to the glass-house to apprehend him ; but he had gone away before they came. He despatched his followers to intercept him, and returned alone to Jamestown, armed only with a sword, not suspecting any danger. In the woods he met the chief of the Pashiphays, a neighboring tribe of Indians, a tall and strong man, who at first attempted by artful persuasion to bring Captain Smith within reach of the ambuscade. Failing, however, in this, he attempted to shoot him with his bow, which Smith prevented by suddenly grappling with him. Neither was able to make use of his weapons, but the Indian drew his adversary by main strength into the river, in the hope of drowning him. There they struggled for a long time, till Captain Smith seized his antagonist's throat with such a grasp as nearly strangled him. This momentary advantage enabled him to draw his sword, at which his foe no longer resisted, but begged his life with piteous entreaties. Captain Smith led him prisoner to Jamestown and put him in chains.

The German meanwhile had been taken ; and, though he attempted to account for his conduct, his treachery was suspected and finally confirmed by the confession of the captive chief, who was kept in custody, and offered to Powhatan in exchange for the faithless Germans whom he had with him. Many messengers were sent, but the Germans would not come of their own accord, neither would Powhatan force them. While these negotiations were going on, the chief himself escaped through the negligence of his guards, though he was in irons. An attempt was made to retake him, but without effect. Captain Smith made prisoners of two Indians, by name Kemps and Tussore, who are described as being "the two most exact villains in all the country." He himself went with an expedition to punish the tribe of Pashiphays for their past injuries and deter them from any future ones, in which he slew several of them, burned their houses, took their canoes and fishing-weirs, and fixed some of the latter at Jamestown.

As he was proceeding to Chickahominy, he was assaulted by some of their tribe; but, as soon as they saw who he was, they threw down their arms and sued for peace, a young man, named Okaning, thus addressing him; "Captain Smith, the chief, my master, is here among us, and he attacked you, mistaking you for Captain Wynne, who has pursued us in war. If he has offended you in escaping imprisonment, remember that fishes swim, the birds fly, and the very beasts strive to escape the snare and the line ; blame not him, therefore, who is a man.   He would ask you to recollect what pains he took, when you were a prisoner, to save your life.   If he has injured you since, you have taken ample vengeance and great-ly to our cost.   We know that your purpose is to destroy us ; but we are here to desire your friend-ship, and to ask you to permit us to enjoy our houses and plant our fields.   You shall share in their fruit ; but if you drive us off, you will be the greatest losers by our absence.   For we can plant any where, though it may cost us more labor ; but we know you cannot live, unless you have our harvests to supply your wants. If you will promise us peace, we will trust you ; if not, we will abandon the country."

This "worthy discourse," as it is justly called by the writer of the narrative, had its desired effect.   Captain Smith made peace with them on condition that they would supply him with provisions.   This good understanding continued so long as Captain Smith remained in the coun-try.

When Smith returned to Jamestown, complaint was made to him, that the people of Chicka-hominy, who had always seemed honest and friendly, had been guilty of frequent thefts.   A pistol, among other things, had been recently stolen and the thief escaped; but his two brothers, who were known to be his confederates, were apprehended. According to the President's usual summary mode of proceeding in such cases, one of these was sent home with a message, that if the pistol were not forthcoming in twelve hours, the other (who meanwhile was imprisoned) should be hung. The messenger came back before midnight with the pistol, but a sad spectacle awaited him. Captain Smith, pitying the poor naked Indian who was shivering in his dark, cold dungeon, had sent him some food and charcoal to make a fire with. The simple savage, knowing nothing of the mysteries of carbonic acid gas,* soon fainted away under its deleterious influence, and was brought out to all appearance dead. His brother, seeing his confident hopes so cruelly disappointed, broke out into the most passionate lamentations, and Captain Smith, to pacify him, told him that he would restore him to life. By the application of brandy and vinegar, he was restored to consciousness; but his faculties remained in such a state of confusion and disorder, as alarmed his brother hardly less than his seeming death. But a night's sound sleep restored him to his senses, and they were both pre-

---

* The English writer was not much wiser; he says the Indian was smothered with the smoke.

sented with a piece of copper and sent home. From this circumstance, a report was spread far and wide, among the Indians, that Captain Smith was able to restore the dead to life.

Another incident took place about this time, which increased the awe in which the English were held. An "ingenuous savage" at Werowocomoco had by some means obtained possession of a bag of gunpowder and of the backpiece of a suit of armor. Wishing to display his superior accomplishments to his countrymen, he proceeded to dry the powder over the fire, upon the armor, as he had seen the soldiers do at Jamestown. Many thronged around him and peeped over his shoulders, to watch the process, when suddenly the powder exploded, killed the unfortunate operator and one or two others, and wounded several more, which gave the whole nation a great distaste to gunpowder. "These and many other such pretty accidents," as we are told, so amazed and alarmed Powhatan and his whole people, that they desired peace from all parts, bringing in presents and restoring stolen articles, which had long been given up in despair. After this, if any Indian was detected in stealing, he was apprehended and sent to Jamestown to be punished, and the whole country became as free and safe to the English as to the Indians themselves.

The English, thus unmolested from without, were enabled to devote their undivided energies to the internal affairs of the colony. They set themselves to labor with industry and success. In the space of three months, they had made a considerable quantity of tar, pitch, and potash; produced a sample of glass; dug a well of sweet water in the fort, an article which they had not had in abundance before; built twenty new houses; new covered the church; provided nets and weirs for fishing; and built a block-house on the isthmus of Jamestown, in which a garrison was stationed to trade with the Indians, and which no one was allowed to pass without an order from the President. Thirty or forty acres of ground were also dug and planted. A block-house was likewise erected on Hog Island, and a garrison stationed there to give notice of any vessels that might arrive. At leisure times they exercised themselves in cutting down trees and making clapboards and wainscoting. About this time Captain Wynne died, so that Captain Smith was left with the whole and absolute power, being both President and council.

Their prosperous and contented industry received a sudden interruption. On examining their store of corn, they found that half of it had rotted, and the rest was nearly all consumed by the rats, which had been left by the ship, and increased in great numbers. This put a stop to all their enterprises and obliged them to turn their whole attention to the procuring of food.

The Indians were very friendly to them, bringing in deer and wildfowl in abundance, and Powhatan spared them nearly half his stock of corn. The river also supplied them with sturgeon and oysters ; so there was no danger of their starving to death. But then food could not be procured without considerable toil and trouble ; and many of them were so intolerably lazy, that, as the narrative says, " had they not been forced *nolens volens* perforce to gather and prepare their victual, they would all have starved or have eaten one another." These men were very clamorous that he should sell their tools and iron, their swords and muskets, and even their houses and ordnance, to the Indians for corn, so that they might enjoy the luxury of idleness.

They endeavored also by all means in their power to induce him to leave the country. Necessity obliged Captain Smith to overlook for a time their mutinous and disorderly proceedings; but, having detected and severely punished the principal ringleader, he addressed the remainder in the following terms. " Fellow-soldiers, I did not think that any one was so false as to report, or that you were so simple as to believe, either that I intended to starve you, or that Powhatan had, at this time, any corn for himself, much less for you, or that I would not procure corn, if I knew where it was to be had. Neither did I think that any were so malicious, as I find many are; but I will not so yield to indignation as to prevent me from doing what I can for the good of my most inveterate enemy. But dream no longer of any further assistance from Powhatan, and do not imagine that I shall not compel the indolent to work, as well as punish the refractory. If I find any one attempting to escape to Newfoundland in the pinnace, let him be assured that the gallows shall be his portion. You cannot deny that I have often saved your lives at the risk of my own, and provided you food when otherwise you might have starved. But I protest, by the God that made me, that since necessity has no power to compel you to gather for yourselves the fruits which the earth yields, I will oblige you to gather them, not only for yourselves, but also for the sick. You know that I have fared like the meanest of you, and that my extra allowance I have always distributed among the sick. The sick shall not starve, but shall fare like the rest of us; therefore, whoever does not gather as much every day as I do, the next day he shall be put over the river and be banished from the fort, until he either alters his conduct or starves."

These orders were murmured against as being extremely cruel and tyrannical; but no one dared to disobey them. All exerted themselves diligently to procure food, so that they not only did not suffer from want, but grew strong and healthy. Many were billeted among the Indians, a fact which shows how much confidence there was on one side, and how much respect, or at least fear, on the other. These last were so well treated by their kind entertainers, that many deserted from Jamestown and took up their abode with them; but the Indians, who knew that they had acted contrary to Captain Smith's orders, received them with great coldness, and finally brought them back to him. He inflicted on them such exemplary punishment, that no one ventured to follow their example. The good conduct of the Indians at this crisis extorts from the writer of the narrative the remark, that there was more hope to make good Christians and good subjects of them, than of one half of those who pretended to be both.

At this period, Mr. Sicklemore returned from his expedition, but without gaining any satisfactory account of Sir Walter Raleigh's lost company or of the silk-grass. Captain Smith, who thought it proper not to abandon a point so strongly urged by the council in England, sent upon the same errand two of his company to the

Mangoags; a tribe of Indians, not subject to Powhatan, who dwelt somewhere on the borders of North Carolina and Virginia. They were furnished with guides by the chief of the Quiyoughnohanocs, a small tribe dwelling on the southern banks of the James River, about ten miles from Jamestown. "This honest, proper, promise-keeping king," as he is styled, was ever friendly to the English; and, though he zealously worshipped his own false gods, he was ready to acknowledge that their God exceeded his, as much as guns did bows and arrows. He would often send presents to the President, in a time of drought, begging him to pray to his God for rain, lest his corn should spoil, because his own gods were angry with him. The result of this expedition was, like that of the former one, entirely unsuccessful.

The Germans, who were with Powhatan, gave them constant trouble. One Volday, a Swiss, was employed to solicit them to return to the colony; but, instead of that, he basely and treacherously entered into a conspiracy with them to cut off the English, and diligently exerted himself to bring it to a successful issue. Seeing that these were obliged to wander about in search of provisions and leave the fort but feebly defended, they endeavored to prevail upon Powhatan to lend them his forces, promising to burn the town, to seize the bark, and make the greater part of the colonists his subjects and slaves.

This plot was communicated to some of the malcontents at Jamestown; and two of them, " whose Christian hearts relented at such an unchristian act," revealed it to the President.   When it became generally known in the colony, the sentiment of indignation was so lively, that several volunteered to go and slay the Germans, though in the very presence of Powhatan.   Two were accordingly sent on this errand ; but, on their arrival, the Germans made such plausible excuses, and accused Volday so warmly, that they were unaccountably suffered to go unpunished.   Powhatan seems to have observed a strict neutrality in this business.   He sent a message to Captain Smith, informing him that he would neither attempt to detain the Germans, nor to hinder his men from executing his commands.   One of these Germans, we are told, afterwards returned to his duty, on promise of full pardon for the past ; the other remained with Powhatan.

The writer of this portion of the History of Virginia, after relating these incidents, and stating that their great security against the treacherous machinations of these foreigners, and their unprincipled coadjutors at Jamestown, was the love and respect in which Captain Smith was held, by all the neighboring Indians, goes on to remark upon his merits in a strain of honest admiration; "By this you may see, for all those crosses, treacheries, and dissensions, how he wrestled and overcame (without bloodshed) all that happened; also what good was done; how few died; what food the country naturally affordeth; what small cause there is men should starve or be murdered by the savages, that have discretion to manage them with courage and industry. The two first years, though by his adventures he had often brought the savages to a tractable trade, yet you see how the envious authority ever crossed him, and frustrated his best endeavors. But it wrought in him that experience and estimation amongst the savages, as otherwise it had been impossible he had ever effected that he did. Notwithstanding the many miserable, yet generous and worthy adventures he had oft and long endured in the wide world, yet in this case he was again to learn his lecture by experience; which with much ado having obtained, it was his ill chance to end, when he had but only learned how to begin."

In the spring of the year 1609, Captain Samuel Argall, afterwards a governor of the colony, arrived at Jamestown. He came to trade with the colony and to fish for sturgeon, in a ship supplied with wine and provisions. This, says Stith, was a prohibited trade, but it was connived at, because Argall was a relation of Sir Thomas

Smith. The necessity of the colony obliged them to take his provisions, by which the object of his voyage was defeated; but as soon as they received supplies from England, they revictualled him home, with letters giving a full account of the state of their affairs. By him Captain Smith received letters, blaming him for his cruel usage of the Indians, and for not sending back the former ships freighted. By him they also heard of the great preparations in England for sending out an expedition, under the command of Lord Delaware, and of the entire change projected in the government of the colony.

CHAPTER XII.

New Charter granted to the Virginia Company. — Expedition despatched to Jamestown. — Confusion which ensues on its Arrival. — Captain Smith returns to England.

THE administration of Captain Smith, and the general course of events from the first, at Jamestown, had been far from satisfactory to the company in England. They had founded the colony solely from selfish motives, in the hope of acquiring great and sudden fortunes by the opening of a passage to the South Sea, or by the discovery of abundant mines of gold and silver. The splendid success of the Spaniards in South America had filled the imaginations of all Europe with golden dreams; and the company were disappointed and irritated, because there had not been found in Virginia the mineral treasures of Peru and Mexico. They chose to visit their displeasure upon the innocent head of Captain Smith, as if he had either been the cause of their extravagant hopes, or had, by some potent magic, banished the precious metals from the soil of Virginia.

Their prejudice against him was increased, undoubtedly, by their extreme ignorance of every thing relating to the history and situation of the colony, which disqualified them from judging of the propriety of his measures. Their minds too had been poisoned by the misrepresentations of Newport, who possessed their entire confidence, and who hated Captain Smith with that untiring and dogged hatred, with which an inferior being contemplates an enemy, who is too much above him to allow the most distant hope of rivalship. They were dissatisfied, among other things, with his treatment of the Indians, thinking it too harsh and peremptory, and that a milder and more conciliatory one would have induced them to discover the hidden treasures, which they were persuaded existed somewhere in the country.

Captain Smith, as the reader must have observed, considered himself bound from the first, to provide for the protection and support of the colony, rather than the pecuniary interests of the council at home. He endeavored to give it a permanent footing in the country, an object about which they cared very little, as is shown by their shameful neglect in supplying it with provisions, as well as by the character of the adventurers whom they sent out.

He perceived at once the futility of any expectations of raising a revenue from Virginia, and dwelt upon it in all his communications to England. He saw that a handful of Englishmen were surrounded by numerous and formidable tribes of Indians, and that there could never be any security to life or property, unless they were promptly overawed by firm and spirited conduct. With great propriety he considered himself far better able to judge of the measures which ought to be adopted for the colony, than a company of gentlemen, three thousand miles distant, who derived their information from imperfect or interested sources. His administration, as we have seen, was vigorous and decided, aiming rather to benefit the colony, than to please the council at home. He was too independent and proud a man to stoop to conciliate those whose favor was not to be won by a steady adherence to duty. He had not a drop of the courtier's blood in his whole body. His intercourse with his superiors in station was marked with dignity and self-respect. His letter to the council, which he sent by Newport, and of which we have given an account, is certainly unmarked by delicate official deference, and little calculated to win or regain favor. All these things had combined to render him and his administration unpopular ; and he, whose services to the colony had been incalculable, was made the victim of their capricious displeasure, and dismissed from an office which he had filled so honorably, so successfully, and with such constant self-sacrifice.

The Virginia company, having induced many persons of rank and wealth to join with them, in order to increase at once their dignity and their funds, applied to King James for a new charter, which was granted, and which bears date, May 23d, 1609. It gave the most ample powers to the council in England and showed the most wanton disregard of the rights and privileges of the colonists who had emigrated on the faith of the first charter, and who had toiled, suffered, and accomplished so much. By virtue of these powers, the new council appointed Lord Delaware, a nobleman of high rank and distinguished character, captain-general of the colony ; Sir

Thomas Gates, lieutenant-general ; Sir George Somers, admiral ; Captain Newport (the only one who had ever been in Virginia), vice-admiral ; Sir Thomas Dale, high marshall ; Sir Ferdinando Wainman, master of the horse. The countenance of so many honorable and distinguished persons made the enterprise fashionable and popular, so that they were able to equip nine ships, in which five hundred persons consisting of men, women, and children, embarked.

The expedition set sail from England in May, 1609, under the command of Sir George Somers, Sir Thomas Gates, and Captain Newport, each of whom had a commission authorizing him, who first arrived, to supersede the existing administration, and to govern the colony by the terms and provisions of the new charter, until the arrival of Lord Delaware with the remainder of the recruits and supplies. By a most extraordinary oversight, no precedence in rank was assigned to either of these gentlemen, and they were unable to settle the point among themselves, neither being willing to resign his chance of being the temporary head.

To obviate this difficulty, they adopted a most injudicious and unfortunate expedient ; they all determined to embark in the same vessel, their weak and childish ambition inducing them to take a step which defeated the very object of this triumvirate division of authority. In their ship were contained also the bills of lading, the new commission, instructions and directions of the most ample nature, and the greater part of their provisions. This vessel, on the 25th of July, parted from the rest of the squadron in a violent storm, and was wrecked on one of the Bermuda Islands; another small vessel foundered at sea; the seven others arrived safely at Jamestown. The President, who was informed of their arrival by his scouts, and who had no expectation of so large a fleet, supposed them to be Spaniards coming to attack the colony, and with his usual promptness put it in a posture of defence. The Indians at this crisis gave the strongest proof of their good-will, by coming forward with the greatest alacrity, and offering to fight side by side with the English against their enemies.

These unfounded apprehensions were soon dissipated, but only to be replaced by substantial evils. With the seven ships came three individuals; of whom the reader has before heard, Ratcliffe (whose real name, as has been stated, was Sicklemore), Archer, and Martin, all of whom were enemies to Captain Smith, and had so prejudiced the minds of their companions against him, that they were prepared to dislike without ever having seen him. Their ships had been greatly shattered in their stormy passage, their provisions were running low, many of them were sick, and they arrived at the season of the year most trying to the constitution. The greater part of the company, moreover, consisted of persons "much fitter," as Stith says, "to spoil or ruin a commonwealth than to help to raise or maintain one." They consisted of dissipated young men, exiled by their friends to escape a worse destiny at home; bankrupt tradesmen; needy adventurers; gentlemen, lazy, poor, and proud; profligate hangers-on of great men, and the like.

A scene of wild confusion took place immediately upon their landing. They had brought no commission with them which could supersede the old one, and no one could, with legal propriety, supplant Captain Smith. The new comers, however, disdained to submit to his authority, prejudiced as they were against him, and looking with contempt upon the little band of colonists, whom they were sent to cast into the shade.

He, at first, allowed them to have every thing in their own way, and in consequence there was an entire end of all government, discipline, and subordination. The new comers, though having neither the authority nor the capacity, undertook to remodel the government. They conferred the chief power first on one and then on another; to-day, they administered the government according to the old commission; to-morrow, according to the new; and the next day, after a new fashion of their own. There was no consistency, no responsibility, and in fact no government; but instead of it a wild anarchy and misrule, to which nothing but chaos could furnish a parallel.

The sensible and judicious part of the community, both of the new comers and of the old settlers, perceived that this state of things, if long continued, would bring the colony to utter ruin, and, justly appreciating the distinguished merit of Captain Smith, entreated him to resume his abandoned authority, and save them from destruction, before it was too late. He was himself so disgusted with the new comers and their proceedings, that, had he consulted his own wishes alone, he would have abandoned the country and gone to England. But there was no alloy of selfishness in his nature. He felt for the colony, of which he was the soul and life-blood, the pride and affection which a parent feels for a favorite child. To its prosperity he was ever ready to sacrifice his private feelings, and he saw plainly, that the present system would end in its ruin.

He felt emboldened too by the conviction of the fact, that he was and had been its legal head, and that no one had any official authority for superseding him. He did not hesitate, therefore, to resume the station, which he had for a short time tacitly resigned, though in doing so he exposed himself to infinite vexations and no little actual danger from the secret and open opposition of his enemies. The most obstinate and refractory of them he cast into prison for safe keeping, until there was leisure for a fair and legal trial. It was thought expedient to divide their numbers, and accordingly Captain Martin was sent with a hundred and twenty men to Nansemond, and Captain West with the like number to the Falls of James River, each receiving a due proportion of provisions from the common stock.

Before these settlements were planted, Captain Smith, having established a regular government, and being near the end of the year of his presidency, resigned it in favor of Martin, who was the only person that could be chosen to the office. He had the good sense to perceive, that he was not qualified for so arduous a station, and, restoring it to Captain Smith in less than three hours, proceeded with his company to Nansemond. His experiment proved a total failure. The Indians were kindly disposed towards him, till his injudicious conduct converted them into determined enemies. They made a successful attack upon him, killing many of his men, and carrying off a thousand bushels of his corn. He made a feeble resistance, and did not attempt to recover what he had lost, but sent to Jamestown for thirty soldiers to aid him. These were promptly despatched, but he made no use of them ; and they soon returned of their own accord, disgusted with his cowardice and imbecility. Martin himself shortly followed them, leaving his company to take care of themselves.

Disasters also followed the settlement at the Falls. It was originally made in a place exposed to the inundations of the river and to other great inconveniences ; and Captain West returned to Jamestown to obtain advice and assistance in the removal of it. Captain Smith immediately purchased of Powhatan the place called by his name, which was a short distance lower down the river, and went up to the Falls himself, to superintend their establishment in their new abode. But the mutinous and disorderly company, seeing him attended with only five men, refused to obey his orders, and, on his attempting to use force, resisted him and obliged him to take refuge on board his vessel, having narrowly escaped with his life.

He remained here nine days, in the hope that they would listen to reason and consult their own interest in putting themselves under his guidance. But they obstinately refused to the last. The Indians, meanwhile, flocked around him with bitter complaints of the treatment they had received from the settlers, saying, that they had robbed their gardens, stolen their corn, beaten them, broken into their houses, and carried off some of their people and detained them prisoners. They offered to assist him in bringing them to subjection by the strong arm of power, and told him, that they had borne these insults and injuries from his countrymen out of respect to him; but that he must forgive them if hereafter they defended themselves to the utmost of their ability, and repelled unprovoked aggressions by force.

Finding his efforts to be unavailing, Captain Smith departed; but his vessel grounded, after she had proceeded about half a league, a very fortunate circumstance, as the result showed. For no sooner was his back turned, than some Indians, not more than twelve in number it is stated, burning for revenge, assaulted the settlers, and, killing several stragglers whom they found in the woods, struck such a panic into the rest, that they sent down in great alarm to Captain Smith, offering to accede to any terms that he would propose, if he would come and assist them. He returned, and, after punishing six or seven of the chief offenders, removed the rest to Powhatan, a place every way adapted to their purposes, as it had been brought under cultivation by the Indians, who had also erected a strong fort there.

As soon as they were settled in their new habitation, Captain West returned and began to undo all that had been done. Captain Smith, unwilling to contend with him, opposed him in nothing, but left him to manage every thing in his own way. By his influence they were induced to return to their former situation, for what reason it is not stated.

Captain Smith met with a most unhappy accident as he was returning to Jamestown. While he was sleeping in the boat, a bag of powder lying near him exploded, and tore and burned his flesh in the most shocking manner. His clothes being on fire, he leaped overboard to quench the flames, and was with difficulty rescued from drowning. In this sad condition he arrived at Jamestown, where things were in such a state as to require all his faculties of mind and body. The time set for the trial of Ratcliffe, Archer, and the others who had been imprisoned, drew near, and their guilty consciences made them shrink from an inquiry, about the result of which they could entertain no doubt. Seeing too the helpless state of the President, they entered into a plot to murder him in his bed; but the heart of the base wretch, who was chosen to be the instrument of their wickedness, failed him at the last moment, and he had not the courage to fire his murderous pistol. Having failed in this, they endeavored to usurp the government and thereby escape punishment. Fevered and tormented by his wounds, Captain Smith became weary of this perpetual struggle against the violence and malice of his enemies, and of supporting his rightful authority by force and severity; and he now determined to return to England, though his old friends, indignant at the treatment he had received, offered and indeed entreated to be allowed to bring him the heads of his foes. But he would not permit the colony to be embroiled in a civil war on his account. His wounds also grew very dangerous, from the want of surgical aid; and he believed that he could never recover, unless he went home as soon as possible to be cured there. He therefore, in the early part of the autumn of 1609, departed from Virginia never to return to it again. He left behind him four hundred and ninety colonists, one hundred of whom were trained and expert soldiers, three ships, seven boats, twenty-four pieces of ordnance, three hundred muskets and other arms, abundance of ammunition and tools, wearing apparel sufficient for all their wants, and an ample stock of domestic animals and provisions.

CHAPTER XIII.

Remarks on Captain Smith's Administration in Virginia.

CAPTAIN SMITH resided a little more than two years in Virginia; during one of which he was President of the colony. The reader, who has gone thus far with me, will be enabled to form a conception of what he accomplished, and the disadvantages against which he contended. It is difficult for those who have been reared on the lap of civilization, and had wants created by the facilities of gratifying them, to have a full sense of the labors and sufferings of the first settlers of a new country. Familiar with the luxuries of artificial life, they are thrown into a situation where animal existence can hardly be supported. Severe and unremitted toil wears down the frame and depresses the mind. Famine often lays siege to them, and new and strange diseases prostrate their strength. A vague sense of apprehension ever darkens their lot, and not a leaf stirs, but makes them start with the expectation of encountering some great and unknown danger.

The bright hopes, with which they began their enterprise, are apt to languish and die; and their hearts faint under the influence of that homesick-

ness, for which there is no medicine but a draught
of the air of one's native land.   To be the successful leader of a band of new settlers under
the most favorable circumstances, requires an
extraordinary combination of powers.   He must
be able to use his hands as well as his head, to
act as well as to command, to show how things are
to be done as well as to give directions to do
them.   He must be able to awe the refractory, to
encourage the distrustful, and to cheer up the
drooping.   He must have courage, fortitude, self-
command, and perseverance ; he must be just,
yet not stern, dignified, yet affable and easy of
approach.

   The Virginia colony, and its head in particular,
had trials and perils of a peculiar nature to encounter, in addition to those which they might naturally have expected.   In the first place, they were
surrounded by numerous and powerful tribes of
Indians, whose occupation was war, and who were
organized into a powerful confederacy under a
ruler of extraordinary resources, the idol of his
people, full of courage and enterprise, rivalling
in dissimulation the most accomplished European
diplomatist ; and, if not the implacable enemy of
the whites, he has been represented as being still
very far from their friend, and, with a prophetic
spirit, apparently realizing from the first, that
their permanent residence and increase would involve the ruin of his own people.

As we have seen, too, Captain Smith had much to contend against in the characters of many of the settlers themselves, whom the old world seems to have shaken off, as being too worthless and desperate to be any longer tolerated at home. They were continually irritating him by their surly opposition, and infecting the well-disposed by their ill example; for labors and hardships are much lightened when they are shared by all. Instead of receiving aid from the council at home, they were to him a source of unmixed vexation and disappointment.

Chagrined by the failure of their visionary hopes, with a truly consistent selfishness they abandoned to unwarrantable neglect the settlers, whom they had sent into a howling wilderness, taking no pains to provide for their wants, and, by their absurd exactions, making the expeditions they sent out to them a tax and a burden. Captain Smith they honored with peculiar dislike, because he preferred the interests of the colony to their own; believing all that his enemies could say of him, giving him reproof where honor was due, and finally depriving him of his command, at the very moment, when, by his extraordinary exertions, he had established the colony upon a firm basis, and could look confidently forward to its steady increase and continued prosperity.

It is hardly possible for Captain Smith's services to the colony to be exaggerated. Nothing but the force of his character could have conducted it through so many difficulties and dangers. Upon his single life its existence hung, and without him the enterprise would have been relinquished again and again, as in the case of the settlements on the coast of North Carolina, and the establishment of a permanent colony in America would have been delayed to an indefinite period, since every unsuccessful attempt would have been a fresh discouragement to such an undertaking. It is easy to be seen that he embraced the interests of the colony with the whole force of his fervid and enthusiastic character. He was its right eye and its right arm. In its service he displayed a perseverance, which no obstacles could dishearten, a courage, which bordered upon rashness, and a fertility of resources, which never left him at a loss for remedies against every disaster, and for the means of extricating himself from every difficulty and embarrassment.

It is curious to observe that he seemed not only to superintend, but to do every thing. His official dignity never encumbered him when any thing was to be done. We find him, at one time, cutting down trees with his own hands; at another, heading an exploring expedition, venturing, with a few timid followers in an open bark, into unknown regions densely peopled with savage tribes; and at another, marching with a few soldiers to procure provisions, and sleeping on the bare ground in the depth of winter. He had the advantage of possessing an iron frame and a constitution which was proof against sickness and exposure ; so that, while others were faint, drooping, and weary, he was vigorous, unexhausted, ready to grapple with danger, and contemplating every enterprise with cheerful confidence in the result.

In the government of his colony he was rigidly impartial, just, and, as might be expected from one who had so long been a soldier, strict even to severity. This was indeed one of the objections made to his administration by the council in England, and it without doubt created him many enemies in Jamestown. But the intelligent reader will find for him a sufficient apology in the desperate character of many of the settlers, and in the absolute necessity of implicit subordination, which their situation required.

The whole power was centred in his own person, and a refusal to obey him was a refusal to obey the laws, upon which their safety and even existence depended. His severity arose from a sense of duty, and no one ever accused him of being wantonly cruel or revengeful. No man was more ready to forgive offences, aimed at himself personally; a striking proof of which is, that we hear of no punishments being inflicted on the dastardly wretches who attempted to assassinate him, as he was lying helpless from his wounds, during the last days of his administration.

His conduct to the Indians, though not always dictated by a spirit of Christian justice or brotherhood, will be found very honorable to him, if tried by the standard of the opinions of his day. Here, too, his apology must be found in the peculiar circumstances in which he was placed. He was not the head of a powerful body, meeting and trading with the Indians on terms of equality, but of a feeble band, whom they, if they had known their own strength, might have crushed in a moment. The passion of fear is the parent of cruelty and of treachery. It was necessary (or at least it was deemed so) to overawe the Indians, to strike terror into them; and, if the means resorted to for accomplishing these ends were not strictly justifiable, there was at least an excuse for them.

The English were also more than once threatened with famine, while their Indian neighbors were generally well supplied with provisions; and reason and experience tell us that starving men will not be very nice in their expedients to obtain food, or coolly examine into the right and wrong of measures, when a fierce animal instinct is goading them on. Captain Smith, by his prudence and firmness, established a most harmonious feeling between the two races.

The respect of the Indians for him hardly stopped short of idolatry. His great qualities were evident to these untutored children of nature, and their reverence was the instinctive homage which is paid to innate superiority. This is alone sufficient to prove that he never treated the Indians, even as they thought, with injustice, cruelty, or caprice; had it been so, he never would have been so admired and honored by a race of men who are proverbial for never forgetting an injury.

The genuine merits of Captain Smith, as a presiding officer, can only be fairly estimated by comparing him with others. We have seen that whenever he departs from Jamestown every thing is thrown into confusion, and that, as soon as he returns, order is restored and the jarring notes of discord cease to be heard. As none but himself could bend the bow of Ulysses, so no one was capable of sustaining the office of President for a single day but Captain Smith. We have seen in what difficulties and embarrassments Captain Martin at Nansemond and Captain West at the Falls severally involved themselves; and from this specimen we may draw "ominous conjecture" of what would have been the fate of the whole colony, had either of these gentlemen been at its head.

Compare also the results of his brilliant expedition to explore the Chesapeake with Newport's pompous march into the country of the Monacans, in which his failure was as wretched as his means of success were ample. The miserable adventures of the colony, too, after he, its ruling and moving spirit, had departed, are in themselves a splendid encomium upon his energetic and successful administration.

The reader may have some curiosity to know what became of the Germans, whose treachery and misconduct we have so often been obliged to record. One of them, by name Samuel, never returned to the English from the time he first left them, but spent his days in Powhatan's service. Another, named Adam, returned, upon promise of pardon, at the time of Volday's conspiracy. During the troubles in the colony after the arrival of the last expedition, he, with another of his countrymen, named Francis, taking advantage of the general confusion, fled again to Powhatan, promising that they would do wonders for him at the arrival of Lord Delaware. But the savage monarch, with that sagacity and elevation of character which were peculiar to him, told them that the men, who were ready to betray Captain Smith to him, would certainly betray him to Lord Delaware, if they could gain any thing thereby, and immediately ordered their brains to be beaten out.

As to Volday, himself he contrived to go to England, where he imposed upon many merchants with stories of the rich mines he had discovered and of how much he could enrich them, so that he was sent out with Lord Delaware ; but, his real character being discovered and his falsehoods detected, he died in misery and disgrace.

CHAPTER XIV.

Captain Smith's First Voyage to New England.

From the time of Captain Smith's departure from Virginia, till the year 1614, there is a chasm in his biography. So active a mind as his could not have been idle during that time, but, unfortunately, no records are preserved of what he attempted or accomplished. We have every reason to suppose that his favorite subject of settling the American continent occupied a large portion of his time and thoughts. His distinguished reputation, and his great knowledge and experience upon that head, would naturally point him out as the most proper person in England to be consulted by those who had any projects of the kind in contemplation, and as the best qualified to take a part in them himself.

In 1614, probably by his advice and at his suggestion, an expedition was fitted out by some London merchants, in the expense of which he also shared, for the purposes of trade and discovery in New England, or, as it was then called, North Virginia. An attempt had been made to establish a colony on the coast of Maine, by the Plymouth company as early as 1607, and forty-five individuals passed the winter there. As the winter of 1607–8 was remarkably severe all over the world, we can easily imagine their sufferings; and shall not be surprised to learn, that they abandoned the enterprise, and returned to England in the first vessel which was sent out to them. They gave a most unfavorable account of the country, describing it as cold, barren, and rocky in the extreme. Disheartened, it would seem, by these representations, the company for some years confined their efforts to one or two voyages, the objects of which were, to catch fish and traffic with the Indians, till, as we have stated, they associated with themselves the enterprising genius of Captain Smith.

In March, 1614, he set sail from London with two ships, one commanded by himself, and the other by Captain Thomas Hunt. They arrived,

April 30th, at the island of Manhegin on the coast of Maine, where they built seven boats. The purposes, for which they were sent, were to capture whales and to search for mines of gold or copper, which were said to be there, and, if these failed, to make up a cargo of fish and furs.

Of mines they found no indications, and they found whale-fishing a "costly conclusion"; for, although they saw many, and chased them too, they succeeded in taking none. They thus lost the best part of the fishing season; but, after giving up their gigantic game, they diligently employed the months of July and August in taking and curing cod-fish, an humble, but more certain prey. While the crew were thus employed, Captain Smith, with eight men in a small boat, surveyed and examined the whole coast, from Penobscot to Cape Cod, trafficking with the Indians for furs, and twice fighting with them, and taking such observations of the prominent points, as enabled him to construct a map of the country. He then sailed for England, where he arrived in August, within six months after his departure.

He left Captain Hunt behind him, with orders to dispose of his cargo of fish in Spain. Unfortunately, Hunt was a sordid and unprincipled miscreant, who resolved to make his countrymen odious to the Indians, and thus prevent the establishment of a permanent colony, which would diminish the large gains he and a few others derived by monopolizing a lucrative traffic. For this purpose, having decoyed twenty-four of the natives on board his ship, he carried them off and sold them as slaves in the port of Malaga.

History, fruitful as it is in narratives of injustice, oppression, and crimes, has recorded few acts so infamous as this. He was indignantly dismissed from his office by his employers, when they heard of his guilt ; but this could not undo the mischief which had been done, nor prevent its evil consequences. The outrage sunk deep into the hearts of the Indians, and, with the indiscriminating vengeance of savage natures, they visited their wrongs in after times upon innocent heads, because they belonged to that hated race with whom their early associations were so tragical.

Captain Smith, upon his return, presented his map of the country between Penobscot and Cape Cod to Prince Charles (afterwards Charles the First), with a request that he would substitute others, instead of the "barbarous names" which had been given to particular places. Smith himself gave to the country the name of New England, as he expressly states, and not Prince Charles, as is commonly supposed. With his request Prince Charles graciously complied, and made many alterations in the nomenclature, which were generally marked by good taste. The name which Smith had given to Cape Ann, was Cape Tragabigzanda, in honor of his Turkish mistress, whom I hope my readers have not forgotten. Those, who have occasion to pronounce the name frequently, will congratulate themselves on the change. Cape Cod, the name given by Gosnold, was altered by the Prince to Cape James, in honor of his father; but posterity has pertinaciously adhered to the old, homely title, in spite of the double claims of the new one, as being the name of a king and bestowed by a prince. With his characteristic modesty, Smith had given his own name only to a small cluster of islands, which the Prince did not alter; but, by some strange caprice, they are now called the Isles of Shoals, a change which has neither justice nor taste to recommend it.

The first port, into which Captain Smith put on his return to England, was Plymouth. There he related his adventures to some of his friends, " who," he says, " as I supposed, were interested in the dead patent of this unregarded country." The Plymouth company of adventurers to North Virginia, by flattering hopes and large promises induced him to engage his services to them. Upon his arrival in London, overtures were made to him by his old employers

the South Virginia company, who had probably, by experience of others, learned to form a
more just estimate of his merits and abilities;
but these, on account of his previous engagement,
he was constrained to decline.   His refusal seems
to have given some offence to those whose good
opinion he valued ; for he takes pains to state,
that it proceeded from no disinclination to them
or their cause, but he considered himself in
honor bound to the Plymouth company.

CHAPTER XV.

*Captain Smith sails a Second Time for New
England. — Is taken by a French Squadron
and carried to France. — Makes his Escape.
— Arrives in England. — Publishes his Description of New England.*

WHEN Captain Smith left Plymouth for London, it was with the understanding that he should
return to the former place at Christmas and
take charge of an expedition of four ships, which
the company were to furnish him.   The London
company made him an offer of the same nature,
which, as we have stated, he was obliged to de-

cline. He endeavored to induce the two companies to fit out an expedition in common, for which there were many inducements.

The Londoners had the most capital, but the men of Plymouth were better acquainted with the art of taking and curing fish, and could more easily fit out vessels for that object; so that it was desirable that funds should be raised in London in behalf of an expedition which should sail from Plymouth. Besides, as Captain Smith says, " it is near as much trouble, but much more danger, to sail from London to Plymouth, than from Plymouth to New England, so that half the voyage would be thus saved." This project, though recommended by reason and expediency, could never be realized on account of the absurd jealousy which the two companies entertained towards each other, and the unwillingness of either to give precedence to the other.

Early in January, 1615, Captain Smith, with two hundred pounds in his pocket, and attended by six of his friends, left London for Plymouth, expecting to find the four ships waiting for him. But his sanguine expectations were destined to be disappointed. The ill success of the expedition, which sailed the June previous from the Isle of Wight, under the command of Harley and Holson, occasioned by the flame of excitement which the outrage of Hunt had kindled in the Indians had chilled the zeal of the Plymouth company.* But by the indefatigable exertions of Captain Smith, and the liberal assistance of Sir Ferdinando Gorges, Dr. Sutliffe, Dean of Exeter, and others, two ships were prepared and equipped, one of two hundred tons, and the other of fifty, in which, besides seamen, there were sixteen men destined to remain as settlers.

They set sail in March; but, after they had gone about a hundred and twenty leagues, they encountered a violent storm, which separated the two vessels, dismasted Captain Smith's, and obliged him to return under a jury-mast to Plymouth. His consort, commanded by Thomas Dermer, meanwhile proceeded on her voyage, and returned with a profitable cargo in August; but the object of the enterprise, which was to effect a permanent settlement, was frustrated.

Captain Smith's vessel was probably found to be so much shattered as to render it inexpedient to repair her; for we find that he set sail a second time from Plymouth, on the 24th of June, in a small bark of sixty tons, manned by thirty men, and carrying with him the same sixteen settlers, he had taken before. But an evil destiny seemed to hang over this enterprise, and

---

* See Prince's *Chronological History of New England,* p. 133, ed. 1826. Belknap's Life of Gorges, in his *American Biography,* Vol. I. p. 358.

to make the voyage a succession of disasters and disappointments. Soon after his departure he was chased by an English pirate, to whom his crew importuned him to surrender without resistance; which however he disdained to do, though he had only four guns and the pirate thirty-six. The apprehensions of all parties were soon agreeably and singularly dispersed; for Captain Smith, on speaking with her, found that her commander and some of his crew had been fellow-soldiers with him (probably in his Turkish campaigns), and had recently run away with the ship from Tunis.

They were in want of provisions and in a mutinous state, and offered to Captain Smith, either to put themselves under his command, or to carry him wherever he desired; but these offers were declined. Near Fayal, he met with two French pirates, one of two hundred tons and the other of thirty. His crew were again panic-stricken, and would have surrendered without firing a gun; but Captain Smith, whose impetuous valor made him disregard the greatest odds against him, told them that he would rather blow up the ship, than yield while he had any powder left. After a running fight he contrived to make his escape.

Near Flores, he was chased and overtaken by four French men-of-war, who had orders from their sovereign to make war upon the Spaniards and Portuguese and to seize pirates of all nations. At the command of the admiral, Captain Smith went on board his ship, and showed him his commission under the great seal, to prove that he was no pirate. The Frenchman (as it was his interest to prevent any settlement of English in New England, who might compete with his own countrymen at Acadia, in their profitable trade with the natives), in open defiance of the laws of nations, detained him prisoner, plundered his vessel, manned her with Frenchmen, and dispersed her crew among the several ships of the fleet. But, after a few days, they gave them back their vessel and the greater part of their provisions, and Captain Smith made preparations for continuing his voyage, though a great many of the crew were desirous of going back to Plymouth.

But before they parted from the French fleet the admiral on some pretence sent for Captain Smith to come on board his ship, which he did accordingly, alone. While he was there, the French ship, seeing a strange sail, gave chase, detaining him on board; and during the next night the disaffected part of his own crew entered into a plot to turn their ship's head homeward, which they accordingly did, the sixteen landsmen, who were going out as settlers, knowing nothing of it, till they found themselves safe at Plymouth again. The abduction of Captain Smith by the Frenchman was undoubtedly intentional, being caused, as Smith himself says, by the calumnies of some of his own crew, who were anxious to be rid of him and return home.

Captain Smith soon found that those who captured him were no better than pirates. The admiral's ship was separated from the rest of the fleet by a storm and followed her fortunes alone. Her cruise was very eventful and lucrative. Captain Smith had the misfortune to see more than one English ship plundered, without any means of preventing it. Whenever they fell in with one of these, they confined him in the cabin; but whenever they had engagements with Spanish ships, they insisted upon his fighting with them. Having spent the summer in this way, they carried him to Rochelle, where, notwithstanding their promises to remunerate him for all his losses by giving him a share of their prizes, they detained him a prisoner on board a vessel in the harbor.

They accused him of having burnt the French settlements at Port Royal in 1613 (which was the act of Captain Argall),* and endeavored to compel him to give them a discharge in full for all demands before the Judge of the Admiralty, threatening him with imprisonment in case he refused. While he was deliberating upon this

---

* See Holmes's *American Annals*, for the year 1613.

proposal, Providence held out to him the means of making his escape, without any violence to his sense of justice, or any degradation to his pride.   A violent storm arose, whose " pitiless pelting " drove all the people below ; and, as soon as it was dark, Captain Smith pushed off from the ship in a boat, with a half-pike for an oar, hoping to reach the shore.   But he fell upon a strong current which carried him out to sea, where he was exposed to great danger, in a small, crazy boat, when the storm was so violent as to strew the coast with wrecks.   Twelve hours he passed in this fearful state, expecting every moment to be swallowed up by the waves ; till by the returning tide he was thrown upon a marshy island, where he was found by some fowlers, nearly drowned and totally exhausted with cold, fatigue, and hunger.   By pawning his boat, he found the means of conveyance to Rochelle, where he learned that the ship which had captured him, with one of her prizes, had been driven ashore, and the captain and one half the crew drowned.

On landing at Rochelle, he lodged a complaint with the Judge of the Admiralty, and supported his claims by the evidence of some of the sailors, who had escaped from the wreck of the French ship.   We are not informed what was the final result of this process ; but he received from the hands of the Judge a certificate of the truth of his statement, which he presented to the English ambassador at Bordeaux. Both at this place and Rochelle he found much sympathy, and received many friendly offices; among others, he says, " the good lady Madam Chanoyes bountifully assisted me." He returned to England, we are not told at what time, but probably in the latter part of the year 1615, and, proceeding to Plymouth, took measures to punish the ringleaders of the mutiny among his crew.

While he had been detained on board the French pirate, in order, as he says, " to keep my perplexed thoughts from too much meditation of my miserable estate," he employed himself in writing a narrative of his two voyages to New England, and an account of the country. This was published in a quarto form, in June, 1616. It contained his map of the country, and the depositions of some of the men, who were on board his ship, when he was detained and carried off by the French, inserted, as he says, " lest my own relations of those hard events might by some constructors be made doubtful, envy still seeking to scandalize my endeavors, and seeing no power but death can stop the chat of ill tongues." As a proof of his indefatigable zeal in the promotion of his favorite object, he spent the whole summer in journeying about in the West of England, distributing copies of this book (seven thousand in

number, according to his own account,) among all
persons of any note, and endeavoring to awaken
an interest in the subject of settling America.
But, he says, "all availed no more than to hew
rocks with oyster-shells," so desponding were
the minds of men on account of the ill-success
which had attended so many enterprises of that
nature. He reaped, however, an abundant harvest of promises, and the Plymouth company, in
token of their respect for his services, formally
conferred upon him the title of *Admiral of New
England*.

Captain Smith's work on New England was the
first to recommend that country as a place of
settlement, and to disabuse the public mind of the
erroneous impressions which had arisen from the
dismal accounts of the settlers, who had returned
after the failure of Popham's expedition, and who
had represented the whole country as a cold,
rocky, and barren waste. It is evidently written
in the spirit of an advocate, and not of a judge,
and is tinged throughout with the sanguine temperament of its author. Still it is never visionary
or wild; it is full of good sense, accurate observation, and a sagacity that sometimes almost assumes
the shape of prophecy. No one can read it without admiration of this extraordinary man, in whom
the powers of action, reflection, and observation
were so harmoniously blended.

CHAPTER XVI.

Visit of Pocahontas to England. — Captain Smith's Interview with her. — Death of Pocahontas.

THE order of events in the life of Captain Smith again associates him with Pocahontas. After his departure from Virginia she continued to be the firm friend of the settlers, as before. In 1610, when Ratcliffe and thirty men were cut off by Powhatan, a boy named Henry Spilman was saved by her means, and lived many years among the Potomacs. We next hear of her in 1612, when Captain Argall, who had gone on a trading voyage to the country of the Potomacs, learnt from Japazaws, their chief, that she was living in seclusion near him, having forsaken her father's dominions and protection.

We are not informed of the reasons which induced her to take this step. It has been conjectured that her well-known affection for the English had given displeasure to her father, or that her sensibility was pained at witnessing the bloody wars which he waged against them, without her having the power of alleviating their horrors. When Captain Argall heard of this, he perceived how advantageous to the settlers it would be to obtain possession of her person, and that so valuable a prize would enable them to dictate their own terms to Powhatan. He prevailed upon Japazaws to lend him his assistance in this project, by that most irresistible bribe in an Indian's eyes, a copper kettle ; assuring him at the same time that she should not be harmed, and that they would detain her only till they had concluded a peace with her father. The next thing was to induce her to go on board Argall's ship, and the artifice by which this was brought about, is curious and characteristic of the Indian race.

Japazaws ordered his wife to affect, in the presence of Pocahontas, a great desire to visit the English ship; which she accordingly did, and acted her part so well, that when he refused to gratify her and threatened to beat her for her importunity, she cried from apparent vexation and disappointment. Wearied at last by her excessive entreaties, he told her that he would go with her if Pocahontas would consent to accompany them, to which proposal she with unsuspecting good-nature signified her assent. They were received on board by the captain and hospitably entertained in the cabin, " Japazaws treading oft on the captain's foot, to remember he had done his part." When Pocahontas was informed that she was a prisoner, and must go to Jamestown and be detained till a peace could be concluded with

her father, she wept bitterly, and the old hypo-
crite Japazaws and his wife set up a most dismal
cry, as if this were the first intimation they had
ever had of the plot. Pocahontas, however, soon
recovered her composure, either from the sweet
equanimity of her character, or because she felt
that her reception and treatment by the English
could not be any thing but kind and friendly.
The old couple were sent home, happy in the
possession of their kettle and various toys.

As soon as Pocahontas arrived at Jamestown, a
messenger was despatched to Powhatan informing
him of the fact, and that she would be restored to
him only on condition that he should give up all
his English captives, swords, muskets, and the
like. This was sad news to Powhatan ; but the
demands of the English were so exorbitant, that
he returned no answer to their proposals for the
space of three months. He then liberated and sent
home seven of his captives, each carrying a rusty,
worn-out musket, with a message, that if they
would give up his daughter, he would make satisfaction for all the injuries he had done, present
them with five hundred bushels of corn, and ever
be their friend. It was not thought expedient
to trust to his promises ; and an answer was
accordingly returned to him, that his daughter
should be well treated, but that they should not
restore her till he sent back all the arms which he

had ever, by any means, obtained from them. This displeased Powhatan so much, that they heard no more from him for a long time.

In the beginning of the year 1613, Sir Thomas Dale, taking Pocahontas with him, marched with a hundred and fifty men to Werowocomoco intending to compel Powhatan to ransom his daughter on the proposed terms. The chief himself did not appear; but his people received the English with scornful bravadoes, telling them, that if they came to fight, they were welcome, and should be treated as Captain Ratcliffe and his party had been. These were not words to "turn away wrath," and the boats were immediately manned, and a party landed, who burned and laid waste every thing they could find, not without resistance on the part of the Indians. After this, much time was spent in fruitless negotiation, and in mutual reproaches and defiance. Two brothers of Pocahontas came to see her, and were very happy to find her well and contented. Two messengers, Mr. John Rolfe and Mr. Sparks, were also despatched from the English to Powhatan. They did not see the chief himself, but were kindly treated by Opechancanough, who promised them to use his influence with his brother to induce him to comply with their wishes. The English returned to Jamestown to attend to their agricultural labors without bringing matters to any definite result.

The troubles between Powhatan and the English were soon to be healed by the intervention of a certain blind god, who, if tales be true, has had a large share in the management of the greatest concerns of the world. A mutual attachment had long existed between Pocahontas and Mr. John Rolfe, who is said to have been an "honest gentleman and of good behavior." He had confided his hopes and fears to Sir Thomas Dale, who gave him warm encouragement; and Pocahontas had also "told her love" to one of her brothers. Powhatan was duly informed of this, and his consent requested for their marriage, which he immediately and cheerfully gave, and sent his brother and two of his sons to be present at the ceremony and to act as his deputies.

The marriage took place in the beginning of April, 1613, and was a most auspicious event to the English. It laid the foundation of a peace with Powhatan, which lasted as long as his life, and secured the friendly alliance of the Chickahominies, a brave and powerful race, who consented to call themselves subjects of King James, to assist the colonists in war, and to pay an annual tribute of Indian corn.

In the spring of 1616, Pocahontas and her husband accompanied Sir Thomas Dale to England. She had learned to speak English during her residence in Jamestown, had been instructed in the doctrines of Christianity, and " was become very formal and civil after the English manner." They arrived in England on the 12th of June, 1616, where her name and merits had preceded her, and secured her the attentions and hospitalities of many persons of rank and influence. As soon as Captain Smith heard of her arrival, he addressed the following letter to Queen Anne, the wife of James the First.

" *To the most high and virtuous Princess Queen Anne of Great Britain.*

" Most admired Queen,

" The love I bear my God, my king, and country, hath so oft emboldened me in the worst of extreme dangers, that now honesty doth constrain me to presume thus far beyond myself, to present your majesty this short discourse. If ingratitude be a deadly poison to all honest virtues, I must be guilty of that crime, if I should omit any means to be thankful. So it is, that some ten years ago, being in Virginia, and taken prisoner by the power of Powhatan, their chief king, I received from this great savage exceeding great courtesy, especially from his son Nantaquas, the most manliest, comliest, boldest spirit, I ever saw in a savage, and his sister Pocahontas, the king's most dear and well-beloved daughter, being but a child of twelve or thirteen years of age, whose compassionate, pitiful heart, of desperate estate, gave me much cause to respect her; I being the first Christian this proud king and his grim attendants ever saw; and thus enthralled in their barbarous power, I cannot say I felt the least occasion of want that was in the power of those my mortal foes to prevent, notwithstanding all their threats.

"After some six weeks fatting amongst those savage courtiers, at the minute of my execution, she hazarded the beating out of her own brains to save mine; and not only that, but so prevailed with her father, that I was safely conducted to Jamestown, where I found about eight and thirty miserable, poor, and sick creatures, to keep possession of all those large territories of Virginia; such was the weakness of this poor commonwealth, as, had the savages not fed us, we directly had starved.

"And this relief, most gracious queen, was commonly brought us by this lady, Pocahontas. Notwithstanding all these passages when inconstant fortune turned our peace to war, this tender virgin would still not spare to dare to visit us; and by her our jars have been oft appeased, and our wants still supplied. Were it the policy of her father thus to employ her, or the ordinance of God thus to make her his instrument, or her extraordinary affection to our nation, I know not. But of this I am sure; when her father, with the utmost of his policy and power, sought to surprise me, having but eighteen with me, the dark night could not affright her from coming through the irksome woods, and with watered eyes gave me intelligence, with her best advice to escape his fury ; which had he known, he had surely slain her. Jamestown, with her wild train, she as freely frequented, as her father's habitation ; and, during the time of two or three years, she next under God was still the instrument to preserve this colony from death, famine, and utter confusion, which if in those times had once been dissolved, Virginia might have lain as it was at our first arrival to this day.

"Since then, this business having been turned and varied by many accidents from that I left it at, it is most certain, after a long and troublesome war after my departure betwixt her father and our colony, all which time she was not heard of, about two years after she herself was taken prisoner ; being so detained near two years longer, the colony by that means was relieved, peace concluded, and at last rejecting her barbarous condition, was married to an English gentleman, with whom at present she is in England ; the first Christian ever of that nation, the first Virginian ever spake English, or had a child in marriage by an Englishman, a matter surely, if my meaning be truly considered and well understood, worthy a prince's understanding.

" 'Thus, most gracious lady, I have related to your majesty, what at your best leisure our approved histories will account you at large, and done in the time of your Majesty's life ; and however this might be presented you from a more worthy pen, it cannot come from a more honest heart, as yet I never begged any thing of the state or any ; and it is my want of ability and her exceeding desert, your birth, means, and authority, her birth, virtue, want, and simplicity doth make me thus bold, humbly to beseech your majesty to take this knowledge of her, though it be from one so unworthy to be the reporter as myself, her husband's estate not being able to make her fit to attend your majesty. The most and least I can do, is to tell you this, because none hath so oft tried it as myself; and the rather being of so great a spirit, however her stature. If she should not be well received, seeing this kingdom may rightly have a kingdom by her means, her present love to us and Christianity might turn to such scorn and fury, as to divert all this good to the worst of evil ; where finding so great a queen should do her some honor more than she can imagine, for being so kind to your servants and subjects, would so ravish her with content, as endear her dearest blood to effect that, your majesty and all the king's honest subjects most earnestly desire. And so I humbly kiss your gracious hands."

Captain Smith gives us a few details of the residence of Pocahontas in England, and an account of his own interview with her, which the reader will probably prefer to read without any alteration. "Being about this time preparing to set sail for New England," he says, "I could not stay to do her that service I desired and she well deserved ; but hearing she was at Branford [Brentford] with divers of my friends, I went to see her. After a modest salutation, without any word, she turned about, obscured her face, as not seeming well contented ; and in that humor, her husband with divers others, we all left her two or three hours, repenting myself to have writ she could speak English. But not long after, she began to talk, and remembered me well what courtesies she had done ; saying, ' You did promise Powhatan what was yours should be his, and he the like to you ; you called him father being in his land a stranger, and by the same reason so must I do you ;' which though I would have excused, I durst not allow of that title, because she was a king's daughter, with a well-set countenance, she said, ' Were you not afraid to come into my father's country, and caused fear in him and all his people but me, and fear you here I should call you father ? I tell you then I will, and you shall call me child, and so I will be for ever and ever your countryman. They did tell us always you were dead, and I knew no other till I came to Plymouth; yet Powhatan did command Uttamatomakkin to seek you and know the truth, because your countrymen will lie much.'

"This savage, one of Powhatan's council, being amongst them held an understanding fellow, the King purposely sent him, as they say, to number the people here, and inform him well what we were and our state. Arriving at Plymouth, according to his directions, he got a long stick, whereon by notches he did think to have kept the number of all the men he could see, but he was quickly weary of that task.* Coming to London, where by chance I met him, having renewed our acquaintance, where many were desirous to hear and see his behavior, he told me Powhatan did bid him to find me out to show him our God, the king, queen, and prince, I so much had told them of. Concerning God, I told him the best I could; the king, I heard he had seen, and the rest he should see when he would. He denied ever to have seen the king, till by circumstances he was satisfied he had. Then he replied very sadly, 'You

---

* When he returned to Virginia, it is stated, that Powhatan asked him how many people there were in England, and that he replied, "Count the stars in the sky, the leaves on the trees, and the sand upon the sea-shore, such is the number of people in England."— *Stith*, p. 144.

gave Powhatan a white dog, which Powhatan fed as himself, but your king gave me nothing, and I am better than your white dog.'

"The small time I staid in London divers courtiers and others, my acquaintances, have gone with me to see her, that generally concluded they did think God had a great hand in her conversion, and they have seen many English ladies worse favored, proportioned, and behaviored; and, as since I have heard, it pleased both the king and queen's majesties honorably to esteem her, accompanied with that honorable lady, the Lady Delaware, and that honorable lord, her husband, and divers other persons of good qualities, both publicly at the masks and otherwise, to her great satisfaction and content, which doubtless she would have deserved, had she lived to arrive in Virginia."

Pocahontas, or the Lady Rebecca, as she was now called,* was destined never to leave the country, which had become her own by adoption, nor to gladden again the eyes of her aged father, whose race of life was almost

---

* Perhaps it is not generally known that her true and original name was Matoax or Matoaka, which the Indians carefully concealed from the English under the assumed one of Pocahontas, having a superstitious notion, that, if they knew her real name, they would be able to do her some mischief. — *Stith*, p. 136.

run.† Early in the year 1617, as she was preparing to return to Virginia, she was taken sick at Gravesend and died, being then about twenty-two years old. The firmness and resignation with which she met her death bore testimony to the sincerity of the religious principles, which she had long professed.

It is difficult to speak of the character of Pocahontas, without falling into extravagance. Though our whole knowledge of her is confined to a few brilliant and striking incidents, yet there is in them so complete a consistency, that reason, as well as imagination, permits us to construct the whole character from these occasional manifestations. She seems to have possessed every quality essential to the perfection of the female character; the most graceful modesty, the most winning sensibility, strong affections, tenderness and delicacy of feeling, dovelike gentleness, and most entire disinterestedness. These beautiful qualities were not in her nurtured and trained by the influences of refined life, but were the native and spontaneous growth of her heart and soul.

Her mind had not been formed and fed by books, or the conversation of the gifted and cultivated; the nameless graces of polished life had not surrounded her from her birth and created

---

† He died in the spring of 1618, probably between seventy and eighty years of age.

that tact in manner and deportment, and becoming propriety in carriage and conversation, which all well-bred people, however differing originally in refinement and delicacy of perception, seem to possess in about the same degree ; nor had the coarse forms of actual life been, to her eyes, concealed by the elegant drapery which civilization throws over them. From her earliest years she had been familiar with rude ways of living, uncouth habits and lawless passions. Yet she seems to have been, from the first, a being distinct from and unlike her people, though in the midst of them. She reminds one of a delicate wild-flower, growing up in the cleft of a rock, where the eye can discern no soil for its roots to grasp, and sustain its slender stalk. We behold her as she came from the hands of her Maker, who seems to have created her in a spirit of rebuke to the pride of civilization, giving to an Indian girl, reared in the depths of a Virginian forest, that symmetry of feminine loveliness, which we but seldom see, with all our helps and appliances, and all that moral machinery with which we work upon the raw material of character.

But in our admiration of what is lovely and attractive in the character of Pocahontas, we must not overlook the higher moral qualities, which command respect almost to reverence.

Moral courage, dignity, and independence are among her most conspicuous traits. Before we can do justice to them we must take into consideration the circumstances under which they were displayed. At the time when the English first appeared in Virginia, she was a child but twelve or thirteen years old. These formidable strangers immediately awakened in the breasts of her people the strongest passions of hatred and fear, and Captain Smith, in particular, was looked upon as a being whose powers of injuring them were irresistible and superhuman. What could have been more natural than that this young girl should have had all these feelings exaggerated by the creative imagination of childhood, that Captain Smith should have haunted her dreams, and that she should not have had the courage to look upon the man to whom her excited fancy had given an outward appearance corresponding to his frightful attributes ?

But the very first act of her life, as known to us, puts her far above the notions and prejudices of her people, and stamps at once a seal of marked superiority upon her character. And from this elevation she never descends. Her motives are peculiar to herself, and take no tinge from the passions and opinions around her. She thinks and acts for herself, and does not hesitate, when thereto constrained, to leave her father, and trust for protection to that respect, which was awakened alike by her high birth and high character among the whole Indian race. It is certainly a remarkable combination which we see in her, of gentleness and sweetness with strength of mind, decision, and firm consistency of purpose, and would be so in any female, reared under the most favorable influences.

The lot of Pocahontas may be considered a happy one, notwithstanding the pang which her affectionate nature must have felt, in being called so early to part from her husband and child. It was her good fortune to be the instrument, in the hand of Providence, for bringing about a league of peace and amity between her own nation and the English, a consummation most agreeable to her taste and feelings. The many favors, which she bestowed upon the colonists, were by them gratefully acknowledged, and obtained for her a rich harvest of attentions in England. Her name and deeds have not been suffered to pass out of the minds of men, nor are they discerned only by the glimmering light of tradition. Captain Smith seems to have repaid the vast debt of gratitude which he owed her, by the immortality which his eloquent and feeling pen has given her. Who has not heard the beautiful story of her heroism, and who, that has heard it, has not felt his heart throb quick with generous admiration? She has become one of the darlings of history, and her name is as familiar as a household word to the numerous and powerful descendants of the " feeble folk," whom she protected and befriended.

Her own blood flows in the veins of many honorable families, who trace back with pride their descent from this daughter of a despised people. She has been a powerful, though silent advocate in behalf of the race to which she belonged. Her deeds have covered a multitude of their sins. When disgusted with numerous recitals of their cruelty and treachery, and about to pass an unfavorable judgment in our minds upon the Indian character, at the thought of Pocahontas our " rigor relents." With a softened heart we are ready to admit that there must have been fine elements in a people, from among whom such a being could spring.*

---

* The child of Pocahontas was left behind in England and did not accompany his father to Virginia, his tender years rendering a sea-voyage dangerous and inexpedient, without a mother's watchful care. He was left in charge of Sir Lewis Steukley, whose treacherous conduct to Sir Walter Raleigh has given him an infamous notoriety. Young Rolfe was afterwards transferred to the care of his uncle, Henry Rolfe, in London. He came to Virginia afterwards, and was a person of consequence and consideration there. He left an only daughter, who was married to Colonel Robert Bolling, by whom she

CHAPTER XVII.

Captain Smith's Examination by the Commissioners for the Reformation of Virginia. — His Death. — His Character.

CAPTAIN SMITH, in his account of his interview with Pocahontas in the early part of 1617, speaks of his being on the eve of sailing for New England. This confident expectation was probably founded on a promise of the Plymouth company to send him out, in the spring of that year, with a fleet of twenty ships. But this promise was never kept, and Captain Smith, so far as is known to us, passed the remainder of his life in England. But, though his body was there, his spirit was in America; and he was unwearied in his endeavors to encourage his countrymen to settle in that country.

---

had an only son, Major John Bolling, who was father to Colonel John Bolling and several daughters. These were married to Colonel Richard Randolph, Colonel John Fleming, Dr. William Gay, Mr. Thomas Eldridge, and Mr. James Murray.

The above is taken from Stith, who adds, "that this remnant of the imperial family of Virginia, which long ran in a single person, is now increased and branched out into a very numerous progeny." Her descendants are numerous in Virginia at this day. Among them, as is well known, was the late gifted and eccentric John Randolph of Roanoke, who was not a little proud of the distinction.

The 27th day of March, 1622, was rendered memorable by the dreadful massacre of the English settlers at Jamestown, by the Indians under the direction and by the instigation of Opechancanough, who had succeeded to Powhatan's power and influence over his countrymen, and who was compounded of treachery, cruelty, and dissimulation. The design had been for a long time formed and matured with deliberate skill and forethought. The English were entirely unsuspicious and defenceless, and three hundred and forty-seven of them were cruelly slain. The massacre was conducted with unsparing and indiscriminate barbarity. Six of the council were among the victims.

This disastrous event threw the whole colony into mourning and gave to its progress and prosperity a blow, from the effects of which it was long in recovering. The news created a great excitement in England, and Captain Smith, in particular, was deeply affected by this misfortune, which happened to a colony, whose recent flourishing condition he had contemplated with so much pride and satisfaction. He was desirous of going over to Virginia in person, to avenge the outrage. He made proposals to the company, that if they would allow him one hundred soldiers and thirty sailors, with necessary provisions and equipments, he would range the country, and keep the savages under subjection and in check.

Upon this proposal there was a division of opinion in the council, some being warmly in favor of it, while others were too avaricious and short-sighted to lay out present money for future and contingent good. The only answer which Captain Smith could obtain from them was, that their capital was too much exhausted to undertake so expensive a plan, that they thought it was the duty of the planters themselves to provide for their own defence, and that they would give him permission to go on such an enterprise, provided he would be content with one half of the pillage for his share. This pitiful offer was rejected with the contempt which it deserved. Captain Smith says he would not give twenty pounds for all the pillage, which could be obtained from the savages in twenty years.

The calamities of the colony in Virginia and the dissensions of the company in England having been represented to King James, a commission was issued on the 9th of May, 1623, under the great seal of England to certain of the Judges and other persons of distinction, seven in number, giving authority to them, or any four of them, to examine the transactions of the company from its first establishment, report to the Privy Council all grievances and abuses, and suggest any plan by which they might be remedied, and the affairs of the colony be well managed in future. Seve-

ral questions were propounded by these commissioners to Captain Smith, which, together
with his answers, he has himself preserved.
These answers are marked by his usual good
sense, sagacity, and perfect knowledge of the
subject. He ascribes the misfortunes of the
colony to the rapid succession of governors, to the
numerous and costly offices with which they
were burdened, and to the fact that their affairs
in England were managed by an association far too
numerous to be efficient, the majority of whom
were bent upon nothing but their own gain.

As is well known, King James, in 1624,
dissolved the Virginia company, arrogated to
himself their powers, and issued a special commission, appointing a governor and twelve coun-
sellors, to whom the whole government of the
colony was entrusted, and making no provision
for a house of representatives. His death
taking place soon after, King Charles immediately upon his accession to the throne, published
a proclamation, in which he signified his entire assent to the changes introduced into the administration of the colony by his father, and his
determination to make its government depend
entirely upon himself. He declared, that the
whole administration should be vested in a
council, nominated and directed by himself, and
responsible to him alone.

The death of Captain Smith occurred in **1631**, at London, in the fifty-second year of his age. We know nothing of the circumstances which attended it, and we are equally ignorant of his domestic and personal history, with whom he was related and connected, where he resided, what was the amount of his fortune, what were his habits, tastes, personal appearance, manners, and conversation, and, in general, of those personal details which modest men commonly do not record about themselves.

From the fact that he expended so much money in behalf of the great objects of his life, and particularly in the publication and distribution of his pamphlets, we may infer that he was independent in his circumstances, if not wealthy. For his labors and sacrifices he never received any pecuniary recompense. In a statement addressed to his Majesty's commissioners for the reformation of Virginia, and written probably about 1624, he says, that he has spent five years and more than five hundred pounds, in the service of Virginia and New England; yet, he adds, " in neither of those two countries, have I one foot of land, nor the very house I builded, nor the ground I digged with my own hands, nor ever any content or satisfaction at all, and though I see ordinarily those two countries shared before me by them that neither have them, nor know them but by my descriptions."

A very superficial acquaintance with the events of Captain Smith's life will be sufficient to convince any one that he was a man cast in an uncommon mould, and formed alike for the planning and conducting of great enterprises. He had that happy combination of qualities, which gave symmetry to his character, and enabled him to assume the most important duties and responsibilities. His constitutional courage was tempered with coolness and self-command. The warmth and enthusiasm of his temperament never perverted the soundness of his judgment. His zeal was not a transient flame, quenched by the first experience of difficulty and danger, but a deep-seated, indestructible principle, which gained strength from opposition and vigor from defeat.

The perseverance with which he prosecuted his enterprises equalled the ardor with which he undertook them. His energy was so great and overflowing, that he could not be confined to any one sphere of duty. We see him at the same time performing the offices of a provident governor, a valiant soldier, and an industrious laborer, capable alike of commanding and executing. He dreaded nothing so much as repose, inactivity, and ease. He seemed to court the dangers, toils, and sufferings, which other men shrink from, or encounter only from a sense of duty. His resources increase in proportion to the extent of the demand

made upon them.   As the storm darkens around
him, his spirit grows more bright and serene, and
that, which appals and disheartens others, only
animates him.   It was his good fortune to have a
vigorous mind seconded by an equally vigorous
body.   He had a "soul of fire" enclosed in a
"frame of adamant," and was thus enabled to
endure and accomplish whatever his adventurous
spirit impelled him to.

If we were called upon to say what was his
ruling and characteristic trait, we should reply,
enthusiasm, using that word in its highest and
best sense, as the quality which leads a man to
devote himself to some great and good object with
courage, constancy, and self-abandonment, and to
exert in its advancement and behalf all the
energies of his nature, undaunted by natural obstacles, unruffled by opposition, and uninfluenced
by the insinuations of the malicious, the open violence of enemies, and the lukewarmness of selfish
friends.   For the first thirty years of his life, we
see him without any predominant object of interest or pursuit, obeying the impulses of a fiery
valor and a restless spirit of enterprise, "seeking
the bubble reputation" in desperate skirmishes in
an obscure corner of Europe, eagerly embracing
every opportunity of exposing himself to danger
and of winning glory, prodigal of life and covetous
of honor.   Yet, in all the scenes of his chequered

career, he is animated by those high and romantic motives, which must extort admiration from even those, who look upon war as a crime and military renown as a worthless bauble. There is nothing selfish or mercenary in his conduct; he does not belong to the Dugald Dalgetty school of heartless and ruffianly adventurers, making a trade of blood and anxious only for pay and "provant." He was a generous and highminded soldier, who fought for the battle and not for the spoils, and who gave to the cause he espoused, not only his sword, but his entire soul and heart.

But, fortunately for himself and for the world, in his early manhood he was induced to devote himself to the settlement of America, an object attractive enough to keep his imagination perpetually kindled, and vast enough to task all his powers, the prosecution of which unfolded in him high qualities of mind and character, that the iron routine of the camp could never have called forth, and which secured him a peaceful glory, far more durable and valuable than the laurels of a hundred victories. Henceforward this great interest absorbed and monopolized him. It supplied the place of friends, kindred, and domestic ties. He embraced it and labored for it with a disinterestedness and a sense of duty, worthy both of himself and of the cause. He never made it the means of securing pecuniary gain or

worldly advancement, being content to point out
to others the way to wealth, while he remained
poor himself.   He never coveted official dignity;
and, when he obtained it, he made it no excuse for
indolence or self-indulgence, and did not regard it
as of so delicate a texture as to render a dignified
and lofty seclusion necessary to preserve it unim-
paired.   He was never actuated by the motives
or spirit of a hireling.

We have seen him in Virginia struggling against
a host of difficulties, contending, not only with
those natural obstacles which he might reasonably have expected, but with mutiny, treachery,
and disaffection in the colony and base injustice
and persecution at home ; yet never abandoning
his post in disgust and despair, but, for the sake
of the settlement, doing every thing and suffering
every thing.   And what was his conduct on his
return ?   He showed no peevish resentment and
betrayed none of the irritation of disappointment.
He never magnified his own wrongs nor the ill-
treatment of the company.   He did not write
pamphlets to beg of the public the consolation of
their sympathy, and to pour into the general ear
the tale of his great merits and great neglect.   His
conduct was magnanimous, dignified, and noble.
Strong in the confidence of innocence, he made
no appeal and attempted no justification.   He
continued, as before, the active and zealous friend

of the colony at Jamestown, and of all similar projects.

He frequently volunteered his own personal services, and twice sailed to the coast of New England. By the writing and distribution of pamphlets, and by personal exertions, he diffused information among all classes upon the subject of America; enforcing eloquently its advantages as a place either for trade or for permanent settlement, and appealing, in its behalf, to avarice, ambition, enterprise, and that noble spirit of benevolent self-sacrifice, which dwelt in bosoms kindred to his own. Never was a scheme for obtaining wealth or personal aggrandizement pursued by any individual with more fervor and singleness of purpose, and never was one crowned with more splendid success, though he himself "died before the sight."

Captain Smith must have been something more than mortal, had he possessed so many brilliant and substantial good qualities without any tincture of alloy. The frankness of his character reveals to us his faults no less than his virtues. He was evidently a man of an impatient and irritable temperament, expecting to find, in every department of life, the prompt and unhesitating character of military obedience. He had keen sensibility and lively feelings, and was apt to regard as studied neglect or intentional hostility, what was in fact only lukewarm indifference. His conviction of the importance of discipline and subordination made him sometimes imperious and tyrannical. ˙ The energy and decision of his character led him sometimes to adopt questionable means to secure a desired result. His high spirit and independence made him perhaps unnecessarily rough and haughty in his communications to his superiors in station and authority.

Nothing is more difficult, than, in our intercourse with those above us in rank, influence, or consideration, to hit that exact medium of deportment, which is demanded alike by self-respect and by respect to others, and which is equally removed from slavish fawning and from the unbending stiffness generated by undue notions of self-importance. We have Captain Smith's own authority that he had a great many enemies. These were undoubtedly made by his haughty bearing, his uncompromising freedom of speech, the warmth of his temper, and the impatience of his blood. His resentments were lively, his antipathies strong, and prudence had never dictated to him to refrain from the expression of them.

There is one circumstance which may serve to palliate some of these weaknesses in Captain Smith. His birth was nothing more than respectable in an age when the greatest importance was attached to nobility. It is easy to perceive that this peculiarity in his fortunes may have produced in him a soreness of feeling and jealousy of temper; may have made him suspicious and fearful, lest he should not receive from others the respect and consideration, which he knew were due to his personal merit. This inequality between one's lot and one's merits and wishes is a severe trial of character, and, in men of high spirit, is apt to beget a morbid sensitiveness and pride, a surly independence of manner, and a painful uneasiness lest their dignity should be ruffled by too familiar contact. To this source is undoubtedly to be ascribed much of that tartness of expression which we find frequently in his writings, and of that haughtiness which we have every reason to suppose was characteristic of his deportment.

Those who have read this biography will, I think, be ready to allow, that the debt of gratitude which we of this country owe to Captain Smith can hardly be exaggerated. With the exception of Sir Walter Raleigh (and perhaps Richard Hakluyt) no one did so much towards colonizing and settling the coast of North America. The state of Virginia is under peculiar obligations to him as its virtual founder; since, without his remarkable personal qualities and indefatigable exertions, the colony at Jamestown could never have taken root.   In reading the history of his administration, we are made to feel in regard to him, as we do in regard to Washington, when we contemplate the events of the American Revolution; that he was a being specially appointed by divine Providence to accomplish the work entrusted to him.   He was exactly fitted for the place which he filled, and not one of his many remarkable gifts could have been spared without serious detriment.

His claims upon the gratitude of the people of New England are hardly inferior.   He was the first to perceive the advantages held out by it as a place of settlement, in spite of its bitter skies and iron bound coast, and to correct the erroneous, unfavorable impressions prevalent concerning it.   Though he himself had no direct share in the settlement of Plymouth, yet without doubt it was owing to the interest which had been awakened by his writings and personal exertions, that the ranks of the colonists were so soon swelled by those accessions of men of character and substance, which gave them encouragement and ensured them prosperity and success.   It was the peculiar good fortune of Captain Smith to stand in so interesting a relation to the two oldest states in the union, and through them to the northern and southern sections of the country. The debt of gratitude due to him is national and

American, and so should his glory be. Wherever upon this continent the English language is spoken, his deeds should be recounted, and his memory hallowed. His services should not only be not forgotten, but should be "freshly remembered." His name should not only be honored by the silent canvass, and the cold marble, but his praises should dwell living upon the lips of men, and should be handed down by fathers to their children. Poetry has imagined nothing more stirring and romantic than his life and adventures, and History, upon her ample page, has recorded few more honorable and spotless names.

NOTE.

Account of Captain Smith's Writings.

It is a proof of the versatility of Captain Smith's powers, that, after having passed so many years in stirring and eventful action, he was able to sit quietly down in the autumn of life, and compose book after book, as if he had never gone beyond the walls of his study. It is fortunate, both for us and for his own fame, that he was able to handle the pen as well as the sword, to describe what he had observed and experienced, and to be at once the champion and the herald.

He published, in 1612, "A Map of Virginia, with a Description of the Countrey, the Commodities, People, Government, and Religion. Written by Captaine Smith, sometimes Gouvernor of the Countrey. Whereunto is annexed the Proceedings of those Colonies since their first Departure from England, with the Discourses, Orations, and Relations of the Salvages, and the Accidents that befell them in all their Journies and Discoveries, &c. by W. S. [William Simons.] Quarto. Oxford." The "Proceedings," &c. is separately printed with a distinct title and paging, and an Address signed "V. Abbay." The above title is copied from Mr. Rich's catalogue. There is a copy of the same work in Colonel Aspinwall's collection.

In 1620, he published a pamphlet entitled " *New England's Trials*, declaring the Successe of 26 Ships employed thither within these Six Yeares." A second edition of the same work was published in 1622 with this title ; " *New England's Trials*, declaring the Success of 80 Ships employed thither within these Eight Years." An extract from this work is contained in Purchas, (Vol. IV. p. 1837.) There is no copy, so far as I am aware, of either of these editions in America.

In 1626, he published the following work ; " *The Generall Historie of Virginia, New England, and the Summer Isles*, with the Names of the Adventurers, Planters, and Governours, from their first Beginning, An. 1584, to this present 1626. With the Proceedings of those Severall Colonies, and the Accidents that befell them in all their Journyes and Discoveries. Also the Maps and Descriptions of all those Countryes, their Commodities, People, Government, Customes, and Religion, yet knowne. Divided into Six Bookes. By Captaine John Smith, sometymes Governour in those Countries and Admirall of New England." There are copies of this work with the dates 1627 and 1632, but Mr. Rich states, that they are apparently the same edition with merely an alteration in the title-page. A great part of it had been printed in 1625, by Purchas in his " Pilgrims." * It is a compilation made up of the previously written tracts of Captain Smith and a great number of journals, letters, and narratives by his friends and companions.

---

* I find in Colonel Aspinwall's CATALOGUE the following work ; " Smith's History of Virginia, fo. cf. gt. front. maps and plts. large paper. Lord Rich's copy. London. 1624." If this date be correct it would seem that the " General History " was published two years earlier than has been generally supposed.

It comprises the whole of the "*Description of New England*," the greater part, if not the whole of "*New England's Trials*," and probably the whole of the work on Virginia, printed at Oxford in 1612. The portions of it written by Captain Smith are thus subscribed; "John Smith writ this with his owne hand." The whole of the second and sixth books are written by him, but to the other four books he stands only in the relation of editor, intermixing occasionally his own observations and reflections with the narratives which he collected and arranged. The third book, which contains the history of the colony at Jamestown during Captain Smith's residence there, and from which I have so frequently quoted, is stated to be "extracted from the authors following, by William Simons, Doctour of Divinitie." It is a little curious, that the narratives in this compilation of Simons's are none of them written by one individual. For instance, a chapter, detailing the events which took place in Captain Smith's first expedition to survey the Chesapeake, is said to be written by Walter Russell, Anas Todkill, and Thomas Momford; and the next one in order, giving an account of the second expedition for the same purpose, is subscribed by Antony Bagnall, Nathaniel Powell, and Anas Todkill. This accounts for the fact, that in quoting from this book, I have not mentioned the name of any author. The work is dedicated to the Duchess of Richmond.

There are a great many copies of commendatory verses, some prefixed to the first, and some subjoined to the third and fifth books of this History, which were written mostly by his personal friends. Some of these are very curious (particularly one by Purchas, which is stuffed full of learning and extravagant conceits), though not very smooth or poetical. In subjoining those to the third book, Captain Smith says, "Now seeing there is much paper here to spare, that you should not be altogether cloyed with prose, such verses as my worthy friends bestowed upon New England, I here present you, because with honesty I can neither reject nor omit their courtesies." His own prose will be found more poetical than his friends' poetry.

This "General History" is reprinted in the thirteenth volume of Pinkerton's Collection of Voyages. A perfect copy should contain an engraved title-page, with the portraits of Elizabeth, James the First, and Charles the First; four maps, one of Virginia, one of Old Virginia, (part of North Carolina) with five plates in the compartments, representing Captain Smith's adventures among the Indians; (these two are reprinted in the Richmond edition;) a map of the Somers' Islands with a view of the forts; and map of New England with a portrait of Captain Smith in one corner; also a portrait of the Duchess of Richmond and another of Pocahontas. Mr. Rich says, "The original portraits of Mataoka (Pocahontas) and the Duchess of Richmond are rarely found in the book, but are sometimes supplied by well executed modern fac-similes." There are two copies of this work in the Library of Harvard University, one with the date 1626 and the other 1632, neither of which is perfect.

In 1630 he published "*The true Travels, Adventures, and Observations of Captaine John Smith, in Europe, Asia, Affrica, and America, from* 1593 *to* 1629. Together with a Continuation of his Generall History of Virginia, Summer Isles, New England, and their Proceedings, since 1624 to this present 1629: as also of the new Plantations of the great River of the Amazons, the Isles of St. Christopher, Mevis, and Barbadoes in the West Indies." In his Dedication to the Earl of Pembroke he observes, that he has been induced to publish an account of his early adventures by the request of Sir Robert Cotton, "that most learned treasurer of antiquity," and that he was the more willing to comply with it, because they had become so notorious as to be publicly acted upon the stage. "To prevent therefore all future misprisions," he says, "I have compiled this true discourse." It is contained in the second volume of Churchill's Collection of Voyages and Travels.

This work, together with the "General History of Virginia," was reprinted in 1819, at Richmond, Virginia, in two octavo volumes, and in a manner very creditable to the printer and publisher. The value of this edition would, however, have been much enhanced, if there had been something in the way of preface, explanation, and description, giving an account of the original editions, &c. As it is, the reader is left without guide or assistance, thrown, as it were, upon a sea of heterogeneous materials without chart or compass. There are no notes, no prefatory remarks, nothing to supply breaks and chasms, nothing but the original works themselves, reprinted word for word. But notwithstanding this, we owe much to the publishers, who have thus given to the public in a cheap and accessible form, works interesting to every American, and indispensable to one who desires to be well acquainted with our early history, which in their original editions are very expensive and difficult to be obtained.

The last thirty or forty pages of the "General History" contained in this edition, are devoted to an account of the settlement at Plymouth; and in the "Continuation" (which is prefixed to his *Travels, Adventures, &c.*, but forms the concluding portion of the Richmond edition) he gives a very brief sketch of their proceedings from 1624 to 1629. In this he says that New England had always been represented as a rocky, barren country, till his account of it was published, which had raised its credit so high that forty or fifty sail had gone there every year to trade and fish ; but that nothing had been done to establish a settlement, " till about some hundred of your Brownists of England, Amsterdam, and Leyden went to New Plymouth, whose humorous ignorances caused them, for more than a year, to endure a wonderful deal of misery with an infinite patience."

Captain Smith, a man of the world and a soldier, loyal in his feelings and probably a member of the Church of England, could not appreciate the motives which led to the settlement at Plymouth. The high religious enthusiasm, made morbid in some instances by persecution, could not appear to him as any thing else than wild fanaticism. But, though not capable of sympathizing with them, he regarded their settlement with lively interest, as is proved by the narrative of their proceedings for the first four years contained in his "General History," and the remarks he makes upon it. He is sanguine in his anticipations of their complete and final success, and says, that if there were not an Englishman left in America, he would begin the colonizing of the country again notwithstanding all he had lost and suffered.

In 1631 there appeared from his pen the following work. *" Advertisements for the unexperienced Planters of New England, or any where. Or, the Pathway to Experience to erect a Plantation.* With the yearely Proceedings of this Country in Fishing and Planting, since the Yeare 1614 to the Yeare 1630, and their present Estate. Also how to prevent the greatest Inconveniences, by their Proceedings in Virginia and other Plantations, by approved Examples. With the Countries Armes, a Description of the Coast, Harbours, Habitations, Land-markes, Latitude and Longitude; with the Map, allowed by our Royall King Charles. By Captaine JOHN SMITH, sometimes Governor of Virginia and Admirall of New England." I have quoted the title at length, since, like most of the titles of those days, it gives a tolerable abstract of the book itself.

This is a curious work, and in literary merit the most finished of his productions. It is rambling and desultory in its character, combining narrative, disquisition, advice, and apology without order or method. Here we have a paragraph in praise of a ship, another in reproof of religious dissensions; — here an account of the discoveries of former navigators, and, near to it, a sketch of the qualities requisite to form a good governor of a plantation. Many paragraphs are borrowed, some with a little alteration, others with none, from his former writings. He takes great pains to justify his own conduct and policy, when he was in Virginia, points out the errors and mistakes of those who had succeeded him, and alludes to the injudicious conduct of the council in England, and to the annoyance which they occasioned him while he was President.

He speaks occasionally in a disparaging and taunting manner of the "Brownists" of Plymouth, "the factious humorists" as he calls them. The pertinacity inspired by religious enthusiasm was offensive to his notions of military discipline, and irritated him not a little. And yet his sense of justice prompts him to do honor to the firmness and constancy, with which they endured their trials and sufferings. He speaks of Governor Winthrop in terms of the highest admiration and respect. He alludes to his "General History" occasionally, in which, he says, one may read of many "strange actions and accidents, that to an ordinary capacity might rather seem miracles than wonders possibly to be effected; which though they are but wound up as bottoms of fine silk, which with a good needle might be flourished into a far larger work, yet the images of great things are best discerned, contracted into smaller glasses."

A further and more extended notice of this work would be superfluous, as it has lately been reprinted by the Massachusetts Historical Society, in their COLLECTIONS (Third Series, Vol. III.), and thus rendered accessible to all who feel an interest in the subject. There is a copy of the original edition of this work, in the Library of Harvard University.

It has been generally supposed that the literary labors of Captain Smith were confined to subjects connected either with his own personal adventures, or with America and the settlements established there; but such is not the fact. In 1626, he published "*An Accidence, or the Pathway to Experience, necessary for all young Seamen;*" and, in 1627, "*A Sea Grammar, with the plaine Exposition of Smith's Accidence for young Seamen, enlarged.*" Of this latter work a second edition was published in 1653, and a third, with additions, in 1692. He alludes to this work once or twice in his other writings. In his "Advertisements," &c., he says, "Of all fabrics a ship is the most excellent, requiring more art in building, rigging, sailing, trimming, defending, and mooring, with such a number of several terms and names in continual not understood of any landman, as none would think of, but some few that know them, for whose better instruction I writ my Sea Grammar." In the Dedication of his "Travels, Adventures, and Observations" to the Earl of Pembroke, he says, "My Sea Grammar (caused to be printed by my worthy friend Sir Samuel Saltonstall) hath found such good entertainment abroad, that I have been importuned by many noble persons to let this also pass the press."

For the account of the two works last mentioned I am indebted to Lowndes's " Bibliographer's Manual." From a sentence in the " Advertisements," &c. (published in 1631, the year of his death,) it seems that Captain Smith was then engaged upon a work, which he calls the " *History of the Sea*," and which, as it was never published, was probably left unfinished at his death. There are two works ascribed to Captain Smith, in Watt's " Bibliotheca Britannica," (the two last in the list,) which were not written by him.

The extracts, which have been made from the writings of Captain Smith, will enable the reader to form a tolerably correct opinion of his merit as a writer. It will be seen, that he writes like a man of sense, observation, and talent, whose acquisitions are by no means contemptible, but who has been trained to the use of the sword and not of the pen. There is a rough vigor and energy in his style characteristic of the man, but it wants the clearness and polish of a practised writer. He betrays in it the irritability of his temperament, and he uses no silken phrases to express his displeasure and disgust. His own unbounded activity made him have no patience with sloth, imbecility, and procrastination. He could not see things going wrong, and be silent. But it is impossible to read any of his works without perceiving that he was largely endowed by nature, a man of lively sensibilities and of easily excited blood, with many of the elements which go to form the poetical character. His writings abound with picturesque and eloquent passages, and with expressions full of a native grace which Quinctilian himself could never have taught.

He was alive to the beautiful and grand in the outward world, as his animated descriptions testify; and, above all, his style is characterized by fervor, earnestness, and enthusiasm. His heart is in every thing which he writes. His mind is warmed and kindled by the contemplation of his subject, and it is impossible to read any of his works (after being accustomed to his antiquated diction) without ourselves catching a portion of their glow. If he has not the smoothness, he has not the monotony of a professed man of letters. His style has the charm of individuality. It has a picture-like vividness arising from the circumstance, that he describes, not what he has heard, but what he has seen and experienced.

Reading his tracts, as we do now, with the commentary which the lapse of two centuries has given them, we cannot but wonder at the extent of his knowledge, the accuracy of his observation, and the confidence, amounting almost to inspiration, with which he makes predictions, which, it is needless to say, have been most amply fulfilled. Had he done nothing but write his books, we should have been under the highest obligations to him; and the most impartial judgment would have assigned to him an honorable station among the authors of his age.

CAMBRIDGE:
CHARLES FOLSOM,
PRINTER TO THE UNIVERSITY.

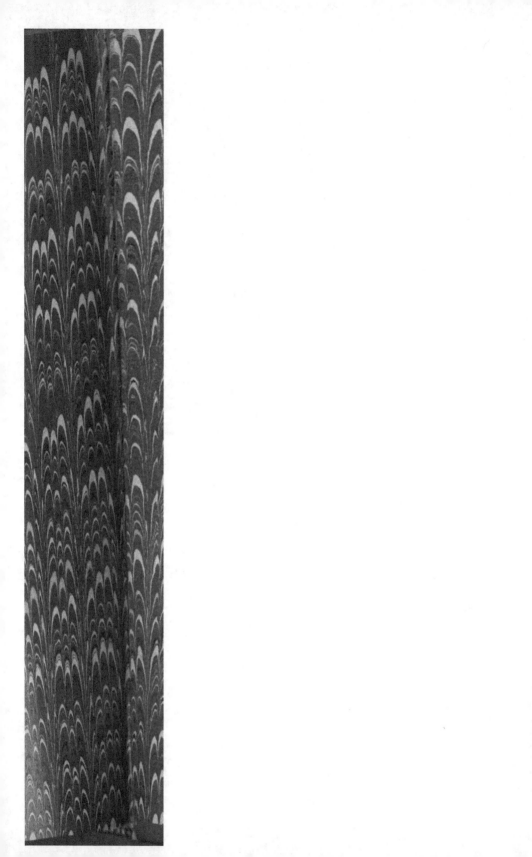

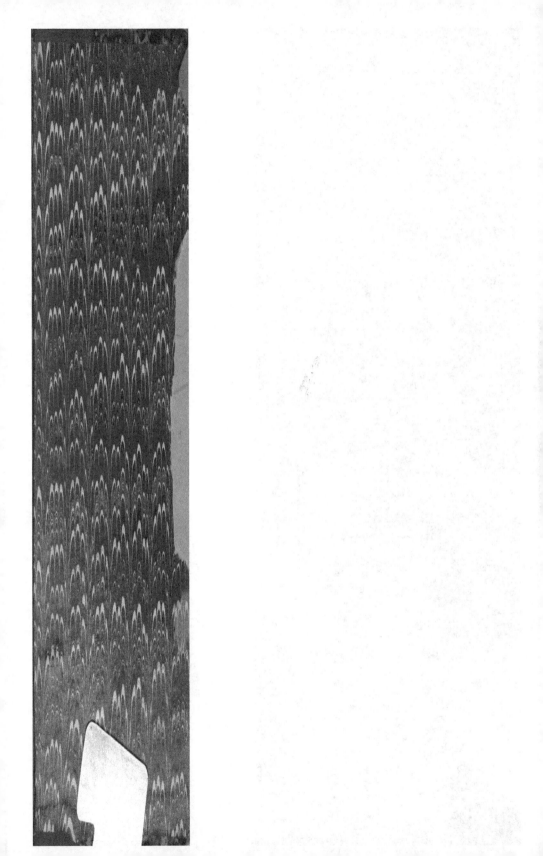

Check Out More Titles From HardPress Classics Series In this collection we are offering thousands of classic and hard to find books. This series spans a vast array of subjects – so you are bound to find something of interest to enjoy reading and learning about.

Subjects:
Architecture
Art
Biography & Autobiography
Body, Mind &Spirit
Children & Young Adult
Dramas
Education
Fiction
History
Language Arts & Disciplines
Law
Literary Collections
Music
Poetry
Psychology
Science
…and many more.

Visit us at www.hardpress.net